CW01368195

MEDIA, RELIGION, CITIZENSHIP

A British Academy Monograph

The British Academy has a scheme for the selective publication of monographs arising from its British Academy Postdoctoral Fellowships, British Academy Newton International Fellowships and British Academy/Wolfson Fellowships. Its purpose is to assist individual scholars by providing a prestigious publishing opportunity to showcase works of excellence.

Kumru Berfin Emre is Senior Lecturer in Communications and Media at London College of Communication, University of the Arts London. Her research on Turkish media has been published in leading peer reviewed journals such as *International Journal of Communication, Media, Culture & Society* and *European Journal of Cultural Studies*. She is the author of the monograph titled *Paramilitary Heroes on Turkish Television*.

MEDIA, RELIGION, CITIZENSHIP

Transnational Alevi Media and Its Audience

Kumru Berfin Emre

Published for THE BRITISH ACADEMY
by OXFORD UNIVERSITY PRESS

Oxford University Press, Great Clarendon Street, Oxford OX2 6DP

© Author 2023
Some rights reserved.

This is an open access publication distributed under the terms of the Creative Commons Attribution Non Commercial No Derivatives 4.0 International licence (CC BY-NC-ND 4.0), a copy of which is available at http://creativecommons.org/licenses/by-nc-nd/4.0/. For any use not expressly allowed in the CC BY-NC-ND licence terms, please contact the publisher.

You must not circulate this book in any other form
and you must impose this same condition on any acquirer

British Library Cataloguing in Publication Data
Data available

Library of Congress Cataloguing in Publication Data
Data available

Typeset by Cheshire Typesetting Ltd, Cuddington, Cheshire
Printed in Great Britain by TJ Books Ltd, Padstow, Cornwall

ISBN 978-0-19-726742-4 (hardback)
ISBN 978-0-19-888884-0 (electronic)

Contents

Acknowledgements	vii
List of Abbreviations	ix

1 Researching Alevi Media — 1
- Situating the Alevi Community — 3
- Research Context and Limitations — 12
- Structure of the Book — 15

2 Transversal Citizenship in the Digital Era — 18
- Multi-spatiality: From Cultural to Transversal Citizenship — 20
- Mediation: Traditional and Digital Media as Co-habiting — 24
- Decolonial Media Studies: Focusing on the Citizenship Acts of Marginalised Communities — 28

3 Transnational Alevi Politics and Alevi Citizenship — 34
- Alevis as 'Aliens' of the Nation — 34
- Transnational Alevi Politics — 39
- Alevi Citizenship Acts — 44

4 Transversal Acts of Citizenship — 51
- Demands for 'Fair Representation' — 52
- Media and Alevi Citizenship Acts — 57

5 Transnational Media, Transversal Imaginaries — 67
- Ethnography and Archiving through Local Programmes — 68
- National Coverage and Multilinguality — 72
- From Transnational to Transversal Imaginaries — 76

6 Alevi Viewership and Transversal Imaginaries — 82
- Personal Stories, Collective Histories — 83
- Exploring Alevism through Media — 87
- Transversal Imaginaries — 90

7 Communicative Ethnocide and Transversal Citizenship	**98**
Ethnocide: The Cultural Annihilation of a Community	99
Communicative Ethnocide: Destroying the Communicative Means of a Community	102
8 Limits of Transversal Citizenship	**113**
Digital Avenues: Fragmentation and Marginalisation	113
Limits of Transversal Citizenship Acts in Media	119
Limits of Transversal Citizenship Acts through Media: Critical Distances	122
9 Transversal Citizenship in a Complex Media Environment	**128**
References	135
Index	153

Acknowledgements

This book would not have been possible without the contribution and support of many people.

First of all, I would like to thank all the participants in this research, the workers and volunteers at Yol TV, TV10 and Can TV who generously shared their stories, perspectives and experiences with me. Experiences of discrimination and violence are intimate, and thus not very easy to share. I am grateful for their trust and openness.

My access and presence in Alevi circles have been facilitated by various activists, such as İsrafil Erbil (British Alevi Federation), Nadide Köroğlu (British Alevi Federation), Zeynep Demir (British Alevi Federation), Mahmut Akgül (Yol TV) and Şükrü Yıldız (TV10/Can TV), and the Alevi organisations of the European Alevi Unions Confederation and the British Alevi Federation. I would like to express my heartfelt gratitude for their ongoing support over the years.

My sincere thanks to Suay Abak, Veli Haydar Güleç and Pirha News Agency, which kindly allowed me to use the photograph from the protest of TV10's closure on the cover of this book.

This project was awarded a Newton International Fellowship (2016) by the British Academy. The scholarship marked a turning point in my academic journey. I hope this book can inspire new academics to apply for fellowship programmes offered by the Academy. I would like to thank Suavi Aydın and Simten Coşar, my colleagues at Hacettepe University, Gholam Khiabani and Dina Matar for their support in my application for the Newton International Fellowship.

The project was hosted by the Department of Media and Communications at the London School of Economics and Political Science. The department was a very rich learning hub and sharpened my critical perspective a great deal. My mentor, Myria Georgiou, was always there for me throughout the project. I am grateful for her supportive guidance, intellectual rigour and critical eye. It has been a privilege to work with her.

The book was mainly written during my sabbatical leave from the London College of Communication, University of the Arts London. I am truly grateful to Pratap Rughani, Rebecca Bramall, Steve Cross and Zoetanya Sujon for supporting my application for the sabbatical. My colleagues at the London College of Communication, Chiara Minestrelli, Sara Marino, Thomas Giakoglou and Zoetanya Sujon, made sure that I was able to focus on the book during my leave. Many thanks to the students of the BA in Contemporary Media Cultures, BA in Media Communications and MA in Media, Communications and Critical Practice (2019–22) for being wonderful learning companions and sharing their views about my research.

Many thanks to Cengiz Güneş, Kaya Akyıldız and Khanna Omarkhali, who kindly shared their publications with me.

I am very grateful to the anonymous reviewer for their constructive comments.

My friend Derrick Wright has proofread the book and made very useful suggestions. He is both a special friend and an amazing person to work with.

I would like to thank Göze (Orhon) for her invaluable support and friendship. Our chats have been thought-provoking and have motivated me more than she is probably aware. Yalçın (Armağan) has been the most generous and open friend I have ever had and a role model for intellectual passion. Special thanks are extended to my friends Berrin (Yaşot), Celia (Jenkins), Chiara (Minestrelli), Derrick (Wright), Ece (Kocabıçak), Esra (Emin), Joep (Meijers), Kate (McNicholas Smith), Maitrayee (Basu), Sara (Marino) and Sevgi (Adak) for sharing the joy and the struggles of life with me. You make me feel that I never walk alone.

I would like to thank my parents, my aunt, Can, and my extended family, who believed in me and supported the choices I have made in my life. I am blessed to have their love, compassion, support and kindness.

Ümit has always been present with his love, care, encouragement and comradeship. His research and our chats on Alevism have been deeply inspiring. My ideas on decoloniality in particular have been shaped by my ongoing conversations with him. Thank you, Ümit, for being an amazing partner and an admirable intellectual companion.

Thank you, Robin, for being the joy of my life. Hope you can find something in this book about your own questions of identity that will come as a child of a migrant Alevi family.

As much as I truly enjoyed writing this book, feelings of loss and mourning have been part of my writing routine. Over the course of writing this book I have lost many family members: Süleyman (Çelik), Hicran (Çimen Özdemir), Haluk (Emre), Abidin (Emre), Alaaddin (Güneş), Kumru (Emre), Atilla (Güneş), Hasan (Güneş) and Nurinisa (Emre). I am sure they would all have been proud of me. This work is dedicated to their loving memory.

List of Abbreviations

BAF	British Alevi Federation
DAF	Democratic Alevi Federation (Federasyona Demokratika Alewi)
DPMP	Democratic Peace Movement Party (Demokratik Barış Hareketi Partisi)
DRA	Directorate of Religious Affairs (Diyanet İşleri Başkanlığı)
JDP	Justice and Development Party (Adalet ve Kalkınma Partisi)
NMP	Nationalist Movement Party (Milliyetçi Hareket Partisi)
PKK	Kurdistan Workers Party (Partiye Karkeren Kurdistan)
PP	Peace Party (Barış Partisi)
TRT	Turkish Radio Television (Türkiye Radyo Televizyon Kurumu)
TUP	Turkish Unity Party (Türkiye Birlik Partisi)

1

Researching Alevi Media

This book is about Alevi media and the ways in which it has generated a particular form of citizenship that I call transversal citizenship. Alevis have been struggling for the right of recognition and equal citizenship in Turkey for decades. Despite this political struggle and its acknowledgement in the field of Alevi studies, their rights claims, with a few exceptions, have not been considered as acts of citizenship. Instead, their demands for equal citizenship have been situated within the framework of 'identity politics' in the post-Cold War context, usually with pejorative undertones. This book examines the contemporary Alevi movement through Isin's (2008, 2009, 2012, 2013) theory of citizenship enactment and argues that Alevi media paves the way for transversal imaginaries and rights claims that embed different spatial levels into Alevi politics.

In this book I also argue that, in order to unpack the socio-political dynamics of Alevi television, we must adopt a community-centred approach and make sense of Alevis' boundary-making practices, political divisions and ethnic diversity. This community-centred approach is mainly influenced by contemporary debates on decolonising that took place in South Africa more than a decade ago and have been increasingly influential in the Global North more recently (Nigam 2020; Meghji 2021; Reiter 2021). We need a community-centred approach not only for an understanding of Alevi media in detail but also for decolonial media studies, which has a great deal to learn from marginalised community media and communications. Umbrella terms such as community media are useful for understanding social conceptions and patterns in relation to media communications but they pose limitations on distinguishing different types of communities (e.g. ethno-religious minorities). They also do not guarantee a critical understanding of the colonial legacies that underpin media studies. For this reason, decolonial media studies is not simply about researching marginalised communities or oppressed or under-represented groups; it is rather a theoretical orientation towards unpacking the legacies of colonialism, while developing a critical dialogue with media studies. A productive approach to this can be found by examining the history of these groups and exploring their emic perspectives, which this research also endeavours to do. A prominent example of this is Richardson's (2020) work on African American citizen journalism. Instead of examining the uses of smartphones by the Black community in recording, disseminating and protesting against police violence in the USA through focusing on devices or platforms, Richardson rightfully situates these within the long history of Black witnessing of racist violence. Another call for cultural specificity comes from Florini (2019), who investigates Black digital networks by grounding her analysis in histories of Black communication and media production. In this book I adopt a similar approach in looking at the history of Alevis and the Alevi movement to understand how Alevi media has engendered a particular form of citizenship.

In doing this I am not suggesting a particularistic approach, which might inevitably lead to essentialism, but rather emphasising that we must unpack the power dynamics in the making of ethno-religious communities in order to understand their motivations, aspirations for and practices of media production. In order to do this, we must also critically engage with the research on the community and wear a decolonial set of goggles in examining them. In other words, a critical engagement with Alevi studies and the decolonial media studies are deeply interrelated in the sense that they require questioning the assumptions and attributions about the concept of 'community', which in the case of Alevis consists of both the producers and the viewers.

The broader aims, therefore, of this study are to contribute, first, to the decolonising of media studies by offering a critical perspective on community media and, second, to the decoloniality of Alevi studies by critically examining some key postulates and unquestioned assumptions about the Alevi community which have been highly influenced by Turkish nationalism. As this book focuses on Kurdish Alevi viewers, studying Kurdish Alevis also requires a decolonial perspective, in particular because of their minority position within the Turkish and Kurdish communities. That is why a decolonial perspective has been doubly employed in approaching the Alevis/Alevism research and media studies. Despite the fact that a great deal of valuable work has been produced on different Alevi communities and the history of Alevism, we can still argue that Alevism is an under-researched area, one where there is still much to uncover. Also, I cannot overstate the decolonising work that has already been done by various studies on Alevism, even if they have not employed the term. With this book I would like to pay respect to this body of work while applying the decolonial perspective. In other words, it takes a collective effort to challenge the established assumptions and this book can be situated within that contingently emerging collective realm.

This process of decolonisation is also an insider's look at unquestioned assumptions and internalised power dynamics, which unravel through encounters with other insiders and through attempts to engender a critical perspective towards one's own study. But it must be noted that an insider position in a persecuted community does not automatically produce a critical understanding of the colonial practices of domination. In Haraway's (1988: 584) words, '[t]o see from below is neither easily learned nor unproblematic, even if "we" "naturally" inhabit the great underground terrain of subjugated knowledges'. Identity is a constant work which is shaped within social encounters with close and distant others (Hall 1990).

Situating the Alevi Community

Alevis constitute the second largest religious group in Turkey with an estimated population of fifteen to twenty million. Aydın (2018) argues that Alevis can be regarded as an ethno-religious group who have primarily defined themselves according to their tribes or the *ocak*s (literally, 'hearth', a reference to a holy lineage) to which they belong. Their ethno-linguistic identity as Kurdish, Zaza or Turkish is a contemporary axis of difference that had been secondary to the Alevi identity until the 20th century. Alevis have suffered persecution since the 16th century either by the state, right-wing groups or religious fundamentalists, and the history of persecution holds a significant place in the Alevi collective memory and is arguably a key reference point for defining Alevi identity. The Alevi migration to cities has also meant that urban Alevism has been able to reunite different Alevi communities under the umbrella of Alevi, even, for example, embedding Nusayris as *Arab Alevis*, despite their differences with regard to this broader identity (Aydın 2018).

Alevi migration to Europe began in the 1960s, mainly to Germany as so-called guest workers (Zırh 2008). In Germany, migrant Alevis were recruited early on into leftist or worker organisations established by the migrants from Turkey and later into Alevi organisations during the 1990s. While Alevis in Turkey had to wait for the de facto ban on the right to organise imposed by the 1980 military coup to be abolished in 1989 for them to be able to establish Alevi organisations in Turkey (Bruinessen 2016), many Alevi organisations across Europe had been able to organise as federations. These federations were united under the umbrella of the European Alevi Confederation in 2002, which currently represents more than 250 organisations across Europe, including in Romania, Norway and Italy. Issa and Atbaş (2017: 193) estimate that the Alevi population is spread out in Europe as follows: 800,000 in Germany, 300,000 in the UK, 200,000 in France, 80,000 in Austria, 30,000 in Switzerland, 12,000 in Sweden and 8,000 in Denmark.

The majority of the Alevis in the UK, and hence by far the majority of the participants of this research, are Kurdish Alevis (White 2003; Gezik 2012, 2018, 2021; Gezik and Gültekin 2019; Sevli 2019; Cetin, Jenkins and Aydın 2020; Gültekin 2022), who can be considered as a 'twice minority' (Cetin 2013) because of both their ethnic (Kurdish) and religious (Alevi) minority position.[1] In Turkey, Kurdish Alevis live mainly in the eastern region of Anatolia (in Maraş, Adıyaman, Malatya, Sivas, Elazığ, Dersim, Erzincan, Erzurum, Bingöl, Kars and Muş) and speak Kurmanci or Zazaki. While Kurdish Alevis in Dersim, Erzincan, Varto and Bingöl predominantly speak Zazaki, in other locations Kurmanci is the main language (Gezik 2021: 562). Notably, notions of Kurdishness and Aleviness are deeply intermingled in the Kurdish Alevi community, whose members often refer to themselves as Kırmanc, thus unifying the ethnic and religious aspects of their identity (Deniz 2012; Gezik 2012; Gezik and Gültekin 2019; Gültekin 2022).

Kurdish Alevi migration to the UK began in the late 1980s. According to Cetin (2013), there are three main reasons underpinning Kurdish Alevi migration to the UK: 1) the rising state violence in Turkey and Kurdish Alevis being forced to join the state's security forces as village guards, set against the context of a burgeoning Kurdish movement; 2) the rising Islamist movement in the Kurdish region; and 3) economic issues. The first wave of migrants mainly came to the UK as refugees and formed an ethnic labour force working in the textile industry as low-paid and low-skilled workers (Jenkins and Cetin 2018). In the late 1990s, many opened corner shops, cafes and restaurants, while the second generation successfully integrated into the broader labour market and within different industries (Issa and Atbaş 2017). More recently, Alevis have been active participants in UK politics, particularly at local level as councillors or mayors (in Haringey in 2016 and Enfield in 2018), and in 2019 a second-generation member of the community was elected to the House of Commons.

Alevis established the London Alevi Cultural Centre and Cemevi[2] in 1993 (Geaves 2003), following the so-called Alevi Revival (Vorhoff 1998) in Europe. Different Alevi organisations were formed across the UK, including in Croydon, Edinburgh, Bournemouth, Doncaster, Nottingham, Sheffield, Hull, Glasgow and the East Midlands, which in 2013 united under a Federation, following other European examples. Today the majority of Kurdish Alevis in the UK are organised under the British Alevi Federation (henceforth, 'the Federation'), while in the rest of Europe, the Federasyona Demokratika Alewi (henceforth, the Democratic Alevi Federation, DAF) is deemed to be the umbrella organisation for Kurdish Alevis who are close to the Kurdistan Workers Party (Partiye Karkeren Kurdistan, PKK).[3] In this regard Kurdish Alevis in the UK are the exception within Europe both in terms of being a majority among Alevis and in generally belonging to the Federation.

---

[1] There is a growing interest in the research of Kurdish Alevis, predominantly focusing on the Dersim region. While this is promising when considering the history of persecution in Dersim, it also comes with the risk of rendering Kurdish Alevis living in other regions invisible.
[2] See Hanoğlu (2022) for the contemporary place-making practices of Alevis in the UK.
[3] The PKK was established as a Marxist organisation in 1978 with the aim of establishing an independent Kurdistan and has been in armed conflict with Turkish armed forces since 1979. See Bruinessen (1991) and Güneş (2012).

The Federation claims that there are 300,000 Alevis in the UK;[4] however, there is no way to verify this estimate. Alevism was included as a distinct religious category in the UK Census 2021 as a result of the successful campaigning by the Federation, and this might be able to provide more reliable data about the Alevi population in the UK in the near future. The Federation has been active in raising Alevis' visibility in the UK. For instance, it has campaigned for Alevism lessons to be included in the school curriculum (following similar efforts by other European federations, notably in Germany) to address community problems pertaining to the second-generation, such as school drop-outs, gangs and suicides (Cetin 2013, 2017, 2020). Consequently, Alevism has been included in the primary and secondary religious education curriculum in the UK since 2011 and the Federation has prepared teaching materials for schools in collaboration with the Standing Advisory Committee on Religious Education, education practitioners and academics (Jenkins and Cetin 2017; Jenkins 2020). The Office for Standards in Education reported that Alevi 'pupils have grown in confidence and self-esteem as well as improving attainment' following the implementation of the Alevism lessons (2012: 6, cited in Issa and Atbaş 2017: 195). The Federation also lobbied for the formation of an All-Party Parliamentary Group for Alevis in the UK parliament; this group was set up in 2015 (Hanoğlu 2021).

Alevis refer to members of the community as *can*. The main religious Alevi ritual is the *cem* ceremony, where members of the community perform a dance called *semah* along with songs called *deyiş* and *gülbang*, which are sang by *dede* or *zakir*.[5] Alevi rituals are led by *dedes*, who also act as the religious leaders of one or more tribes. Alevis were organised under the so-called *ocak* system where single or multiple tribes follow an *ocak* who provides spiritual leadership to ordinary Alevis (*talip*). Each *ocak* is considered to come from the holy lineage of the Prophet Ali and serves as a *talip* to other *ocaks*. In this way, rather than following a vertical organisational order, each *ocak* is also responsible for another. Endogamy is still a wide practice among Alevis; only an individual who is born to Alevi parents and later attends a specific *cem* ceremony to be accepted into the community (*ikrar cemi*) is deemed to be Alevi.[6]

While we have defined Alevis as an ethno-religious community, it is interesting to note that researchers argue that Alevism has taken a more religious turn recently by more clearly defining itself as a religion. According to Dressler (2008: 284),

---

[4] See http://www.alevinet.org/Default.aspx; last accessed 2 May 2022.
[5] See Sökefeld (2002a) on the role of *dedes* in the German diaspora and Coşan-Eke (2021) for the changing role of *dedes* in the transnational Alevi movement, from purely religious leaders to political actors representing the community.
[6] Being Alevi is based on two key criteria: being born to Alevi parents and attending the *ikrar cemi*. Although being born to Alevi parents is still deemed a necessary criterion, in the present day attending and being accepted in the community through *ikrar cemi* is not widely practised. Salman Yıkmış (2014: 174) argues that being born to Alevi parents is now considered sufficient for being Alevi.

Alevism has been transformed along three axes: 'first, secularization understood as decline of religious beliefs and practice; second, a turn to leftist ideologies; and third, a cultural and religious reorientation'.[7] Yıldırım (2017a) takes a similar approach and identifies four principal layers which compose modern Alevism: traditional lore; a Kemalist[7]–secularist world view; a socialist ideology; and recently conciliation with religion. For both scholars these turns in Alevism also correspond to a historical trajectory which interact and shape one another. This then raises the question of how we can address Alevis on the basis of citizenship. Here I shall answer the question by looking at the lines drawn between the fields of culture and religion by the Turkish state and by Alevis themselves.

There is no doubt that Alevi emic definitions differ at the community and individual levels including whether Alevism is regarded as a religious, ethno-religious, political or cultural identity. It is important to note that these self-definitions are not necessarily static but are relational (depending on the interactions and connections with intimate and distant others) and situational (depending on the historical and cultural contexts) (Fenton 2010). Alevi citizenship stands at the nexus of these different identities in relation to the different rights claims of Alevis in different national and historical contexts. For instance, while many Alevi organisations have been campaigning for secular education in Turkey, Alevi organisations in Germany and the UK have secured the inclusion of Alevism in the religious curriculum in primary and secondary schools (Jenkins and Cetin 2017; Jenkins 2020); therefore, their rights claims on the basis of religion are not aligned either at the transnational or national level.

While being a 'primordial' identity, Alevism is currently shaped by discourses of citizenship and right claims. According to Aydın (2018), the Alevis' position against the Turkish state has deeply shaped their political identity. They regard the state as a 'Sunni apparatus' and a means of oppression. Yıldırım (2017a) notes that the establishment of the Turkish Republic had serious implications for Alevis as a religious community. Alevis gave up their cosmology, religious and ritual practices in order to be modern secular citizens of Turkey. A similar critique comes from Alevis themselves who point to the Alevi support and membership of leftist organisations in the 1970s as detrimental to Alevi identity. Both these claims imply a tension between being a citizen who participates in the making of Turkish politics and having an Alevi (religious) identity.

Despite being an ethno-religious minority Alevis have been reluctant to associate their rights claims within the category of minority rights (Dressler 2014; Şen 2020; Karademir and Şen 2021). Karademir and Şen (2021) examine the legal

---

[7] Kemalism is the generic term that refers to the founding ideology of the Turkish Republic and derived from the name of the founder Mustafa Kemal Atatürk. It may be considered as an ideology or an indoctrination or the combination of two. It is a posthumous name coined by the followers of Mustafa Kemal and ideologists.

and cultural meanings of being a minority focusing on the Lausanne Peace Treaty (1923) which provided religious minorities such as Christians and Jews with minority rights in Turkey. They contend that '"enjoying" minority rights in Turkey amounts to being a silent, apolitical, foreign, divisive, isolated, and invisible legal entity' (Karademir and Şen 2021: 159). As such Alevis have not been keen to carry the negative socio-cultural connotation of being a minority group in the Turkish context. Furthermore, being regarded as a minority would legally bind Alevis to a certain definition which would mean eliminating the diversity that exists within the community (Karademir and Şen 2021). Indeed, the possibility of defining Alevis as a minority was also a concern of the Turkish officials during discussions on the Lausanne Treaty (Kurban 2006; Tambar 2014).

Alevis do not constitute a politically coherent community as they have actively engaged with different political movements and types of activism particularly in Turkey (Güneş 2020). Alevi politicians have established political parties, the Turkish Unity Party (TUP) in 1966 and the Peace Party (PP) in 1996, which were supported by the Alevi Federation in Germany (Sökefeld 2008a: 223) with the aim of mobilising the Alevi vote. However, neither of them gained significant support from community members in Turkey (Sökefeld 2008a; Ertan 2017; Massicard 2017). Focusing on the PP, Ertan (2017) argues that the ambiguity of Alevi identity and Alevis' fear of making themselves an open target by engaging with party politics that could lead to further massacres served as barriers to Alevi engagement with the PP. According to Massicard (2017), this indicates that Alevis are unable to unite under a political organisation because that they cannot agree on what Alevism is. However, one can argue that Alevis are not necessarily interested in being defined by their political identity and are inclined to fix their political position to their Alevi identity rather than vice versa. Alevi political subjectivity emerges around specific rights claims, most of which cuts across different political views (leftist, Kemalist, Kurdish) and different definitions of Alevism (including as a sect, a religion, real Islam and a culture).

The struggle for recognition is inherently a cultural claim in the broadest sense which is able to accommodate different perspectives, political orientations and self-definitions within a particular community. Nevertheless, to regard Alevi identity as cultural does not mean proposing a culturalist version of Alevism, as is suggested by leftist interpretations which aim at eliminating its religious character. Instead, I consider culture as a useful concept for including different interpretations of Alevism and accommodating various forms of boundary-making (Akdemir 2017). In this sense, Alevi citizenship includes the religious rights claims of the community, which, as demonstrated by Dressler, cannot easily be divorced from demands for secularisation. That is to say, I do not consider fields of religion and culture as exclusive, but as interconnected and situational. Sökefeld (2004: 151) also acknowledges that the distinction between religion and culture is not always easy to draw as 'the diversity of ideas and identification, related to each other in a process of contestation, becomes itself an essential aspect of Alevi culture'. Moreover, as demonstrated by Sökefeld (2008a) and Dressler (2011), religiosity is far from identifying contemporary Alevism but secularism is a key demand and world view for many Alevis. In other words, rights claims for recognition of Alevism do not necessarily indicate piety among Alevis since this claim is also adopted by organisations who distance themselves from the religious nature of Alevism and by individuals who call themselves 'atheist Alevis'.

Sökefeld (2008b: 294) asks a crucial question in his examination of the transnational Alevi movement and claims for recognition: 'recognition as what?' It is important to note that Alevis face this question when they come to negotiate their rights with official bodies and thus it is a 'power question'. I argue that by claiming rights to recognition, regardless of whether as a religion or not, Alevis are demanding equal citizenship. Drawing on Mamdani (2003), Akdemir (2015) stresses that in Turkey the government of the Adalet ve Kalkınma Partisi (Justice and Development Party, JDP) over-emphasises differences and internal conflicts among Alevis, an often used colonialist and ethnocentric strategy, and one that ignores the fact that identities are fluid and contingent. Such an approach also underpins some Alevi research which adopts a Eurocentric approach in searching for a homogeneous self-definition of Alevism or for a 'unified' Alevi movement. In other words, religion and culture are useful as analytical categories but in terms of rights claims they may also be limiting. As Isin (2013: 22) says, 'people do not often mobilise and rise for abstract or universal ideals', nor do they fight for pre-conceived categories. Alevis might define religion differently, vote for different parties, speak different languages and have different world views; nevertheless, this does not pose an obstacle to their self-identification as Alevi and to be seen as Alevis, a distinct group, by distant 'others'. This is why Alevis are able to make rights claims as a collective group, which is what makes Alevi citizenship possible.

However, there are certain limits to what Alevi citizenship can accommodate. For instance, despite being involved in the national politics of the host countries, Alevis do not necessarily demonstrate the same level of engagement and enthusiasm for politics in Germany or the UK compared to their engagement in Turkish politics. In other words, Alevis can be regarded as 'active citizens' at the national level in European countries as they vote, pay taxes and engage with their civic duties, whereas they are 'activist citizens' at a transnational level when claiming their cultural rights. Active citizenship draws the boundaries of Alevis in belonging to a national polity as Turkish, German or UK citizens, while activist citizenship expands these boundaries to include transnational contexts and the regional borders of Europe.

The first explicit presence in the media of Alevis as a persecuted community occurred on Alevi radio channels during the unregulated media environment of Turkey in the 1990s. The neoliberal economy of the era, along with the discourses of 'being free' (meaning free from state regulations), allowed various radio stations to flourish (Algan 2003; Kaya and Çakmur 2010). Alevis were able to establish their presence, raise their voice and reach a broader public than could be achieved through various Alevi magazines and books that were published at the time. However, an Alevi presence on television came relatively late and had to wait until the 2000s. This is mainly because the invisibility of Alevi identity in Turkish society had until then not allowed the development of a sustainable financial system to support the Alevi media. Due to the fear of persecution in Turkey, Alevis had been unable to organise in large numbers and to represent themselves through associations and non-governmental organisations. This lack of community resources, along with the fear of Alevi individuals, such as business people, who might have held sufficient economic resources to finance media organisations, held back investment in Alevi media. However, the Madımak massacre of 1993, where thirty-seven people, including two assailants, died in a hotel that had been set on fire, proved to be a turning point for Alevis and was a major boost to the so-called Alevi Revival, a reference to the increasing visibility of Alevis through publications and public events that had already started in the Alevi community in Europe in the late 1980s (White and Jongerden 2003; Sökefeld 2008a). This can be taken as a turning point for the Alevi media and paved the way for the establishment of Alevi television, which was born out of a burning necessity felt by Alevis to become more visible in the public sphere and out of a need for the self-exploration of their identity.

The 2000s can be seen as an experimental period for Alevi business people and organisations who explored the use of satellite broadcasting, mostly through Europe-based stations. Among the stations that were established were TV Avrupa (based in Germany), Dem TV (based in the UK), Su TV (based in Germany and later in France), Düzgün TV and Kanal 12 (both based in Germany), Cem TV (based in Turkey), Yol TV (based in Germany and later in Turkey) and TV 10 (based in Germany and in Turkey) (Emre Cetin 2018a). Most of these television stations had only a brief existence, largely as a result of economic factors, along with the political disagreements amongst the owners, which reflected the different political orientations within the Alevi community. More recently, there have also been political pressures and under the state of emergency declared by the Turkish government after the attempted coup on 15 July 2016, TV10, which had been on air since 2011, was closed in September 2016; Yol TV, which had been broadcasting since 2006, was suspended in late 2016. Both have returned to broadcasting, Yol TV on the internet and through IPTV (Internet Protocol Television), while TV10 has been re-established as Can TV. Can TV has been on air via the internet and Hotbird satellite. Currently, only Cem TV, which has been on air since 2005, remains as an Alevi station broadcasting from Turkey.

What distinguishes these channels from each other is their different interpretations of Alevism and their different political orientations, as well as their ownership by different organisations and individuals. TV10 is owned by a group of individuals who, in my interviews with them, emphasise their commitment to representing the ethnic, religious and political differences within the Alevi community. TV10 is also distinguished by its close ties with the Kurdish movement and is, therefore, primarily regarded as the voice of Kurdish Alevis. On the other hand, Yol TV is run by individuals who act on behalf of the European Confederation of Alevi Unions, which owns the station. It is interesting to note that Cem TV, the only station not forced by the Turkish government to suspend its broadcasting, fits in with the Turkish state's attempts to define Alevism within Turkishness. This is most likely explained by the fact that, as I have observed elsewhere, '*Cem TV* is run by the Cem Foundation which espouses an Islamic understanding of Alevism, regarding it as a sect of Islam within the *sufi* tradition, and also emphasises its Turkish origins' (Emre Cetin 2018a: 7).

As this research was conducted in a period when television stations had to close, I have been able to identify the survival and resistance strategies of these stations – the second main contribution of this book. The key survival strategy has been a rapid shift to online streaming and a switch to IPTV technology, both of which have made the internet indispensable for the existence of Alevi television. The stations have endeavoured to co-exist both in the digital and televisual realm and succeeded in doing so. Such a co-existence has required thinking of traditional and digital forms of media production and consumption as co-habiting, something which has been largely ignored in media studies so far since the main axis of distinction has been established between online and offline or digital and non-digital. However, such a distinction does not allow us to make sense of how community media can use both realms strategically. In other words, the Alevi case forces us to think of the media environment in its full complexity and situates digital within the realm of other forms of media production and consumption. That is why I prefer to use 'Alevi television' and 'Alevi media' interchangeably in this study. While Alevi television stations were born as television stations, they turned to social media and online streaming during the time of closure and thereafter. Therefore, the term 'television' no longer fully defines their media production. However, their organisation, production and content, and the fact that they are both available online, via IPTV (Yol TV and Can TV) and satellite (Can TV), does not allow us to fully abandon the term 'television' in addressing them. Hence, I shall use both 'Alevi television' and 'Alevi media', often interchangeably, in this book to remind the reader of the relevance of both television and media in understanding the Alevi case. In his work on Netflix, Lobato (2019) makes a case for situating online streaming within television studies despite new forms of production and consumption offered by subscription on-demand services such as Netflix, Amazon Prime, Apple TV and others. This is also relevant for Alevi media, though only partially as they continue or are willing to switch to broadcasting through Turkish satellites.

Throughout this book, I argue that Alevi television stands as a significant case for understanding how citizenship is enacted through media and for understanding the emergence of transversal citizenship, which consists of different spatial dimensions, including the local, national, transnational and regional in the making of citizenship acts. Moreover, Alevi media and transversal citizenship enable us to see the community media of those who are a minority across different countries and stateless communities in a different light. For such groups, community media becomes the main space in which a transversal imaginary, consisting of different spatial levels beyond the national and transnational contexts, can emerge. Alevi media also highlights the limitations of the 'transnational' as a binary concept that mainly refers to ties and connections across sending/receiving or home/host countries and helps us to address the complexities of transnationalism underpinned by multiple spaces, ethnic and religious diversity, and extra-territorial bonds and imaginaries. Furthermore, Alevi media is very significant for Alevis living in Turkey as they are a key target audience group for the channels. In other words, the transnationalism of Alevi media has a strong link not only from Europe to Turkey but also from Turkey to Europe as Alevis in Turkey are among the imagined audience of the channels. This point is particularly important for an understanding of how Alevi media enables transversal citizenship since the transversal connections also require a strong viewer base in Turkey. Alevi media connects an audience based in Turkey, in Europe and elsewhere and constructs what I call a 'transversal imaginary' by including different localities from these spaces (as discussed in Chapter 5).

Maksidi (2002) criticises the binary notion of Western imperialism versus non-Western resistance and argues that '[i]n an age of Western dominated modernity every nation creates its own orient' (768). He introduces the concept of Ottoman Orientalism to address the 19th-century Ottoman reforms which explicitly or implicitly associated the West with progress and the East with backwardness: 'Through efforts to study, discipline, and improve imperial subjects, Ottoman reform created a notion of the pre-modern within the empire in a manner akin to the way European colonial administrators represented their colonial subjects' (Maksidi 2002: 769). While Maksidi's analysis focuses on Mount Lebanon, Çakmak (2019) argues that Ottoman Orientalism is also relevant for understanding the Ottoman Empire's approach to Kurdish Alevis. Aydın (2018), Çakmak (2019) and Akpınar (2016) suggest that the policies of the Empire towards Alevis from the Hamidian Era (1876–1909) on were launched as part of a 'civilising' process, later identified with Turkification. Using the concepts that I develop in this book, such as transversal citizenship and communicative ethnocide, my aim is to unpack this colonialist perspective towards Alevis and how it has shaped Alevis' rights claims in and through media. The fact that the majority of the participants of this research are Kurdish Alevis and that the research took place in this ethno-religious realm requires a step further in decoloniality by reason of their 'twice minority' position

(Cetin 2013) as being both within the Alevi and the Kurdish communities and within the broader Turkish society. Therefore, engagement with the literature on Alevis has often required me to question widely accepted assumptions that exist within Alevi studies, even those that have adopted a more critical perspective.

Research Context and Limitations

This book is based on my ethnographic research within the Alevi community in London during the period 2016 to 2019 (although it is difficult to give a precise end date as I continue to be part of the community and share the same social spaces). It also uses interviews with Alevi media workers from Yol TV and TV10 (later Can TV) based in Cologne and London, as well as the thematic and discourse analyses of television programmes and thematic analysis of programme schedules. As part of this research, I conducted sixty-five interviews, not including a number of follow-up interviews at different times with the media workers. While twenty of the interviews are with media workers, the rest are with community members and leaders, who are also viewers of Alevi media. Sometimes, it is difficult to draw the boundaries between media workers and viewers since some of the community members occasionally contribute to Alevi media content as guests or participants to the talk shows or community event programmes. Both first- and second-generation migrants have contributed almost equally to this study through my interviews with them.

My research was conducted during my Research Fellowship at the London School of Economics and Political Science (2016–19) and sponsored by the British Academy as part of the Newton Fellowship scheme. The initial project aimed to focus on three Alevi television stations, Yol TV, TV10 and Cem TV, and to include interviews with viewers based in Turkey. My primary goal was to find out the extent to which Alevi media has been able to engender a transnational public sphere in which Alevis negotiate their identity and their rights claims and shape their imaginaries. However, the instability of Turkish politics and the rising authoritarianism in the country, particularly following the failed coup attempt in 2016, reshaped this research. First of all, I have not been able to travel to Turkey and conduct part of my fieldwork there due to security concerns and the risk of the confiscation of my passport by Turkish authorities under the state of emergency. I signed a petition,[8] along with 1,047 academics, criticising the government for the

---

[8] Academics for Peace was founded in 2012 following a statement in support of the demands for peace of Kurdish prisoners who went on hunger strike. Later the initiative called for a petition in 2016 which requested peace, criticising the Turkish government for its disproportionate use of violence against civilians. The signatories of the petition were 'fired from their jobs, their passports were cancelled and confiscated, they were prevented from finding jobs, several were physically and verbally threatened, others were taken into custody, four of them who read a press statement condemning these violations were imprisoned, hundreds were robbed of their right to work in the public sector through governmental decrees' and all of them faced individualized court proceedings. See https://barisicinaka demisyenler.net/node/1, para. 4; last accessed 2 May 2022. Also see Aydın (2020).

violent measures taken against civilians living in the Kurdish regions. This resulted in the labelling, targeting and arrest of signatories and dismissal from their jobs; some of these individuals were my ex-colleagues and friends, while I personally found myself 'stuck' in London and unable to travel to Turkey freely. I decided to revise the scope of my study and focus on Alevis and their media in Europe, including Yol TV and TV10, and limit my research to media workers based in Germany and the UK, while excluding their offices in Turkey. Furthermore, the fact that I had been publicly labelled as 'pro-Kurdish' at best and as a 'terrorist' at worst because of signing the petition could have caused potential participants who adopt a nationalist or pro-state stance to distrust me as a researcher. For instance, it is unlikely that conducting my research with media workers from Cem TV would be productive because of distrust and presumed ideological differences whereby they would likely situate me within their 'oppositional political camp'. Cem TV was established by the Cem Foundation, which adopts a pro-state and at times nationalist perspective towards Alevism, considering it as 'true Islam' and Alevis as genuine allies of the state. Nevertheless, Cem TV has been a recurring theme in my informal conversations and interviews with viewers. The second reason why I had to reframe my research stems from what happened to the Turkish media environment following the failed coup attempt in 2016. Along with many other media outlets which can be positioned within the alternative media spectrum, Alevi television channels, with the exception of Cem TV, were closed down as a result of decrees issued under the state of emergency (2016–18) (Çelik 2020; Yanardağoğlu 2021). Shortly after the failed coup attempt, TV10 was closed down by decree and Yol TV's broadcast was suspended by the Radio Television Supreme Council in Turkey.

It must be noted that the heterogeneity of the Alevi community does not allow for the making of generalisations, while the limited number of studies on different Alevi communities makes it difficult to produce specific arguments about particular Alevi communities. Therefore, although they are problematic, generalisations become inevitable in studying Alevism at this time, despite the problems associated with such generalisations. While I use the word 'Alevis' often in this book, I invite the reader to keep this problematic issue in mind. In other words, I am hoping that the reader is able to draw their own critical conclusions where the analysis does not allow room for further elaboration. In this, I am following in Haraway's (1988: 583) footsteps and her approach to feminist objectivity, which she contends is not about the division between subject and object but about limited location and situated knowledge.

My Kurdish Alevi identity has provided me with an insider position,[9] which is a complex amalgamation of affiliation, knowledge, memory and affect. Throughout

---

[9] See Özkul (2014) and Zırh (2017a) on conducting research with Alevis as an outsider.

the research, I have had to question my own assumptions about the community and about its collective identity and how individuals have experienced it in their personal lives. An insider position was also challenging in terms of being forced to take sides in community politics as an Alevi individual while endeavouring to sustain my critical distance and autonomy as a researcher. This has meant that being an insider and conducting ethnography 'at home' has come at a personal 'cost'. Indeed, I am not the same Alevi individual in terms of how I live and make sense of my collective identity that I was before this research. Also, as an educated, middle-class woman working as an academic, I hold a privileged position in relation to the community members who generously contributed to this research. The majority of the first-generation participants of this study come from a rural background, have little education and have been working in the informal ethnic market in the UK as textile workers, waiters/waitresses and so on. In this regard I cannot possibly be regarded as an 'absolute insider'. Dwyer and Buckle (2009) rightfully criticise insider and outsider positions as fixed in a researcher's identity and suggest a dialectical approach in acknowledging the 'space between'. They contend that membership in a group does not denote complete sameness, and that the opposite does not indicate complete difference. Insider and outsider positions are not inherently held by the researcher; rather, they are negotiated with the participants throughout the fieldwork. Hence, insiderness/outsiderness is also produced by situated knowledges (Haraway 1998) as a process. A dialogical approach is required with the reader of my book as I invite readers to think about my insiderness/outsiderness as a process rather than a fixed position and as a way of acknowledging the limits of self-reflexivity in research.

Gender equality is a hotly debated topic among Alevis as many of them would argue that Alevis have reached gender equity as there is no 'man' and 'woman' in Alevism; instead, there is a notion of 'soul' (*can*), which is genderless (Akkaya 2013; Okan 2016, 2018). In fact, Alevi social spaces are mostly gender mixed and women and men participate in the *cem* ceremony together, something which is presented as proof of gender equality in the community. Although there are various women activists in the Federation and *cemevi*s, I have observed that the community has a clear gender division of labour. For instance, while women organise and participate in cooking and cleaning activities during the community events, it is rare to see a man involved with such chores. Women were less willing to participate in the study as interviewees, often due to their insecurities around talking in a rather formal setting and their concerns about their 'knowledge' and the value of their perspectives. As a result, the number of women participants remained relatively low compared to men, with two thirds of the interviewees being male in this study. Transgender and lesbian visibility are still taboos in the community, even though gay men in particular are not treated as outcasts. This does not mean, however, that gay men are not discriminated against, although they do receive a certain level of acceptance as long as they do not outwardly express their sexual identity. In this research I have been fortunate to hear their perspectives; however, I am cautious in not providing numbers or other details pertaining to gay participants due to concerns of confidentiality. For this reason the study overall is unable to provide a balanced account of gender and sexuality. Therefore, the voices in this study are predominantly those of heterosexual men. Intersectionality and giving voice to marginal identities within the community remain unfulfilled ideals.

Structure of the Book

Transversal citizenship draws on research on media, citizenship, decoloniality and Alevism. The following chapter of the book, Chapter 2, discusses this theoretical backdrop and introduces the concept of transversal citizenship in detail. It outlines the concept, focusing on three key dimensions: multi-spatiality, mediation and decoloniality. The concept helps us make sense of the spatiality of citizenship acts and demonstrates that spatiality matters in shaping and pursuing rights claims. It enables us to acknowledge the relevance of the local in the national, transnational and regional contexts without collapsing each spatial level into the other. It also indicates that different levels of space might be embedded in rights claims to varying degrees, depending on the citizen subject's situatedness and the media's ability to connect the levels. Transversal citizenship is mediated because such complex ways of embedding spatialities at a collective level are only possible through mediated communications. Despite the contemporary emphasis on the democratic potential of digital media, the concept demonstrates the relevance of thinking of traditional and digital media as co-habiting within the same media environment and that communities might turn to either by using their resources strategically, particularly in times of crisis. Finally, Chapter 2 argues that the endeavour of theorising in media studies requires a decolonial focus, which proposes situating a community's rights claims within the broader history of the community rather than simply approaching it as a version of European citizenship.

Chapter 3 outlines the national and transnational dynamics of the Alevi movement and explains why we should consider Alevi rights claims within the framework of citizenship. Alevi rights claims can only be understood in relation to their position 'against' the political power, and vice versa in relation to the state's approach towards the community. In order to make sense of how Alevis emerged as a political subject, the chapter provides an overview of the long history of discrimination and persecution of Alevis and unpacks both the Ottoman and Republican states' approaches towards the community as 'heretics', despite the nuances and discursive changes in this long history. Alevi migration and transnationalism is another key dynamic which has influenced and defined Alevis' rights claims both in Turkey and abroad. Chapter 3 also focuses on Alevi transnational social space in order to make sense of the transnational dynamics of their citizenship acts. The final section of the chapter applies Isin's (2008, 2009, 2012, 2013) theory of citizenship enactment to understand the Alevi case and examines the events, sites and scales of their rights claims. This chapter demonstrates that community media is a significant site for Alevi citizenship acts, one which paves way for the mediated form of transversal citizenship.

Chapter 4 examines Alevi 'demands for fair representation' which emerge in the broader field of cultural production, including literature, films and television programmes. While each of these forms of cultural production consistently reproduces offensive representations of Alevism, Alevis also intervene in this field through protests and demands for a 'fair representation' of Alevis(m). Community media emerges against this historical and cultural backdrop and enables transversal citizenship. In this chapter, I distinguish between two main forms of acts in and through media in the making of transversal citizenship. While citizenship acts in media are mainly accomplished by the media workers who provide information on Alevi history, rituals and the diversity of the community, transversal citizenship through media also results in the involvement of the viewers in protests and campaigns facilitated by the community media.

Transversal citizenship consists of two main components: imaginaries and acts. Transversal citizenship acts are enabled through the members' capacity to imagine themselves as part of an extra-territorial community.[10] Chapter 5 examines how the Alevi media construct transversal imaginaries incorporating different levels of spatialities, including the local, national, transnational and regional. I examine the programme content and schedules and focus on local, national and transnational levels of imaginaries constructed through village programmes, political talk shows and programmes on community events. The analysis of the programmes demonstrates that transversal imaginaries amalgamate different spatial levels and put a particular emphasis on localities in presenting villages as 'authentic' sources of Alevism, while promoting contemporary forms of 'lived Alevism' in Europe through the reporting of community events.

Chapter 6 shifts the focus to Alevi viewership and examines to what extent the histories and narratives of the community enable transversal imaginaries to emerge. My findings demonstrate that Alevi viewers situate their own experience of discrimination and violence within the collective history of the community and that this frames their engagement with community media. Alevi viewers consider community media as a necessary means to tackle discrimination, to learn about Alevism and the community, to make their rights claims and to situate themselves within the broader extra-territorial realm of Alevis. Chapter 6 looks at the viewers' transversal imaginaries, examining their transnational bonds and connections, which are reinforced through visits to the home country, villages

---

[10] See Soğuk (2008) on the relationship between aterritoriality and transversality, with a particular focus on Euro-Kurds.

and other extended family members living in different countries in Europe. This demonstrates that transversal imaginaries also have a relevance beyond mediation.

The closure of Alevi media outlets has had serious implications for Alevi rights claims and this deserves particular attention. Chapter 7 draws on the early period of closure in 2016 and develops the concept of communicative ethnocide in order to unravel how the silencing of Alevi media stems from the ethnocidal policies of the Turkish state towards the community. The concept draws on Clastres's (2010) concept of ethnocide and Yalçınkaya's (2014) use of it in understanding the state's contemporary policies towards Alevis. Here I build on my earlier version of this concept (Emre Cetin 2018b) and demonstrate that communicative ethnocide is part of a systematic approach, one which also includes the displacement of the community, the destruction of its locality and geography, the destruction of the memory of the community and the displacement of the community's rituals and performances. Communicative ethnocide hinders a community's communicative means and capacity, either through direct intervention or by means of a subtle but systematic approach by the state. In this chapter, I particularly examine the infrastructural, audience and transversal dimensions to illustrate the consequences of communicative ethnocide for the Alevi media. I also demonstrate that the concept is useful in understanding the state's approach to the Kurdish community and their media.

Chapter 8 looks at the limits of transversal citizenship, focusing on the digital divides and critical distances of the viewers towards community media. The closure of Alevi television stations has accelerated a move towards digital media in an attempt to survive during the state of emergency in Turkey. The stations have heavily relied on online streaming through their websites, social media, IPTV (Yol TV) and eventually the Hotbird satellite (Can TV) in order to sustain their audience base and as a response to political pressures and uncertainty. This chapter examines how the rapid shift to digital transmission has impacted Alevi television and how it has changed viewer demographics as a result of the digital divides. The Alevi viewers' approach towards community media is far from uniform, with some viewers feeling a clear distance from Alevi television stemming from their different political stance and their unfulfilled expectations of professionalism and a diverse media content. Chapter 8 also looks at how critical distances limit transversal citizenship and demonstrates that transversal citizenship requires political alignment among the members of the community.

Chapter 9 concludes the book by demonstrating the relevance of the concept of transversal citizenship for an understanding of stateless communities dispersed across different geographies. It makes the case for decolonial media studies through theorising and concept-making that focus on cultural specificities and 'learning to unlearn' the coloniality of knowledge (Mignolo 2007, 2021).

2

Transversal Citizenship in the Digital Era

Throughout this book I argue that the transnational Alevi community practises transversal citizenship. This concept is used as a basis for analysis in this study for several reasons. First, the Alevi community's rights claims and their endeavours to create their own public sphere as well as enclaves renders this concept useful for examining contemporary Alevi politics and its relationship with media. Secondly, the use of the concept is promising in terms of developing an understanding of the relationship between online and offline participation, identity-construction and boundary-making, and the broader engagement with the concept of culture. Thirdly, the concept is useful in addressing questions of cultural inclusivity within the complexities of transnationalism, connectivity and belonging, regardless of whether diasporic, migrant or other communities are being examined.

This chapter introduces the concept of transversal citizenship in order: 1) to provide an understanding of how different spatialities are embedded in citizenship acts; 2) to aid the theorising of the media environment that accommodates traditional and digital media as co-habiting; and 3) to demonstrate how the concept is embedded in the decolonial perspective. Globalisation raises a number of questions about the integrity and significance of the nation-state as an institution of governance and about issues concerning 'cultural cohesion' and the problems of living in diverse, multicultural and connected societies. While recent discussions on different forms of citizenship and acts, such as data activism and digital citizenship, have brought broader questions about political subjectivity and participation onto the agenda, neither of these advancements has paved the way for similar outcomes for ethnic minorities and migrant communities. Transversal citizenship focuses on minorities dispersed across various nation-states and aims at addressing their diversity within this environment.

Previously transversal citizenship has been mentioned by Yuval-Davis (1997, 1999) in the context of a dialogical politics that challenges an assumed homogeneity and unity and instead enables specific positionings. Transversal dialogue is about social messages rather than the social identities of those who circulate the messages. Her approach acknowledges a multi-layered membership of different sub-, cross- and supranational collectivities, and takes these layers into account in the making of political subjects. Yuval-Davis (1997, 1999, 2007) also introduces the concept of multi-layered citizenship, which aims to address the intersectionality of political subjects that places 'people as citizens simultaneously to more than one political community' (2007: 562). However, rather than drawing on Yuval-Davis's notion of transversal dialogue and citizenship, the theoretical backdrop of my work develops in dialogue with the concepts of cultural and digital citizenship (Rosaldo 1994, 1997; Stevenson 1997, 2003, 2010; Delanty 2002, 2003; Hintz *et al.* 2019; Isin and Ruppert 2020) in order to enable us to theorise the Alevi case by focusing on their cultural rights claims and how they mediate these in the digital age. The emphasis on a dialogue between the two concepts of cultural and digital citizenship paves the way to overcoming the limitations of each. For instance, cultural citizenship does not allow us to think beyond the context of the nation-state or the binaries of transnationalism. It is not productive in addressing the complexities of stateless migrant communities, those who are minorities in both the home and host countries, because it mainly focuses on the national context of the country of arrival. In a similar vein, digital citizenship does not take the question of identity or the struggle for recognition into account as it mainly focuses on rights pertaining to the uses of technology and the outcomes of usage.

For this reason, neither of the concepts on their own are useful in fully addressing the complexity of the Alevi case. For instance, although we can identify Alevis' rights claims as cultural, the concept of cultural citizenship does not help us to move beyond the context of transnationalism and the need to explicate Alevis' connectedness to various localities. Equally, while digital citizenship can help us understand how Alevi citizenship acts are mediated through digital media and technologies, it does not allow room to include other spaces of mediation, such as television, which have been highly significant for Alevi transnational connections and rights claims. Therefore, the concept of transversal citizenship is developed in order to overcome the limitations of cultural and digital citizenship and to address multi-spatial mediated citizenship acts in a complex media environment. Transversal citizenship enables us to overcome the theoretical limitations of using cultural citizenship by thinking beyond the context of the nation-state and the binaries of transnationalism, while also addressing the shortcomings of digital citizenship by situating digital rights in the broader context of media and communications. As demonstrated in Chapter 1, Alevis are a minority group both in their home and host countries, and they are ethnically diverse. Transversal citizenship enables us to make sense of the similar struggles of minority groups for recognition in various national contexts, while acknowledging the diversity within since it situates spatiality at the heart of understanding mediated citizenship acts.

In this study, I examine transversal citizenship in the context of the struggle for recognition, cultural rights and citizenship. However, transversal citizenship is not limited to issues of cultural rights but is also applicable to economic, social and political rights claims. It is able to work across classical rights categories as they are often interrelated in terms of media and communications. For instance, during the Covid-19 pandemic the access to digital technologies was not solely experienced as a question of cultural rights but was underlined by economic and social constraints as digital access issues stemmed from the politics of location and the unequal distribution of resources. Hence, transversal citizenship helps us to see the digital as more than simply a technology or medium but also as a space and infrastructure through which resources and services are distributed and accessed (un)equally.

Transversal citizenship encompasses social imaginaries and citizenship acts in and through media. I examine these in detail in Chapters 4 and 5, focusing on the Alevi case while I introduce the theoretical basis of the concept here. In this chapter I first critically engage with theories of cultural citizenship and demonstrate why we need to contextualise cultural rights claims as multi-spatial and translocal. I then examine digital rights claims as transversal, as is suggested by Isin and Ruppert (2020), by arguing that digital citizenship acts should be situated within a broader media environment and by discussing how transversal citizenship can help us understand the complexities of online and offline citizenship acts. In the final section of this chapter, I demonstrate that transversal citizenship draws on the tenets of the decoloniality. All these sections address the tripartite framework that defines transversal citizenship as multi-spatial, mediated (concomitantly via traditional and digital media) and decolonial.

Multi-spatiality: From Cultural to Transversal Citizenship

The concept of cultural citizenship has developed as a critique of T. H. Marshall's (1992) seminal work on citizenship, which defines political, economic and social categories for understanding the rights and obligations of modern citizens in Britain. This is alongside various criticism of Marshall's work concerning the ambiguity about the relationship between capitalism, civil society and citizenship (Turner 1993), its limits for understanding civic participation beyond 'Western' countries (Isin 2002) and the emphasis upon the relationship between city and citizenship (Holston and Appadurai 1996). Those who proposed the idea of cultural citizenship aimed to address issues concerning the participation in the making of culture, the means and opportunities of access to it and the state's role and responsibility in defining and executing cultural policy. These issues involved in defining cultural citizenship emanate from the idea that culture is a political field and therefore raises questions of who shapes this field and through what means, and who is left aside. This brings cultural citizenship as a concept much closer to the idea of citizenship status as something derived from participation rather than membership where the areas of education, cultural policy, the arts and media are of key interest. The main body of work on cultural citizenship centres around questions of identity, diversity and inclusion that are inspired by academic debates on globalisation and multiculturalism (Kymlicka 1998), which problematise the culturally homogeneous notion of citizenship as defined by membership of a nation-state.

Pawley (2008) distinguishes three distinct strands in cultural citizenship theory: multiculturalism; the politics of cultural texts; and dialogical communication. According to Pawley (2008), the strand of multiculturalism is exemplified by Rosaldo's (1994, 1997) work, in which he formulates cultural citizenship as the 'right to be different and to belong in a participatory democratic sense' (1994: 402), and by Kymlicka's (1998) theory of multicultural citizenship. The second strand, the politics of cultural texts, looks at how cultural texts construct cultural identities and emphasises a need for different forms of political engagement on the basis of diverse representations (see Miller 1998). Finally, the consideration of dialogical communication is considered a prerequisite for political participation and cultural recognition, which can be distinguished as the third strand in cultural citizenship theory (see Ong 1996; Stevenson 2003).

Cultural citizenship is usually situated within a holistic political project of emancipation (see Stevenson 1997, 2003, 2010; Delanty 2003; Vega and van Hensbroek 2010). According to Stevenson (2010: 289),

> the struggle for a democratic society that enables a diversity of citizens to lead relatively meaningful lives, that respects the formation of complex hybrid identities, offers them the protection of the social state and grants them the access to a critical education that seeks to explore the possibility of living in a future free from domination and oppression.

According to Delanty (2003), cultural citizenship is a learning process. He argues that 'culture and citizenship must be seen as connected in a cognitive relationship by which learning processes in the domain of citizenship are transferred to the cultural dimension of society' (604). In his view, learning can empower people to further their self-understanding, recognition, sense of belonging and identity. Therefore, cultural citizenship is about learning about oneself as well as others. Previously, Parsons (cited in Turner 1993: 7) had introduced a similar vision to Delanty as he describes cultural citizenship as 'the social right to participate in the complex culture of a particular society through educational reform'. In this way, the role of learning and education feeds into representation through the emphasis upon active participation in the field of cultural production (Pakulski 1997; Isin and Wood 2002). Participating in the field of culture through production is a form of intervention in identity politics and, as Isin and Wood (2002) argue, requires cultural capital.

For Pakulski (1997: 80), understanding cultural citizenship is 'a matter of symbolic representation, cultural-status recognition and cultural promotion', where inclusion and recognition require asking 'who is silenced, marginalised, stereotyped and rendered invisible' (Stevenson 2003: 336); or to put it in Rosaldo's (1999: 260) words, 'who needs to be visible, to be heard, and to belong'. Vega and van Hensbroek (2010: 249) follow a similar path in arguing that cultural citizenship needs to be seen as 'a tool for addressing issues of cultural and social dominance rather than lack of rights'. From their perspective, cultural recognition does not guarantee diversity; therefore, acts of citizenship should go beyond simply the demand for recognition and should problematise 'the marginalisation of certain social practices' (Stevenson 2003: 337). Miller (2007) raises a critical voice in addressing the politics of cultural identities and invites political economy to enter the debates on cultural citizenship by looking at the detrimental impact of neoliberalism in erasing 'political' notions of cultural citizenship and replacing them with consumerism and 'self-governance'. In this regard, he emphasises the role of (consumerist) culture in shaping the ideas and practices of cosmopolitanism. His analysis demonstrates that there is no clear-cut parallel between diverse representations and cultural recognition within the existing neoliberal capitalist framework.

As Hall and Held (1989: 175) argue, '[f]rom the ancient world to the present day, citizenship has entailed a discussion of, and a struggle over, the meaning and scope of membership in the community in which one lives'. Therefore, it is useful to look at social imaginary and the sense of belonging in order to better address cultural citizenship. Cultural citizenship can be regarded as a politicised form of cultural identity where cultural identification and membership engender a political consciousness by which the members of a cultural community imagine themselves as part of a political entity. In other words, political action and participation in a political community emerge through a cultural sense of belonging. In this sense, cultural identity overlaps with a political one, as Rosaldo (1994) argues in his work on cultural citizenship and education. Delanty (2002: 172) also says that political community is not a derivative of cultural community but is reflexively shaped by it. This is also true for sexual citizenship, where an individual or a group claim rights on the basis of their sexual identity, or for ecological citizenship, where the human species is imagined as a political entity with regard to its relationship with nature and other species. Therefore, establishing a social imaginary through which members share a sense of belonging is a prerequisite for participation in a political community.

Cultural boundaries also shape the social imaginary as it is not only internally but also externally defined. Drawing on Taylor's (2004) seminal work on social imaginaries, Stevenson (1997: 48) says that the struggle for recognition is a dialogic process negotiated with intimate and distant others. In other words, the construction of a social imaginary is not necessarily an internal process conducted by the members of a cultural community but is constantly negotiated with others. The right to recognition not only entails the relationship between individuals, groups and the state as the legal order, but also includes informal and cultural engagement. Cultural citizenship requires social encounters, engagements and negotiations, as well as consisting of political acts since we cannot define the political beyond the social. However, the social imaginary that cultural citizenship presupposes adheres to the cultural boundaries drawn by the nation-state following the binary division between mainstream national culture versus multiple ethnicities. As such, cultural citizenship does not accommodate the intersectionality of identities, nor does it capture the complexities of ethnicity. A similar critique is also oriented towards Kymlicka's multiculturalism since it considers culture as homogeneous and monolithic, synonymous with 'nation' or 'people' (see Joppke 2001). Transversal citizenship offers an alternative to this conception by situating the relevance of spatiality at the heart of citizenship acts and by introducing the inter-relationality of local, national, transnational and regional levels in constructing social imaginaries. Therefore, transversal imaginaries emerge as a prerequisite for transversal citizenship acts.

In this study, I construe transversal citizenship as political subjecthood that emerges through making claims for the right to recognition, inclusion and self-determination in the sense of a person or a group holding individual or collective power to define, practise and experiment with cultural identities. What distinguishes transversal citizenship is its emphasis upon multi-spatiality and mediation in making cultural right claims. Claims to cultural rights can be made on the basis of participation and a sense of belonging; hence, they are not bound by the spatial and legal boundaries of the nation-state. Instead, borrowing Isin and Ruppert's (2020: xiii) notion, they are transversal and beyond legal frameworks:

> making rights claims traverses multiple political borders and legal orders that involve 'universal' human rights law, international law, transnational arrangements, and multiple state and non-state actors. The rights of the political subject emerging across such borders and orders, and their aggregation and integration, are distinctly and irreducibly transversal and cannot be contained within existing orders and borders.

Isin and Ruppert (2020) focus on digital citizenship acts while examining transversality. I suggest that transversality also applies to migrant communities, particularly those dispersed across the boundaries of different nation-states and particularly those who are minorities in their countries of origin, such as Alevis. In this vein, their cultural rights claims are also *transversal* because the political subjects who make a particular right claim are not necessarily homogeneous. They might be situated within different local contexts and might have different past experiences, or to put it in Kymlicka's (1998: 87) words, 'cultural boundaries may not coincide with political boundaries'.

Transversal citizenship helps us to overcome the limitations of cultural citizenship, which apply mainly to elucidate the nation-state contexts in addressing cultural diversity and multiculturalism. It also questions the binaries of home/host, sending/receiving and departure/arrival in the context of transnationalism by introducing locality and cultural diversity, both in the country of origin and the country of settlement. Elsewhere (Emre Cetin 2020a), I criticise the homogenising of the concepts of Turkish and Kurdish migrant which over-emphasises the common ethnic qualities of these communities and eliminates differences and other cultural tensions. For instance, what happens if 'Turkish migrants' primarily define themselves as Muslim or Alevi in the context of transnational migration? Sobande (2020) also rightly argues that we cannot talk about a uniformly shared identity for the digital Black diaspora. While Black people share systemic oppression under the global force of White supremacy, this collective experience is not fixed and 'does not solely define what it means to be Black' (Sobande 2020: 8). In a similar vein, Gajjala (2019) highlights exclusionary assumptions interwoven into the term 'Indian' which often leaves Muslims or Dalits outside of the national identity in the context of Indian digital diasporas.

In this regard, transversal citizenship enables us to challenge methodological nationalisms (Wimmer and Schiller 2003) in approaching and defining migrant communities by carving out room for different forms of boundary-making and citizenship acts. Furthermore, it also enables us to address migration as multi-routed and hence multi-sited, and to see diasporic communities as connected (Diminescu 2008; Diminescu and Loveluck 2014) to several socio-cultural spaces. In this sense, transversal citizenship proposes a translocal approach in understanding migrant communities. For instance, in the case of Alevis, translocality helps us to make sense of controversial rights claims in different nation-states (for example, claims for recognition as a religious community in its own right in Turkey and as part of Islam in Germany), rather than simply addressing them as strategic or opportunistic. If we solely focus on Alevis' struggle for recognition in Germany and situate Alevis within the category of 'Turkish migrant', we miss the connectivity of transnational Alevi movements across Western Europe and Turkey and turn a blind eye to the tensions around ethnicities of Turkishness and Kurdishness among Alevis. Transversal citizenship offers us the theoretical room to accommodate the complexities of transnational migration as translocal and multi-spatial, inviting a closer look at various national contexts and acknowledging the complexities of cultural identity and boundary-making within a particular community.

Mediation: Traditional and Digital Media as Co-habiting

Transversal citizenship is mediated because such inter-relationality of citizenship acts and social imaginaries between different spatial levels of the local, regional, national and transnational require communication and media technologies. In other words, multi-spatiality embedded in transversal citizenship necessitates connecting and interacting through media. At this point, I would like to look at the debates on digital citizenship briefly in order to demonstrate that transversal citizenship acts might emerge through traditional and digital media which simultaneously co-habit the same media environment. Isin and Ruppert (2020) aptly state that it is not possible to draw the boundaries of digital citizenship acts based on the social organisation of space or geographical territories. This is what makes digital citizenship transversal. However, instead of considering transversality as a characteristic of digital citizenship, I would like to conceptualise it further as a mediated form of citizenship that emerges in and through both traditional and digital media. Therefore, this section aims at demonstrating the relevance of transversal citizenship for making sense of mediated citizenship acts in a complex media environment.

One can distinguish two key approaches to the relationship between citizenship acts and digital media and communications. In the first body of research, the digital has been considered a productive space for political activism and civic participation (Banaji and Buckingham 2013; Herrera and Sakr 2014; Uldam and Vestergaard 2015; Boulliane and Theokaris 2018). These studies are mainly interested in how online engagement transforms and mobilises political participation and civic engagement. According to this body of work, traditional forms of civic participation are reshaped by digital technologies which provide new opportunities for political engagement and bottom-up politics. Contemporarily, digital activism has been used more widely to address online political engagement and arguably as a result civic participation has relatively lost the attention of researchers. The second approach regards the digital not only as a sphere *of* political participation but also a sphere *for* political participation where specific rights claims on access, privacy, use and representations can be made (Mossberger *et al.* 2008; McCosker *et al.* 2016; Hintz *et al.* 2019; Isin and Ruppert 2020; Henry *et al.* 2021). The extent to which digital technologies shape social fields as infrastructure and practice leads these scholars to mark the digital as of political significance. Such an approach also enables the concept of citizenship to be applied to different aspects of digital technologies, such as data and algorithms (Carmi *et al.* 2020; Calzada 2022). For instance, the right to be forgotten, the right to anonymity and claims for digital rights for cities appear to be novel forms of citizenship rights which are among the main concerns of 'digital citizens'.

The distinction between conventional rights (including economic, political, social, cultural and sexual ones) and digital rights is usually difficult to discern. Isin and Ruppert (2020: 175) contend that data and digital rights claims often cross over with or consist of conventional rights. They invite us to think of a broader political subject which exists within a continuous space, beyond the separation of digital and non-digital. For instance, the campaigning and lobbying by the Digital Freedom Fund, which claims digital rights as human rights, encompass various non-digital networks that organise events, talks and workshops. Thus, digital political subjects have a presence beyond the technological realm and where digital citizenship acts do not necessarily take place online. Therefore, in this way of thinking, space is defined on the basis of technology, which becomes a prerequisite for digital citizenship acts, whether enacted within a digital space or not. The 'digital' emerges as one space and the non-digital as another, albeit in connection. However, physical space – that is, place – is often lost in digital citizenship theory. Understandably, as a mediated space, the digital blurs the boundaries between physical and online presence or, to a certain extent, deems the physical situatedness of digital citizens unimportant. This is also because digital citizenship emerges through acts rather than being a status acquired. It is a process where the political subject is realised through enactment, a category which is not automatically assigned to every presence in digital space.

Nevertheless, the physical situatedness of political subjects matters even in the digital realm, for several reasons. First, digital citizens might suffer the consequences of their digital acts in offline spaces. Secondly, legal rights claims require engagement with a national or supranational jurisdiction or regulatory bodies, as in the case of Cambridge Analytica, which impacted Facebook users across the globe, although the legal action against the breach of privacy was brought in the UK and USA judicial contexts (Hintz et al. 2019). Thirdly, digital infrastructures, connectivity and participation might be a necessity for digital citizenship, if not a demand. This means there is always a place-related material basis for digital connection which is often framed by social inequalities. Hence, as much as it is about access and connection, digital citizenship is also about a digital disconnect (Helsper 2021).

Holston and Appadurai (1996: 188–9) contend that 'place remains fundamental to the problems of membership in society, and that cities (understood here to include their regional suburbs) are especially privileged sites for considering the current renegotiations of citizenship'. In today's world, smart cities push us to rethink the relationship between the city as a spatial political formation and the citizen as a dweller (Calzada 2020). Political manifestos such as the *Declaration of Cities Coalition for Digital Rights* (2019) and the *Manifesto in Favour of Technological Sovereignty and Digital Rights for Cities* (2019), which problematise top-down and corporate re-organising and re-imagining of the space, offer a transparent and participatory vision for smart cities. In smart cities, political acts should not only be mediated through digital technologies but should also be a direct form of participation as the use of space and technology cross over. There is also the question of how digital technologies are used by governments and private enterprises to surveil, sort, control and manipulate citizens and non-citizens, which is yet another dimension to consider while thinking about the extent to which digital technologies penetrate and reshape existing structures and infrastructures.

Eubanks's (2018) timely analysis of the algorithmic classification of the poor and resource distribution that draws on technological profiling in the USA demonstrates how online rights are likely to cross over with offline inequalities as digital technologies become infrastructures of administrative and governmental operations. Isin and Ruppert (2020: 179) point out how we currently witness digital acts that re-signify political subjects, such as migrants and refugees, enabling them to perform as yet-to-be citizens. They reference recent work on how refugees in Europe are framed as pedagogical yet disciplinary subjects by communication infrastructures and discourses (Chouliaraki and Georgiou 2017, 2022; Leurs 2017; Tazzioli 2018; Stavinoha 2019; Zaborowski and Georgiou 2019). Digital technologies employed at borders not only operate as a way of surveilling, sorting and controlling refugees, but also serve to distinguish 'us' from 'them', 'members' from 'strangers' and 'citizens' from 'non-citizens'. In a similar vein, Marino (2021: 64) argues that this double-faced framing has further implications for not only defining who refugees are but also what constitutes European citizenship as a territorial and cultural identity. Despite being a global trend, the digital surveillance and sorting of citizens and non-citizens take place in national settings which are often bound by national or supranational legal frameworks. Such examples demonstrate that despite transcending places of connection and engagement, the digital shapes and is shaped by spatial situatedness.

Transversal citizenship enables us to take the spatial situatedness of political subjects into account by focusing on the local, regional, national and transnational and to examine how different levels of situatedness enable or disable citizenship acts (for example, how transnational migration facilitates diaspora communities' citizenship acts, how local citizenship acts are mediated through social media and embedded in national discourses, how national contexts enable regional mobilities and supranational citizenship acts, and so on). It offers a useful framework for addressing the complexities of space in two ways. First, transversal citizenship acknowledges the limits and opportunities brought by the spatial situatedness of citizens as political subjects. Secondly, transversal citizenship transgresses local and national boundaries, whether enacted online or not; however, this does not mean that citizenship acts are ubiquitous and that all these spatial levels collapse as a result. On the contrary, different spatial levels are at play to various degrees in the making of transversal citizenship. For instance, local demands can initiate transnational citizenship acts, and unrecognition or oppression in a national context can lead to supranational legal citizenship acts. In relation to this point, transversal citizenship considers the digital as part of a broader media environment where citizen subjects use different forms of media, while mediating their citizenship acts.

The relationship between online and offline often assumes a distinction between digital spaces/presence and physical spaces/presence. For instance, Gajjala (2019) distinguishes 'digital streets' from streets in digital activism, acknowledging that political practice needs to take place in both of these spaces. Offline encompasses a broad range of activities, practices and spaces, considering the messiness of everyday life and social structures in the making through everyday practices. Traditional media is often lost within the broad category of 'offline' as a declining form and technology. Transversal citizenship is a conceptual invitation to think about traditional and digital media as co-existing and as a critique of the linear progressive historiography of media, as encapsulated by the expression 'from analogue to digital', which can be regarded as an implicit form of technological determinism that celebrates or overestimates emerging technologies.

This study questions the assumptions about the separation of digital media from the broader media environment and seeks to consider digital media and communications as relational in terms of their relationship to (and uses of) other media and technologies. Significantly, the Alevi case demonstrates a continuum between satellite television and online streaming in terms of the state's nuanced attitudes towards different Alevi media outlets, as Chapter 7 will demonstrate. This also requires identifying similarities between regulation, control and censorship online and on air, rather than simply celebrating the 'digital breakthrough'. Traditional and digital media co-exist for marginalised communities, individuals and relatively older age groups, as demonstrated by studies on digital divides and inequalities (Helsper 2012, 2021; Van Dijk 2020). Such groups draw on different forms of media, depending on their affordances, and might strategise switching between them. In that sense, transversal citizenship proposes a decolonial framework, critically distancing itself from perspectives which over-estimate the digital take-over as applying in the same way to different communities. The following section discusses the relevance of the decolonial perspective for transversal citizenship.

Decolonial Media Studies: Focusing on the Citizenship Acts of Marginalised Communities

As discussed in the previous section, cultural citizenship in its varying definitions attempts to tackle questions of recognition, participation and cultural identity (Rosaldo 1994, 1997; Stevenson 1997, 2003, 2010; Delanty 2002, 2003; Hintz *et al.* 2019; Isin and Ruppert 2020). Although it is not identified as such, decoloniality has been a core strand that has nurtured the concept. At a very early point in the history of the concept, Rosaldo (1994) linked decolonising to debates about the curriculum at Stanford University in the USA and called for a revised education curriculum that recognised cultural differences and embedded them in teaching. Cultural citizenship can be considered an attempt to address the complexities of multi-ethnic and multicultural encounters and is deeply embedded in the histories and effects of colonialism and imperialism. It might be fair to say that, as a concept, cultural citizenship has developed as a response to the problems arising from Europe's racist and colonial past and the subsequent entangled cultural encounters. As Turner (1993: 12) demonstrates: 'the growth of citizenship in the West depended upon the legacy of the Abrahamic religions which contained values relating to the person, universal social membership and a particular view of history as requiring or involving social change' and is situated within histories of colonialism.

Decoloniality, as part of the citizenship studies agenda, remains an 'unfinished project' (Isin 2012), one which also has more specific implications for cultural citizenship. Isin (2002: 117) considers orientalism as the first fundamental characteristic of the 'Western' conception of citizenship, 'a way of dividing the world into essentially two "civilizational" blocs, one having rationalized and hence modernised, the other remained "irrational", religious and traditional'. His examination of Weber's work also identifies synoecism, 'a way of seeing the polity as embodying spatial and political unification', as the second fundamental characteristic which defines citizenship. Lee (2014) distinguishes between exogenous and endogenous critiques of coloniality carried in the conceptual backdrop to citizenship. The exogenous critique considers colonial aspirations and development as outside of citizenship; therefore, the decolonial version of global citizenship is a project that can be realised. The endogenous critique, however:

> aims to decolonize global citizenship through a different route: it views colonial and capitalist relations of power as being tangled with, or embedded within, citizenship itself; therefore, the discourse of global citizenship is already implicated in the hegemonic system and cannot be disentangled or transcended from such power configurations. (79)

Nevertheless, this contrasting approach can be usefully combined by always having the exogenous vision at heart, 'while acknowledging such vision can only be realized endogenously in democratic politics, and can never be fully completed' (84). Therefore, 'the political project of decolonizing global citizenship must take the radical impossibility of a fully achieved decolonization as its precondition' (77). Isin (2012) also describes decolonising as ongoing and problematises the orientalist assumption that citizenship is a European invention. He emphasises that in order to reconceptualise citizenship as a new political subject, we need to undo, uncover and reinvent citizenship. This is similar to Mignolo's (2007, 2021) proposal of delinking from the totality of Western epistemology, which in underpinned by coloniality, in order to build other epistemologies. Transversal citizenship is such an attempt at delinking, undoing, uncovering and reinventing citizenship by focusing on minority and marginalised positions. Delinking or undoing citizenship is to unpack the colonial histories and epistemologies that shape the conceptualisations of citizenship, while uncovering citizenship is about revealing the discourses which deem certain political acts and rights claims as disqualifying for citizenship. Reinventing 'requires analysis of how people enact citizenship through "acts" of citizenship that invent new ways of becoming political subjects as citizens' (Isin 2012: 567).

Remarkably, the literature on cultural citizenship has flourished within a plethora of interdisciplinary approaches that includes the political sciences, history, cultural anthropology and media studies, all of which have contributed towards the decolonial perspective (see Santo 2004; Ginsburg 2005; Cupples and Glynn 2013; Wang 2013; Apter 2016; König 2016; Lopez 2016; Şanlı 2016. These studies demonstrate that cultural citizenship is performative and emerges within a complex sphere consisting of networks, festivals, celebrations, gatherings, and media production and consumption. For instance, in an examination of the way Black and African festivals create a discursive space for what it means to be Black, Apter (2016: 313) argues that the 'political stakes of black cultural citizenship were neither trivial nor ephemeral, but emerged within a transnational field of symbolic capital accumulation'. This field encompasses various actors and movements, including Black Panthers in Algeria, liberation movements in Africa and the socialist regimes of the 1970s, in 'establishing transnational solidarity between the racially disenfranchised and dispossessed' (322). In a similar vein, Ginsburg (2005: 81) examines indigenous film-making in Australia as a cultural citizenship practice and emphasises that it has emerged as a result of a 'two-decade long effort on the part of indigenous media activists to reverse that erasure of Aboriginal subjects in public life and making their representations known and visible to a global audience through festivals'. Wang's (2013) research examines how the category of cultural citizenship has shaped cultural policy in Taiwan as a result of indigenous movements, such as those of the Hakkas, who from the late 1990s onwards established a civic consciousness and the practice of multicultural rights. As these examples indicate, cultural citizenship is often shaped by bottom-up movements of marginalised and oppressed groups, whose rights claims are re-appropriated by governments eventually in order to 'deal with' cultural and ethnic diversity.

In this study, I wish to take a different approach than that taken in the studies discussed in this section (Santo 2004; Ginsburg 2005; Cupples and Glynn 2013; Wang 2013; Apter 2016; König 2016; Lopez 2016; Şanlı 2016) and to contribute to the ongoing decoloniality 'project' by developing the concept of transversal citizenship through my research on Alevis. Contrary to usual practice, I wish to reverse the process by learning from the knowledge produced about and by Alevis in order to make sense of citizenship, rather than primarily drawing on the citizenship literature in order to understand Alevis. With this proposal, my aim is to unpack the concept through the experiences of a marginalised community and demonstrate the relevance of the concept despite its possible limitations. Another aim of such an approach is the endeavour towards decolonial media studies not only by focusing on a marginalised community but also by prioritising the research produced by, on and with them as an epistemological and 'political' choice. Therefore, here more briefly, but in Chapter 3 in detail, I shall draw on the Alevi studies literature in order to approach citizenship from a decolonial perspective and critically re-utilise it for an understanding of the contemporary Alevi community. This approach also presents a challenge to the coloniality of media studies. Hence, for this purpose, I shall benefit not only from the use of my own data to critically examine citizenship but also from the literature on Alevi studies.

This approach, however, also has its limitations because research on Alevis is not a unitary field but is diverse in its approach to Alevis and in relation to the social sciences and humanities in general. Also, the majority of research on Alevis does not engage with the agenda of decoloniality per se. On the contrary, there is a considerable body of work in Alevism studies which takes colonialist assumptions about the community for granted. The reason why I align this body of work with colonialism is because of its external anthropological gaze, which does not allow room for a variety of bottom-up self-definitions within Alevism, and its attempt to create a monovocal version of Alevism with reference to its main 'rival', (Sunni) Islam, as a way of eradicating differences and contradictions. Instead of framing the relationship between Islam and Alevism as relational, this colonising approach considers Alevism as a historically 'deviant' form of Islam. This perspective has been canonical and, although there are more recent exceptions, it still mainly defines what Alevi studies are as a field. Nevertheless, what we can learn from studies on Alevism, the transnational Alevi movement and Alevi citizenship has theoretical implications for transversal citizenship more broadly.

Meghji (2021: 96) says that decolonial sociology is a sociology of conversations, an idea inspired by the Zapatista motto 'walking while asking questions', used as a critique of the Western commitment to 'walking while preaching'. Following Meghji (2021: 127) and Bhambra's (2014) 'connected sociologies', my aim is to seek to build 'connections, and to look for already existing connections that we have already collectively erased'. I would like to initiate such a conversation in this book and search for links, relations and connections between different conceptions and appearances of citizenship. The work on Alevis by Yalçınkaya (1996, 2005, 2014, 2020) and Sökefeld (2008a) provides fruitful ground for such links, relations and connections. In his seminal work, Sökefeld (2008a) defines Alevi transnational social and cultural spaces as mutually constitutive and bi-directional, by which the Alevi movement in Germany is shaped with reference to both Turkish politics and the Alevi movement in Turkey. His study demonstrates that cultural rights claims take place within complex transnational networks, although the nation-state is addressed as the main guarantor of rights. These networks also determine how the state approaches and redefines its policies towards ethnic, religious and cultural minorities. In other words, transnational spaces not only define and shape cultural rights claims, but also impact on who is deemed appropriate by the state to make such claims on behalf of the community. Sökefeld's work on Alevism is helpful in understanding the role of transnational spaces in the making of Alevi cultural citizenship. Yalçınkaya's (1996, 2005, 2014, 2020) analysis of the relationship between Alevis and the state also help us to formulate the formal and legal aspects of transversal citizenship. He argues that Alevis have been subjected to ethnocide since the late 19th century as part of a political programme aimed at eliminating Alevism (if not Alevis themselves) as a cultural and ethno-religious identity. This perspective informs Chapter 7, where I explore how the state intervenes in cultural rights claims in a brutal but carefully measured manner, which also produces a disruption in the transnational social space.

In this book, I also open up a channel for a 'pluriversial' debate on citizenship, that is, 'a process of knowledge production that is open to epistemic diversity' (Mbembe 2016: 37), by drawing on these and other works on Alevism. This, according to Mbembe (2016: 37), is 'a process that does not necessarily abandon the notion of universal knowledge for humanity, but which embraces it via a horizontal strategy of openness to dialogue among different epistemic traditions'. As argued by Mbembe (2016), we need to create a 'less provincial and more open critical cosmopolitan pluriversalism – a task that involves the radical refounding of our ways of thinking and a transcendence of our disciplinary divisions' in order to pursue the task of decolonising the university. Hence, interdisciplinarity can be a strong ally by inviting in non-Western knowledge production from different disciplines and epistemic differences.

We need pluriversality in media studies for several reasons. First, it is needed to tackle the over-emphasis upon histories and uses of media in the Global North at the expense of considering the complex and various audience experiences in the Global South. Dutta (2020: 229) argues that whiteness sets up 'normative values of white culture as universal (in this case, the white academic structure Communication Studies), while simultaneously marking the articulations from elsewhere/peripheries as the outside of Communication'. Currently, this is further emphasised by the ubiquity of digital media and the role of super-platforms in setting the scene, which frames audience experiences and engagement with digital media as a 'unifying' experience for audiences located in different geographies. As such, Lobato's (2019) work on Netflix, which situates online streaming studies in relation to television studies, can be seen as a promising exception to such an approach. Secondly, digital divides are often underestimated or overlooked, instead of being taken into account as an overarching presence through which digital media ownership, content creation and user experience are defined. I argue that a key tenet of decolonial media studies is the need to recognise digital divides as a basis upon which the co-existence of traditional and digital media for the communities of the Global South can be taken into account. This is one of the key tasks of this book in examining transversal citizenship in the digital era. Thirdly, examining the media practices of marginalised and oppressed communities requires a dialogue with emic perspectives in order to avoid the reproduction of the colonialist framework. In other words, etic perspectives can only emerge and be developed in dialogue with emic perspectives if they are to distance themselves from the authoritative and oppressive external gaze of the colonial. This understanding is pursued throughout this book. Instead of looking into the case of Alevi television solely through the lens of media studies, which are predominantly produced in the Global North, I shall draw on the emergent body of work on Alevis in Turkey and abroad to examine and theorise the case of Alevi transversal citizenship. By doing so, I hope that this book will contribute to the decoloniality project, with a particular focus on transversal citizenship.

3

Transnational Alevi Politics and Alevi Citizenship

Unlike the majority of researchers on Alevism, Koçan and Öncü (2004) situate the Alevi movement within debates on citizenship rather than debates on the rise of identity politics. They argue that 'what Alevis seek is a revised citizenship model in terms of a system of rights assuring the condition of neutrality among culturally diverse individuals' (464). This is in response to the Turkish model of 'secular' citizenship, which has been culturally exclusionary (472). Özmen (2011) also considers Alevi rights claims as a claim to multicultural citizenship and suggests that constitutional change would secure rights and freedoms for all segments of society in a globalised world. Unfortunately, this conceptual insight into Alevi citizenship has not been explored in further research. Here I would like to pursue this and situate Alevi political subjectivity within theories of citizenship. Therefore, this chapter focuses on Alevi cultural citizenship and how transnational Alevi politics has carved out spaces for citizenship to emerge. First, I look at how Alevis have been excluded from Turkish citizenship and how this has eventually engendered the emergence of Alevi citizenship. I then define the key dynamics of transnational Alevi politics, which have expanded the scope and scale of Alevi citizenship, including transnational and regional dynamics. In the final section, I demonstrate how citizenship enactment theory helps us to see the Alevi movement in a light different from that suggested in other studies on Alevism. Drawing on Isin's (2008, 2009, 2012, 2013) theory of enacting citizenship, I focus on Alevi citizenship acts and situate them within the framework of events, sites and scales. Therefore, this chapter addresses Alevi cultural citizenship in non-media realms, before focusing on media and transversal citizenship.

Alevis as 'Aliens' of the Nation

In this section, I consider the two facets of Alevi citizenship – as a top-down status defined by membership of the nation-state, and as a bottom-up movement claimed by the community. Here I argue that Turkish citizenship is based on the exclusion of Alevi identity, while that exclusion has paradoxically paved the way for the birth of Alevi citizenship. Thus, the casting of Alevis as 'aliens' (Isin and Wood 2002; Isin 2009) or 'heretics'[1] (Ateş 2011) from the perspective of Turkish citizenship has led them to become claimants to an Alevi citizenship. In this section, I shall critically engage with research that focuses on how Turkish nationalism defines citizenship and the Alevis' place within it. Finally, I shall look at how Alevis make rights claims that create the Alevi political subject and hence the Alevi citizen.

There are two seminal studies that examine how Alevis are situated within discourses of Turkish nationalism (Ateş 2011; Dressler 2013). Ateş's (2011) work focuses primarily on the official nationalism of the early Republican period (1923–50), whereas Dressler (2013) refers to the late 19th-century Ottoman era, when Alevis began to 'enter the gaze of nationalists'. While these studies look at how Alevis are seen by the state and from the point of view of hegemonic Turkish nationalisms, studies investigating Alevi citizenship from a bottom-up approach are limited (Koçan and Öncü 2004; Özmen 2011). There might be several reasons for this. First of all, the discriminatory approach towards Alevis has also infiltrated academic research, where studying Alevis has not been given much value. One can also argue that academic research on ethnic or religious minorities has always been a risky route to take in Turkey. The second reason is how in Turkey citizenship is defined with reference to ethnic and religious categories. Historically, the two significant 'other' categories in relation to Turkish national identity, the Kurds and Armenians, could be clearly identified as 'ethnic' categories, whereas it was difficult to categorise Alevis due to their multi-ethnicity (Turks, Kurds) and Alevism's different associations with Islam as a sect, a syncretic religion, a heterodox version of Islam or as 'real Islam'. Furthermore, the ethno-religious character of Alevism, paradoxically, makes it difficult to situate Alevis as a whole, including Kurdish Alevis, within or against Turkish nationalism. All these reasons have rendered Alevis invisible in their attempts at defining themselves as citizens. There has also been a strong stream in Alevism studies that situates Alevi movements within identity politics (see Bruinessen 2016; Massicard 2017; for a combined approach of identity politics and citizenship, see Ertan 2017).

According to Açıkel and Ateş (2011) and Ateş (2011), Turkish nationalism has an ambivalent relationship with Alevism. Ateş distinguishes between religious and secular nationalisms, which, according to Ateş, can be considered hegemonic. Both hegemonic forms of nationalism regard Alevis as heirs of an authentic culture of Turks originating in Asia, and thus Alevism is seen as an 'authentic' ethnic component of national identity.

---

[1] Yıldırım (2017b: 43) says that 'heretic' (*mülhid*) has been used to address Kızılbaş/Alevi communities as outsiders of the Islamic circle for more than four hundred years. They have been the only group who were not assigned any rights before the 19th century. See also Çakmak (2019).

But, at the same time, Alevis are deemed to be heretics who are difficult to situate within Islam due to the 'syncretic' character of their faith (Ateş 2011: 20-1). Akpınar (2016) and Çakmak (2019) demonstrate that the perception of Kızılbaş/Alevis[2] as heretics dates back to the Hamidian Era (1876-1909). They were regarded as a security risk to the Ottomans during this period since their ethno-religious diversity was perceived to be a rising threat to the unity of the Empire. Hence, attempts at systematic modernisation, which had begun during the Hamidian Era, marked Alevis as 'others' who had to be dealt with. Zırh (2008: 111) says that there was no place for Alevis in the Ottoman millet[3] system as 'the Kızılbaş Alevis occupied an inferior place to non-Muslim groups such as Christians and Jews simply because they refrained from fully acknowledging the authority of the state's official orthodox Sunni Islamic theology' (Açıkel and Ateş 2011: 727). Such a view continued during the Republican era (1923-50). Açıkel and Ateş (2005, 2011) draw attention to the parallels between nationalist discourses on Kurds and Alevis. While the Turkish nationalism of the Republican period and later post-1980 coup defined Kurds as backward 'mountain Turks' who would be civilised through Republican policies of Turkification, Açıkel and Ateş say that a similar view was evident in the designation of Alevis as 'mountain Muslims', although this term was never employed officially.

According to Dressler (2013), in romanticised accounts of Turkish nationalism, the Islamisation of the Turks is identified as the historical point when the nomad communities of Turks settled in Anatolia in the 11th century and converted to Islam. From this perspective, Alevis represent nomad communities (Turcomans) who preserved their Turkish origins and integrated shamanism into Islamic tenets. Dressler (2013) echoes Ateş's analysis of Turkish nationalism and its interplay between 'difference' and 'sameness' in the way it frames Alevis as either heretics or authentic Turks.[4] He demonstrates that the Turkification of Alevis began in the period of the Young Turks (1908-18) as a way of gaining the loyalty of the Kızılbaş/Alevi tribes. However, Dressler (2015) adopts a critical approach to the term 'Alevi' as a homogenising concept and argues that the 'modern concept of Alevism is rather new, barely a hundred years old, [and was] formed in the context of the Turkish nation-building process and developed within a semantic framework akin to that of the nation' (15). However, Kehl-Bodrogi (2012) and Çakmak (2019) argue that the term 'Alevi' has been used since the 16th century by the Kızılbaş themselves.

---

[2] Kızılbaş literally means red-headed and refers to the 15th century red headwear that Alevis used to wear in order to distinguish themselves from non-Alevis. Kızılbaş is still widely used to as an umbrella term to address Alevis.
[3] The system in the Ottoman Empire which defined people according to their religious affiliation. While Muslims were first-class citizens, other religious groups such as Jews and Christian were organised into separate millets. Poulton (1997) says that the origin of the millet system remains uncertain.
[4] However, Dressler's analysis also differs from Ateş's in the critical distance he adopts towards binary concepts such as 'orthodoxy' and 'heterodoxy' that associates Alevism with the latter.

Dressler (2013: 231) argues that Markussen's (2012) study of the Alevi Centre in Istanbul demonstrates that Alevis draw on an etic mainstream historiographical discourse concerning Alevism by adopting terms such as shamanism, heterodoxy and syncretism, albeit with positive connotations. However, this perspective implicitly assumes an 'authentic' identity formation that existed prior to the emergence of the nation-state, which was then submerged by the overwhelming power of the state apparatus. It makes more sense to acknowledge a dynamic relationship between state discourses on Alevis and their self-definitions. Such a perspective also comes with a risk of undermining emic definitions of Alevism, barely leaving room for Alevi agency in defining the boundaries of the broader imagined Alevi community. It is also important to take into account the existence for hundreds of years of the relationships established between Alevi *ocak*s across Anatolia and the Balkans, which are still part of the Alevi collective memory and practices (see Karakaya-Stump 2015; Yıldırım 2017b, 2019). For instance, the use of the term Kızılbaş, with its negative connotations of heresy, to describe Alevis was used long before the 19th century (Yıldırım 2017b), although Alevis have more recently reclaimed this term and rejected its negative associations. Also, Çakmak's (2019) study demonstrates that the state's policies on Alevis became more systematic and comprehensive during the Hamidian Era (1876–1909).

Massicard (2017) argues that Alevism was partially accepted as a culture but excluded as a religion during the nation-building process. It is important to emphasise that in the early years of the Republic, Alevis were not excluded from the nation-building process per se as Kemalists actively sought their support. However, in this process there was no room for Alevi political subjectivity within Turkish citizenship, as the latter aimed to exclude any religious identity other than Sunni Islam. Kemalists adopted a utilitarian approach to their relationship with Alevis. They formulated a definition of Turkish citizenship premised on a necessary link between Islam and Turkishness, while also controlling religious practice through the Diyanet İşleri Başkanlığı (the Directorate of Religious Affairs, DRA),[5] which has been criticised by Alevis for representing only Sunnis and for not recognising Alevism as a religion, despite also being sponsored through Alevi taxes. This view was clearly stated when, in 1994, the head of the Diyanet said: 'Alevism is not a religion. Nor is it a sect of Islam. Alevism is a culture complete with its own folklore' (*Turkish Daily News*, 7 January 1994) (Şahin 2005: 481). Nearly a decade later, in 2003, Prime Minister Tayyip Erdoğan, when visiting Berlin, gave the following reply to the demand, raised by the General Secretary of the Germany Alevi Federation, that Alevi places of worship (*cemevis*) should have equal legal status with Muslim mosques: 'One is a house of prayer, the other is a culture house' (Sökefeld 2008b: 292). Erdoğan expressed a similar opinion in

---

[5] For a detailed discussion on the Diyanet's approach to Alevism, see Lord (2018).

2013, recalling a common nationalist trope that Alevis are really a type of Muslim, a comment which was widely criticised by Alevis, when he said: 'Doesn't Alevism love His Holiness Ali? Aren't Alevis Muslims? Sunnis are Muslims too. If Alevism is to love Ali, I am a proper Alevi' (*Milliyet*, 17 July 2013).

As indicated by these statements, and as argued by Ateş (2011), the state holds an ambiguous position towards Alevis, one which oscillates between regarding it as a 'culture' and as a 'religion'. In this formulation, Alevism can be regarded as a culture in its own right but as a religion can only be viewed as part of Islam. Şahin (2005) and Massicard (2017) point out that Alevi organisations and events were financially supported by the Ministry of Culture during the 1990s, even though the governments of the time did not officially recognise Alevis. Such ambiguity is also demonstrated when looking at the role of the Diyanet. At the same time as casting Alevism as a cultural phenomenon, until 2009 the state also regulated its relationship with Alevis through the Diyanet, after which the Alevi Opening (see Soner and Toktaş, 2011; Ecevitoğlu and Yalçınkaya, 2013; Özkul, 2015) created a temporary change in attitudes. Lord (2018: 32) argues that 'the Diyanet has played a crucial role in providing a more favourable environment for Islamist mobilisation and has delimited the nation's boundaries along religious lines through its engagement with and rejection of Alevism'. In other words, the exclusion of Alevis has also be used in the battle to define what the Turkish nation and Turkish citizenship are and are not since 'Alevis at least for two decades [have] systematically challenged limits of secularism and citizenship in Turkey' (Boyraz 2019: 768).

In 2009 the government of the JDP launched a series of workshops with a number of Alevi leaders, intellectuals and representatives from different organisations, along with researchers, journalists, theologians and non-governmental organisations, which became known as the Alevi Opening (Özkul 2015). Even though a similar attempt was planned by the state in 1961, it was not realised until the JDP's initiative (Ata 2007; Yalçınkaya 2020). The Alevi Opening had the aim of resolving ongoing tensions with Alevis and addressing Alevi rights claims. This can be considered part of the JDP's broader move to create a consensus for the 2011 referendum, which proposed a number of changes to the Turkish constitution. Bardakçı *et al.* (2017: 108) emphasise that the Alevi struggle for recognition, through protests, demonstrations, court cases and lobbying of the EU, along with the European Commission's progress reports, which identified discrimination against Alevis as a problem for Turkey's European Union membership process, played a significant role in the JDP's initiative. Notably, the Alevi Opening was the first serious move in which members of the Alevi community were invited to the discussion table with the government, which therefore meant a formal acknowledgement of 'the Alevi citizen' as an addressee. Soner and Toktaş (2011: 429) see the Opening as a turning point in the rapprochement between the government and Alevis, even though Alevis remained suspicious and critical of the government. During the workshops,

> [t]he Alevi representatives, despite the differences of these institutions in their political views and opinions on Alevism, agreed on the following matters as their core demands: giving legal status to cemevis, the abolition of mandatory religious education classes, turning the Madımak Hotel into a museum, stopping the mandatory construction of mosques in Alevi villages and sending away the appointed imams, and finally leaving the places of Alevi faith to Alevi institutions (Alevi çalıştayları önraporu 2010). (Akdemir 2015: 66)

Akdemir (2015: 64) argues that this communication with Alevis gradually broke down because the government tried to impose its own definitions and policies concerning Alevism. Hence, although it was the first official move to include Alevis as a party for 'resolving the Alevi issue', the workshops did not in the end result in any rights gains. In fact, the Alevi Opening ended with the government re-addressing Alevis as the cause of the problem, as a heterogenous and uncompromising party that had not been able to produce a unified position. Alevis were publicly portrayed as a group of people who refused to negotiate (Akdemir 2015: 68) and the religious, political and ethnic diversity of the community was problematised. Previously, the government had already used the diversity of the community, the multiplicity of Alevi organisations and the disagreements within organisations as to what Alevism constituted as an excuse not to negotiate with them on the basis of 'being unable to find an addressee which represents Alevis as a whole'. An alternative view to the government's formal concluding report on the negotiations with Alevis was prepared by the Hacı Bektaş-ı Veli Anatolian Culture Foundation, which produced a detailed and critical account of the workshops in which they argued that the state had imposed its own definition of Alevism upon Alevis (Ecevitoğlu and Yalçınkaya 2013). In the end, despite the Alevi Opening, under the JDP administration Alevi disenfranchisement only deepened through their top-down Islamisation, intensified sectarianism and use of a divisive discourse (Karakaya-Stump 2018).

Transnational Alevi Politics

Alevi political subjectivity, which emerges through a complex set of relations, acts and connections, is often examined through its relationship with the state (Bozkurt 1998; Jongerden 2003; Kehl-Bodrogi 2003; Keiser 2003; Koçan and Öncü 2004; Poyraz 2005; Öktem 2008; Göner 2017b; Karakaya-Stump 2018; Tekdemir 2018; Boyraz 2019) and Alevi membership and support for leftist organisations in Turkey (Sinclair-Webb 2003; Erman and Göker 2006; Küçük 2007; Ertan 2019; Yalçınkaya and Karaçalı 2020). Here I would like to suggest a different approach from these two perspectives and consider Alevi politics as a form of cultural citizenship. This is because Alevism is not a homogeneous identity but consists of a variety of interpretations, as discussed in Chapter 1. In addition, Alevi politics often does not limit itself to identity politics but includes broader claims for equality and diversity. These claims, which since the 1960s have crystallised in their demand for a new constitution, cannot simply be explained with reference to the Alevi inclination towards the politics of the left; rather, it is a form of citizenship which juxtaposes the notions of 'rights for Alevis' with 'rights for "others"'. In order to understand how the Alevi political subject emerges in the form of citizenship, we first need to unpack the dynamics of transnationalism.

There are two key moments which define the emergence of the transnational Alevi movement (Sökefeld 2008a; Massicard 2017): the establishment of the Hamburg Alevi Culture Group in Germany, soon followed by the Alevi Culture Week; and the Madımak massacre in Turkey, which was followed by another massacre in the Gazi neighbourhood of Istanbul. According to Sökefeld (2008a: 220–8), the Alevi Culture Group operated as a 'germ cell' of transnational networking and went on to produce the Alevi Declaration in 1989, something that has been influential in shaping Alevi intellectual thinking and politics both in Germany and Turkey. The Alevi Declaration publicly claimed the right to recognition in Turkey and Germany and was followed by other detailed publications written and distributed in Turkey. The Alevi Culture Group then organised the Alevi Culture Week, which was attended by numerous Alevi musicians and intellectuals from Turkey, so establishing an ongoing transnational practice (Sökefeld 2008a). But, arguably, Alevi transnational space emerged long before the late 1980s when Alevi migrants in Germany worked closely with the first political party established by Alevis in 1960s (Ata 2007). Undoubtedly, the connectedness and scale of this early transnational space was far more restricted than the enthusiasm and impact facilitated by the Alevi Culture Week and the Declaration of 1989.

Collective memories of persecution have been highly formative in the development of Alevi identity (Poyraz 2013; Ertan 2017; Çavdar 2020; Temel 2021); they are deeply enmeshed within Alevi myths and history, going back to the Kerbala massacre of 680 and the death of Hüseyin,[6] one of the twelve imams in Alevism, from whom the *ocak*s are believed to be descended (Kehl-Bodrogi 2008; Göner 2017b; Dressler 2021). The massacres during the Ottoman period (Kehl-Bodrogi 2017; Yıldırım 2017b), the Koçgiri and Dersim massacres of the pre- and early Republican period (Keiser 2003), the more recent Ortaca (1966), Sivas (1978), Kahramanmaraş (1978) and Çorum (1980) attacks (Jongerden 2003),

---

[6] According to Kehl-Bodrogi (2008: 44–5), 'the event of Kerbela is of crucial importance for Alevism: its members see in their allegiance to "the people of the house" (*ehl-i beyt*) the birth of their community. For them Kerbela became an origin myth. Kerbela is the place where, in A.D. 680, in the Islamic month of Muharrem, Ali's son Hüseyin, together with his family members and followers, were slaughtered by the soldiers of the Caliph Yezid in an unequal battle fought for the Caliphate. Traditionally the anniversary of the tragedy was commemorated with ten to twelve days of mourning (*matem*), consisting of fasting, abstaining from shaving, washing, changing one's clothes, sexual intercourse, and the like. In memory of the agony of thirst that Hüseyin and his family suffered in the desert of Kerbela, during the mourning period the Alevis in particular refrained from drinking water.' Also see Solieau (2017).

and the persecution and large-scale imprisonment of Alevis following the 1980 military coup (Sökefeld 2008b) have created a collective memory around violence and annihilation which culminated in a public outcry after the Madımak massacre of 1993. The collective memory of massacres has created a sense of continuity in Alevi history and has played a significant role in politicising Alevis (Ertan 2017: 171).

In this regard, the Madımak massacre was decisive in the emergence of an organised Alevi movement at the national and transnational level. Alevis from the urban neighbourhoods of Istanbul, Ankara and other cities had gathered at the Pir Sultan Abdal Festival in Sivas in 1993. The Madımak Hotel, where the festival attendees were staying, was set ablaze by a large mob shouting Islamist slogans, while the police and gendarmerie looked on (Bruinessen 2016). The massacre resulted in thirty-seven deaths, including of Alevi community members, Alevi and non-Alevi artists and intellectuals, two of the hotel workers and two of the attackers, while more than fifty people were severely injured. Two years later, in the Alevi neighbourhood of Gazi in Istanbul, a violent incident took place in a coffeehouse which resulted in police shootings that targeted members of the Alevi community (Vorhoff 1998; Jongerden 2003; Bruinessen 2016). Within a few days, nineteen people were dead and many injured, and a member of the community, Hasan Ocak, disappeared while in police custody – his dead body was later found in a village.[7] Including those who also died after protests in other cities following the Gazi massacre, a total of thirty people were killed (White 1997, cited in Jongerden 2003: 86). Sökefeld (2008a: 222) argues that although the Madımak and Gazi massacres were local events, they can be regarded as transnational because they facilitated the spaces and means for Alevi collective memory to emerge through the number of commemorative events inside and outside of Turkey that followed with invited speakers from Turkey. For instance, 100,000 people attended the funeral of the Madımak victims in Istanbul and 50,000 attended protests in Cologne (Massicard 2017: 45). This transnational impact is still alive in the UK even more than two decades later. At the Madımak commemoration that I attended at the Sivas Massacre monument in the park at Stoke Newington Common in London in 2018, a father who had lost his children in the massacre was invited to speak at the event about his loss and the gravity of the massacre for the Alevi community.

Sökefeld (2004: 138) notes that the first Alevi organisation was established in Munich in 1973–4, along with a branch in Hamburg following the Maraş massacre of 1978, where more than 100 Alevis were lynched by fascists and locals.

---

[7] Hasan Ocak was a young teacher of Dersim origin who was taken into custody after the Gazi Mahallesi incidents and was murdered during his custody in 1995. His dead body was found in a potter's field in Beykoz, Istanbul. Ocak's mother, Emine Ocak, is one of the Saturday Mothers – more recently called Saturday People – who gather in Taksim in Istanbul every Saturday to protest against the murder or forced disappearance of their relatives by the state.

In a similar vein, the Madımak massacre led to new organisations in Germany during the 1990s, which then mushroomed across Europe in countries to which Alevis had migrated. Many of these organisations gathered under the umbrella of countrywide federations and the European Confederation, with the Alevi Federation Germany being the most influential in defining transnational Alevi politics (see Coşan-Eke 2014, 2017, 2021). On this point Coşan-Eke (2017: 153) notes that:

> the main binding feature of all Alevi organizations in Europe remains their place of origin, the shared history related to this, and fundamental principles of Alevism which they all share. Yet Alevis have developed with multiple identities rather than a single national identity, related to just one country.

Many researchers on Alevism now agree that Alevi politics takes place on a transnational scale and is one of the key forces that shapes Alevi politics in Turkey (see Sökefeld 2008a; Coşan-Eke 2014, 2017; Issa and Atbaş 2017; Karagöz 2017; Massicard 2017; Uçar 2017). Transnationalism in the case of Alevis does not simply refer to bonds and connections between 'sending' and 'receiving' countries, but is a multi-country connection. This growing form of transnationalism is evidenced by the European Alevi Unions Confederation, an umbrella organisation for Alevi Federations based in different European countries, and Alevi television stations, which produce programmes depicting the lives of Alevis in different countries.

One can distinguish several underlying dynamics of Alevi transnational politics. The first dynamic is Europeanism, European identity and Turkey's process to become a member of the European Union, which have influenced the legal, political and identity dynamics of Alevism (Hurd 2014; Çalışkan 2020). The second dynamic consists of the different actors and movements within politics in Turkey, where 'the growth of political Islam, and the struggle of the Kurds, gave an impulse to turn towards Alevi identity' (Sökefeld 2008a: 221). This view is also shared by Çamuroğlu (2008), Massicard (2017) and Ertan (2017), who draw attention to how the escalation of identity politics in Turkey and abroad has also given impetus to the development of the Alevi movement. The third dynamic has two dimensions which stem from the community's own history and the way it characterises itself. First, some Alevis have strong symbolic and political associations with the programme of Kemalist modernisation that anchored Westernisation as essential to the development of Republican Turkey after the demise of the Ottoman Empire. Some Alevis shared this Kemalist vision, as indicated by their support for the secular young Republic and the fact that they have been regarded as its 'true guards' (Massicard 2017).[8] This support was based

---

[8] Keiser (2001: 109) notes that the Alevis' categorical support for Kemalism is a neo-Kemalist invention of 1960s which has been developed as a reaction against the Sunni revival of the 1950s and the support of Alevi youth for leftist politics.

on the hope that the Kemalist project would result in the secularisation of Turkey and would guarantee a socio-cultural space for Alevis free from violence and oppression. Secondly, along with this historic association with Kemalism, Alevi political discourses define the community as inherently modern and progressive, citing the fact that both women and men attend and participate in the *cem* and that education is a key priority for Alevis.

The fact that many Alevis have close connections to each other through family, kinship and birthplace across different countries in Europe also supports transnationalism, although no doubt this does not necessarily mean that it results in equal degrees of engagement and connectedness. However, to an ever-greater extent it has become possible for Alevis to 'expand' their imagination to encompass Alevis living in countries different from their own. That is why I argue that Alevi cultural citizenship is not only transnational but also transversal as it cannot be contained within national borders and legal orders and is also defined by a regional identity. I choose to draw on both the concepts of transnational and transversal as they identify different degrees of dispersion across national borders which may apply differently to various Alevi communities. For instance, Alevi citizenship in Germany is likely to be transversal due to the leading role played by the Alevi Federation Germany in establishing and shaping the European Confederation, whereas Alevi cultural citizenship in the Netherlands is likely to be more transnational because of the bi-national links between the Netherlands and Turkey. In a similar manner, the Cem Foundation in the Balkans is likely to have strong regional connections across Greece, Bulgaria, Macedonia and Albania, rather than two-way transnational connections with Turkey, making them more characteristically transversal. Hence, cultural citizenship may take different forms of the transnational and transversal depending on the population and the organisation and connectedness of the community. As Sökefeld (2008a: 227–8) rightly contends:

> mobilization for transnational concerns, the imagination of diaspora, and sentiments of community among 'ordinary' Alevis cannot simply be taken for granted but need permanent re-creation. Such sentiments and imaginations are constantly invoked and reconstituted in the discourse produced by the agents of the movement.

Nevertheless, we must bear in mind that what constitutes a transnational imaginary is not only discourses about shared identity but also social interactions and connectedness on a transnational scale. In other words, a transnational imaginary is not only culturally constructed but also socially generated, and 'transnational social and cultural spaces are intricately interwoven' (228).

It is argued that the growing sense of an Alevi community is a consequence of migration to the diaspora. For instance, Sökefeld says that the Alevi diaspora is able to accommodate the classical understandings of diaspora defined by loss and traumatic experience. He cites the strong sense of community among migrants such as Italian Americans in the USA and Turks in Germany and that such 'a sense of community is very strong among Alevis in Germany' (2008a: 219). This argument is valid but incomplete because Alevis in Turkey also have a strong sense of community and therefore whether a strong sense of community stems from migration per se is debatable. With this in mind, we need to carefully distinguish between migrant communities which are a majority in their home country and those which are a minority. Therefore, being a religious minority in Turkey, Alevis already had a strong sense of community and sense of belonging, yet the transnational social space created by Alevi migration to Western Europe has operated as a significant force in Alevi collective identity formation.

Alevi Citizenship Acts

This study does not limit itself only to passive forms of citizenship such as voting but focuses on active forms of citizenship, including acts such as campaigning, litigating and advocating for particular rights claims. Nevertheless, it is still useful to look at how Alevis are situated within the Turkish political party landscape and which parties they have supported since Alevi organisations in Turkey and abroad have shaped the so-called Alevi parties. Identifying a particular community with a political party and worldview has essentialist undertones; however, we know that some Alevis widely supported leftist organisations during the 1970s, which must have translated into votes for leftist parties in the following decades. Alevis have also been considered as the 'guards of secularism' in Turkey as some have widely supported the Kemalist modernisation project and its secularism. Massicard (2017) rightfully questions the assumption that Alevis have overwhelmingly supported the Kemalist Republican People's Party. Despite their high support for the party, it is difficult to associate Alevis with a particular Turkish political party. Massicard (2017) questions such an attempt and underlines the lack of data and limited research about the Alevi vote. In addition, Alevi religious leaders and individuals have been members of the Turkish Parliament across different parties since the early years of the Republic (Salman Yıkmış 2014). It should also be noted that Alevi politicians and later an Alevi businessman also established political parties that have not been widely embraced by Alevis themselves (Ata 2007; Ertan 2017).

The relatively liberal political climate following the 1960 constitution led the state to address the inclusion of Alevis. The president of the time, Cemal Gürsel, invited a group of Alevi leaders to meet him, which resulted in the establishment of the Hacı Bektaş associations and a proposal for the Diyanet to have representatives from the Alevi community. The proposal sparked a discourse of hate against Alevis in the Turkish press, which was followed in 1963 by the very first Alevi public manifesto written by a group of undergraduate students (Ata 2007: 49). Yalçınkaya (2020, 92) highlights this moment as the birth of the Alevi movement;

more importantly, he argues that the hate discourse circulated in the press later paved the way for the Ortaca massacre in 1966 (also see Ata 2007).[9] Ertan (2017) says that the Ortaca massacre reinforced the disappointment felt among Alevis and facilitated the emergence of the Unity Party, which was later re-branded as the TUP. The party has been associated with Alevism because it employed Alevi symbols such as the lion, a symbol of the Prophet Ali, and was established by Alevi individuals, members of parliament and *dede*s (Ata 2007; Ertan 2017). The TUP was not able to appeal to the majority of Alevi voters and has been accused of engaging in divisive politics on the basis of sectarianism and dividing the votes of the leftist parties (Ata 2007). Nevertheless, eight members of parliament from the TUP were elected in 1969 and two other members of parliament joined the party later. But the following elections were disastrous for the party as there were no elected members of parliament and the leading politicians were divided in terms of political differences and opportunistic political moves. The TUP eventually was wound up after the 1980 military coup.

Ertan (2017) says that cultural rights were a key theme for the Democratic Peace Movement, which evolved into an Alevi party, the Democratic Peace Movement Party (DPMP) in 1996. The DPMP was established by an Alevi businessman and was later supported by Alevi organisations in Turkey and Germany because some, such as the German Alevi Federation, found Alevi associations ineffective in getting their cause onto the broader public agenda and were looking for alternatives, such as an Alevi party (Ertan 2017). However, later Alevi organisations in Turkey ceased to support the DPMP and, furthermore, the movement did not receive much support from the broader community. In the meantime, the DPMP was accused of breaching political party law by including the demand to abolish the Diyanet in its programme. The case for closure paved the way for the establishment of the PP by the same politicians, community leaders and members. The DPMP had been critical of the cultural formation of the state, which based itself on Turkishness and Sunniness, and argued that the cultural rights of Kurdish, Alevi and non-Muslim groups must be constitutionally guaranteed (Ertan 2017: 251). The DPMP had proposed a 'constitutional citizenship' to address the cultural rights of different ethnic and religious communities (252). Strikingly, as with their predecessor, the TUP, both the DPMP and PP emerged following Alevi persecutions (the Madımak and Gazi massacres), but the PP's political life was much more short-lived. The party only received 0.25 per cent of the votes in the 1999 election and as a result of this failure dissolved itself, donating all of its financial and material assets to the ministry of education.

[9] Yalçınkaya (2020) provides a critical analysis of key Alevi manifestos publicised between 1963 and 2017, and argues that the state has shaped Alevi political agency throughout. He criticises the liberal framework adopted by Alevis in situating the state at the heart of their rights claims, which has resulted in negotiating the definition of Alevism imposed by the state and leaves no room for Alevi autonomy and various adaptations of it.

According to Ertan (2017: 233), the difficulty of mobilising Alevis around a single party stems from Alevi heterodoxy and the multiple meanings attributed to Alevism. However, as Ertan rightfully argues, Alevis do adhere to a secular political party system and think that Alevi demands can be implemented within other political parties' programmes. This is significant in understanding Alevi citizenship and challenges the widely held assumption that the Alevi movement is built around identity politics. Alevis demand their rights on the basis of equal citizenship and a secular society which does not require a particularistic political agenda that can be implemented by a single political party. Instead, Alevi political agency emerges as an active form of citizenship where rights claims do not necessitate a political party affiliation and can be contained within the Alevi movement.

At this point, I draw on Isin's (2008, 2009, 2012, 2013) framework of citizenship as enactment and examine the acts, sites and scale of Alevi cultural citizenship. According to Isin (2009: 383), '[c]itizenship is enacted through struggles for rights among various groups in their ongoing process of formation and reformation. Actors, scales and sites of citizenship emerge through these struggles.' Isin develops four methodological propositions that constitute acts: 1) events; 2) sites; 3) scales; and 4) durations. Unlike actions, which may be routine and ordinary, 'events are actions that become recognizable (visible, articulable) only when the site, scale and duration of these actions produce a rupture in the given order' (Isin 2012: 131). In other words, events have power to initiate a change, a rights claim for addressing an injustice. Events take place within sites both as physical and imaginary spaces based on their strategic value for advancing rights claims; thus, they can be temporal and temporary. For instance, in 1994 feminist activists in London campaigned for a memorial to the Madımak massacre to be erected in Hackney and occupied a space in front of Hackney Town Hall until their demands were met (Savaşal 2021). The tent they erected became the site for this event and defined this space as a site of struggle. Isin (2013: 25) contends that '[s]cales also stretch and permeate sites', enabling 'enactments across borders and boundaries'. Sites and scales are connected and sometimes overlap. In the case of the Madımak memorial, the scale of the event was local as it took place in a particular London borough to demand the placing of a monument in a local place. Nevertheless, despite its local siting, the demand concerned a transnational community and the remembrance of a massacre which took place outside the national borders of the UK. Finally, in relation to duration, Isin (2012: 135) says that the 'duration of the act cannot be reduced to the moment of performance'; the time required for its subsequent interpretation also constitutes duration. For instance, the duration of an act of litigation to exempt Alevi pupils from compulsory religious culture and morality lessons in Turkey would also include the aftermath of the court decision, how it is implemented by the ministry of education and how parents respond to it by opting their children in or out of the lessons. Similarly, the duration of the

Transnational Alevi Politics and Alevi Citizenship

Alevi Cultural Citizenship		
Event	**Site**	**Scale**
Litigation	Courts	Local (villages, towns)
Media activism	Media	National/transnational (Turkey, Germany, UK, etc.)
Commemorations	Streets, conference rooms, festivals	
Demonstrations		Regional (Western Europe, Balkans)
		Transversal

Table 1 Alevi Cultural Citizenship

Alevi Festival in London is not solely confined to the days of the event; rather, it stretches beyond to include the sustained transnational political connections which are carried beyond the site (see Salman 2020). Drawing on Isin's theory of citizenship as enactment, Table 1 identifies events, sites and scales of Alevi cultural citizenship.

Alevi rights claims in Turkey do not constitute a 'coherent' list of demands because of the different perspectives concerning what Alevism is and the various political agendas and priorities that different Alevi organisations adopt. This fact is often seen as a problem by Alevi organisations, members of the community and even Alevism researchers (see Massicard 2017). Naturally, Alevis do not constitute a homogeneous body, no more than any other ethno-religious group, and their understanding of Alevism differs depending on various factors, such as ethnicity, socio-economic background and political orientation (as discussed in Chapter 1). It can also be argued that Alevis advance and prioritise different rights claims depending on the political context and their different priorities. Nevertheless, it is possible to identify distinct rights claims that are sought by Alevi organisations and made by Alevi individuals through citizenship acts such as litigation. These can be summarised as follows:

- Recognition of Alevi identity
- Absolute secularisation of the state
- Abolition of the DRA/inclusion of a board for Alevis on the DRA[10]
- Abolition of compulsory religion lessons/implementation of Alevism within the curriculum[11]

---

[10] This is the first key division among Alevis of different political perspectives about the Diyanet. While the Cem Foundation demands Alevi representation on the Diyanet (in line with the earlier proposals of the state in 1960s), other Alevi organisations demand the abolition of Diyanet to ensure secularism and to save the community from any official form of state interference.

[11] This is the second key division among Alevis of different political perspectives. While the Cem Foundation advocates the implementation of Alevism within the existing religious lessons framework,

- Recognition of *cemevi*s as places of worship
- Return of the management of the Hacı Bektaş Lodge and care to Alevis
- Establishment of a museum at the site of the Madımak Hotel to commemorate the Madımak massacre
- Ending the definition of Alevism by the state and the production of 'state Alevism'
- Prevention and punishment of hate crimes against Alevis
- Ending the building of mosques in Alevi villages
- Abolition of the religion category on national identity cards[12]
- Diverse representation of opinions and identities in public broadcasting[13]
- Revision and correction of stereotyping and misrepresentation of Alevism in school materials, vocabularies and encyclopaedias
- Self-regulation of the media to eliminate content that provokes religious intolerance
- New democratic constitution based on consensus, participation, pluralism, equality and freedom in the light of international law and human rights
- Revision and elimination of discriminatory laws
- Equality before the law in practice[14]

During the 1990s, at the peak of the armed conflict between Kurdish guerrillas and the state, Alevi organisations in Turkey issued reports on human rights violations in Alevi villages which were later submitted to the European Court of Human Rights (ECtHR) (Zırh 2008: 118) and since 2008, in relation to their demands, Alevis have been campaigning for the abolition of compulsory religion lessons in schools in Turkey (Ecevitoğlu and Yalçınkaya 2013). In 2008 and 2009 they organised various demonstrations in Ankara, Istanbul and Izmir in order to make this claim more visible. Alevis organised a Demonstration for Equal Citizenship in 2010 where tens of thousands of Alevis from across Turkey gathered in Ankara

---

other Alevi organisations, such as the Alevi Bektaşi Federation, strongly argue against religious lessons and demand a secular curriculum.

[12] Each Turkish citizen is given an identity card at birth. The identity card had a religion section until 2016 and 'Alevi' was an option. Sinan Işık officially demanded his religion to be stated as Alevi on his identity card, which was refused by officials and then the Turkish courts. Işık took the case to the ECtHR, which found the religion section to be against the freedom of religion and conscience. Following the ECtHR decision, Turkey removed the religion section from the identity cards, albeit it is still visible to officials since the section is encoded in the identity card microchip (https://hudoc.echr.coe.int/app/conversion/pdf/?library=ECHR&id=001-119501&filename=001-119501.pdf&TID=ihgdqbxnfi; last accessed 22 December 2021).

[13] Ecevitoğlu and Yalçınkaya 2013; http://www.alevifederasyonu.org.tr/abfhakkindadetay.php?id=5, 2021)

[14] This claim has been on the agenda of Alevis since the late 1960s. For instance, Ata (2007: 315) says that the leader of the Peace Party, Hüseyin Balan, sued the public broadcasting company, the Turkish Radio and Television Corporation (TRT), on the basis that the Peace Party coverage by the institution was partial.

(Zırh 2012a). They also initiated various court cases in Turkey and the ECtHR,[15] mainly on the basis of religious discrimination. According to Dressler (2011: 193), Alevis have employed the courts as a major arena for contesting secularist legal discourse in Turkey.[16]

Commemorative events are also prominent in the making of Alevi cultural citizenship. With regard to their other demands, Alevis have organised demonstrations and commemorative events to remember the Madımak and Maraş massacres and to keep them on the political agenda as reminders of the oppression of Alevis (Solieau 2017). Alevi festivals (Massicard 2003; Solieau 2005; Salman 2020; Coşan Eke 2021) also play a key role in transversing local and national boundaries, gathering Alevis from different towns, cities and countries, and serving to practise boundary-making. Salman (2020: 115) identifies the two longest-running cultural activities in recent Alevi history as the celebration of Hacı Bektaş-ı Veli (1964), which was reclaimed by the state in 1990s as an official celebration (Massicard 2003; Poyraz 2005; Ertan 2017; Salman 2020), and of Pir Sultan Abdal (1978); both of these activities are named after two symbolic figures in Alevism. Geaves (2003) notes that young Alevis based in London were attending Hacı Bektaş festivals in large numbers in the early 2000s. With the festivals, Alevis gained a great deal of public visibility following decades of secret worship (Sener 1992, cited in Solieau 2005: 101). In this regard, Solieau draws attention to the continuity of rituals. such as performances of the *semah*, the singing of *deyiş*, the venerating of saints (particularly in village festivals) and the emergence of new practices such as talks, political debates and presentations. Salman (2020: 119–20) also highlights the role that such events play in creating what Solieau calls 'continuity':

> Alevi communities have had temporary, transitory and nomadic festivities such as a gathering at a *ziyaret* for a sacrifice ritual, oblation or a prayer for abundance once or a few times a year. These rituals (known in Turkish as *ziyaret, birlik kurbani, adak* and *bereket duasi*) are experienced as both festivals and a form of worship by the rural community (Yıldırım 2018). Mélikoff (2011) cites three festivals celebrated by Anatolian Alevis in January, February and March: Kagant, Hizir and Haftamol.

Bin Yılın Türküsü, which was organised by the Germany Alevi Federation in Cologne in 2000 and later in Istanbul in 2002, where 1,000 people played the *bağlama* and performed the *semah*, was a key event for Alevi transnational politics

---

[15] See Çalışkan (2020) for a detailed analysis of ECtHR cases on Alevis.
[16] Dressler (2011: 194) defines four intertwined issues which have dominated court cases initiated by Alevis: '(1) the question of Alevi representation within the state system of religious administration, that is, the DRA, and the related question of receiving material support by the state; (2) the issue of representation of Alevism by the state, most fiercely contested in the context of mandatory religious school education and the presentation of Alevism in textbooks; (3) the question of who has the authority to signify Alevism, that is, the right to identify the meanings of Alevi symbols and practices; and (4) the question of the relationship of Alevism to Islam'.

(Sökefeld 2008a; Massicard 2017). Religious rituals, cultural performances and political manifestations are interwoven in Alevi festivals. One can argue that following the Madımak massacre, which is commemorated during the Pir Sultan Abdal Festival, Alevi festivals themselves have become a political statement, a way of stressing the presence of Alevis and their ability to gather as a community, despite previous threats of persecution. For instance, Solieau (2005: 99) mentions that in the year following the Madımak massacre, even though the Pir Sultan Abdal Festival did not take place in the Sivas town centre, it was held in Pir Sultan's village. Alevi festivals are ways of celebrating and affirming the community while accommodating 'others' as spectators of such a public representation (Massicard 2003). Festivals enable face-to-face contact among Alevis of different origin while reinforcing a broader social imaginary beyond local contacts and lineage. Therefore, festivals serve as a space for Alevi identity making as well as being a form of citizenship enactment through commemoration (of massacres) and political debates.

In this chapter, I have demonstrated that Alevis strive for their cultural rights and struggle for recognition as a community in their own right. To put it bluntly, Alevi citizenship is cultural citizenship. However, the way they mediate their rights claims through media as multi-spatial and the way they imagine themselves as part of a broader yet connected community across localities and borders enable us to identify transversal citizenship as a particular form of cultural citizenship. In the following chapter, I turn the focus towards Alevi media and acts of transversal citizenship.

4

Transversal Acts of Citizenship

As a mediated act, transversal citizenship emerges in and through media. The use of traditional and digital media by Alevis in claiming their cultural rights and equal citizenship constitutes different but related appearances of transversal citizenship. While they demand the impartiality of public media institutions in representing Alevis and other religious groups, Alevis also aspire to be free from discourses of hate and explicit and implicit forms of otherisation in media. These claims and demands originate from, and primarily target, Turkey; however, some of them take place in a transversal space and include claims beyond specific national contexts. Furthermore, Alevis do not only regard media as an area of contest over representations and public constructions of Alevism, but also utilise community media in citizenship acts for learning about Alevis and other cultural and political communities and for campaigning, including street demonstrations. The fact that Alevi media is strongly embedded in Alevi organisations enables television to emerge as a means and a sphere of political action. In other words, transversal citizenship in the case of Alevis is pre-determined by a strong transnational network of organisations and even the outlets that are the subject of this book can be regarded as another form of such organisations. In addition, the lack of a voice in the mainstream media underlines Alevi media as the main space for enacting transversal citizenship and as a relatively free one. If Alevi media emerges as a means and a sphere of transversal citizenship acts, this is due to the exclusion of Alevis from mainstream media (both as individual media professionals and in terms of the cultural representations of community) and the organic relationship (in the Gramscian sense) of Alevi media outlets with the transnational Alevi organisations. Therefore, this chapter examines Alevi transversal citizenship acts, first, by focusing on three significant events which crystallise Alevis' rights claims in media. In the following sections, it looks at Alevi television and investigates how citizenship acts emerge in and through media.

Demands for 'Fair Representation'

Interestingly, Turkish nationalists' claims of Alevis as the original Turks (discussed in Chapter 3) have not infiltrated much into the media realm and to date remain marginal. Therefore, Alevi demands that fair representation is developed as a response to the historic conception of Alevism as incompatible with Sunni Islam and of Alevis as heretics. As mentioned earlier, Alevi rights claims consist of demands for fair representation and for freedom from the discourses of hate in the media. Claims relating to the media initially focused on public broadcasting (partly paid for by Alevis as taxpayers), which regularly produces programmes on Islam, particularly during the period of Ramadan. As historical prejudices began to appear more frequently in newspapers and private broadcasting, demands for fair representation became focused on content and on the ways that Alevis and Alevism were represented. Being visible in the media, on the other hand, is not as widely problematised by the community as their rights claims. In order to understand the dynamics of Alevi cultural rights claims in relation to media, we need to examine how Alevis see the Turkish media landscape. Examining Alevi representations in Turkish media enables us to situate Alevi rights claims in terms of the media, hate speech and 'fair representation'. Here I would like to discuss three key events where Alevi cultural rights claims in relation to Turkish media crystallised. These incidents were often recalled by my interviewees and emerged as a reference point in justifying the need for Alevi media. Therefore, focusing on particular incidents enables us to better understand citizenship acts in and through Alevi television.

Mum söndü is a derogatory reference to the Alevi/Kızılbaş community and their religious practices. It is deeply embedded in the cultural repertoire on Alevis and has historical roots dating back to the 16th century (Çakmak 2021). While examining the genealogy of *mum söndü* would be very useful in unpacking cultural forms of Aleviphobia, this would go beyond the scope of this study. Here I shall briefly address two significant media events that emerged as a result of the use of the expression on Turkish and German television in order to contextualise Alevi rights claims about cultural representation. *Mum söndü* implies that Alevis blow out the candles that they light during their *cem* ceremony and engage in incestuous relationships (Karolewski 2008). It is noteworthy that such a labelling strategy has not only been used specifically about Alevis but has been used about different communities, including Christian, Jews and others, in different national contexts (Adorján 2004), and as a deeply rooted cultural reference has appeared in different realms of cultural production. To give some examples: *mum söndü* and its variations were used by writers of the late Ottoman period and early Republic such as Ömer Seyfettin (1884–1920), Hüseyin Rahmi Gürpınar (1864–1944), Yakup Kadri Karaosmanoğlu (1889–1974), Reşat Nuri Güntekin (1889–1956) and Peyami Safa (1899–1961) (see Erseven 2005; Çakmak 2019, 2021), and until recently the expression could be found in some dictionaries. A theatrical play titled *Mum Söndü* (1930) by Musahipzade Celal (1868-1959) has been staged in public theatres since the 1930s while Erseven (2005: 185) notes that a film, *Boğaziçinin Esrarı* (Dir. Muhsin Ertuğrul 1922), based on Yakup Kadri Karaosmanoğlu's novel on Bektaşis,[1] *Nur Baba*, led to protests and that its filming was disrupted and delayed as a result of attacks by Bektaşis, who objected to the references to *mum söndü* in the film. Reference to incest within the Alevi community was also made in a Turkish television series called *Aşkı Memnu* ('Forbidden Love') in 1975, despite the fact that there were no references either to incestuous relationships or to Alevis in the novel by Halit Ziya Uşaklıgil (1866-1945) on which the series was based. The renowned director Halit Refiğ added new lines to the series, thus insulting Alevis (Ata 2007: 266). The leader of the Alevi Peace Party, Mustafa Timisi, protested about this reference in the series, raising a parliamentary question and bringing a lawsuit against the public broadcasting company, Turkish Radio Television (TRT) (Ata 2007).

Almost 20 years after the *Aşkı Memnu* incident and few months after the Madımak massacre, a popular television presenter, Güner Ümit, caused a storm of protest from Alevis after he had spoken disparagingly about Alevis in a quiz show broadcast on the private channel Star TV on 9 January 1994. In the programme Ümit referred to the Kızılbaş community as incestuous. Before I had even asked about it, one of my interviewees described the event as one of his childhood traumas in relation to Alevism, along with the Madımak massacre. *Mum söndü*, even if the term was not used explicitly by Güner Ümit, has been a widespread cultural indicator defining Alevis as 'other'. Following the Güner Ümit incident, more than 10,000 Alevis gathered at Star TV headquarters in Istanbul (Ertan 2017: 102) and protests lasted for two weeks. Later Güner Ümit apologised and eventually the show was cancelled. The incident also ended Ümit's television career. Ertan (2017: 102) argues that the protests demonstrated the Alevis' ability to organise and make themselves visible at very short notice. For Yalçınkaya (1996: 212), the Güner Ümit incident indicates how Alevis are critical of the 'discourses of brotherhood' which are circulated by the government in order to calm the community backlash. According to Yalçınkaya, Alevis are well aware of their 'difference' from others and continue to consider non-Alevis as different. In this way, such incidents, where there is the use of symbolic violence in media, reinforce the boundaries between Alevis and non-Alevis. Arguably, as well as shaping public discourses, such incidents filter into the collective memory of Alevism and underline the distrust against media in terms of how Alevism

---

[1] Bektaşis are the disciples of Hacı Bektaşi Veli (13th century) who has been considered the *serçeşme*, that is, the *mürşit* of many *ocak*s in Turkey. The Çelebi branch of Bektaşis claim to descend from Hacı Bektaş and therefore follow the holy lineage system of *ocak*s. The Babagan branch of Bektaşis claim that Hacı Bektaş did not have any descendants and they organise in a way similar to Sufi *tariqa*s in selecting their own leader.

is represented. A similar incident to that of Güner Ümit happened in 2010. A popular television personality, Mehmet Ali Erbil, used the term *mum söndü* while talking to a family on the phone in a competition show. While the protests were not as intense as in the Ümit case, nevertheless he was later fined by a local Turkish court (Zırh 2013).

Remarkably, the incest stereotype has also infiltrated German television through a long-standing popular crime series *Tatort* (Kosnick 2011). In an episode called 'To Whom Honour Is Due', an Alevi father is found to have sexually assaulted both of his daughters, killing one of them, despite the 'prime suspect' having been the Sunni Muslim husband of the victim. While the episode attempted to challenge the Turkish Muslim stereotype around the themes of honour killing, veiling and forced marriage, it resurrected the Alevi stereotype about incest (Kosnick 2011). The series also suggested that Sunni Islam offered protection from the threat of Alevi incest as one of the incest victims preferred to marry a Sunni Muslim, while the other chose to wear a veil as a 'piece of protection' (104). The episode resulted in public unease among Alevis, and led eventually to 30,000 gathering in Cologne to protest at the misrepresentation and stereotyping in *Tatort*, and to the writing of a letter to the German Minister for Domestic Affairs describing the programme as 'a direct attack upon all integration efforts to which Alevi immigrants were contributing' in Germany (106). In my interview, Onur from Yol TV emphasised the role of the channel in campaigning against the discriminatory Alevi representation in *Tatort*:

> If I remember it right, it was back in 2007, *Tatort* on NDR [Norddeutscher Rundfunk] had brought up incest in Alevis. Through television broadcasting on this, we have been able to gather, in our opinion, 50,000 people in Dom Square [to protest against the series].

Alevis from Turkey, the Netherlands and Belgium also attended the protests, either in person or virtually through videos they had recorded and uploaded to YouTube (Kosnick 2011).

The third protest was against a drama series featuring a rare instance of a reference to Alevism on Turkish television. The reaction began even before the series was broadcast on the public channel, TRT, in 2013. The trailer for *Kızıl Elma* ('Red Apple'), in which an Alevi *deyiş* was played in the background and the Zülfikar (the sword of the Prophet Ali) was used by the protagonist, who is an intelligence officer, led to the public perception that the series would be about Alevis and their relationship with the state. Arguably, this perception was reinforced by the fact that *Red Apple* was produced by a team led by a Turkish nationalist, Osman Sınav, who also produced and directed the renowned Turkish series *Kurtlar Vadisi* ('Valley of the Wolves'), about a paramilitary hero (Emre Cetin 2015). Before discussing *Red Apple*, it is necessary to give some background on *Valley of the Wolves* and its depiction of Alevis.

Valley of the Wolves and its spin-offs were on air for more than a decade and depicted controversial topics around such issues as the 'Kurdish question', all from a nationalist-(para)militarist perspective (Emre Cetin 2015). The last of the series led to widespread protests by viewers who logged thousands of telephone complaints with the Turkish regulatory body, the Radio Television Supreme Council, expressing the fear that the nationalist depiction of the 'Kurdish question' would contribute to the escalating conflict and violence against Kurds. As a result of this public unease, the channel decided to pull the series and it was not broadcast. A subsequent version of the series, *Valley of the Wolves Ambush* (2007–16), also depicted Alevism from a nationalist perspective through one of the main characters Zülfikar Ağa. In the series, Zülfikar Ağa works as a close ally of Polat Alemdar (the paramilitary hero and the main protagonist of the series) and tries to keep the Alevi community out of trouble and from causing any 'provocations'. The series can be seen as the first explicit and longest depiction of Alevis in television fiction and despite the nationalist framing of Alevis and Alevism in *Valley of the Wolves Ambush*, the community did not publicly denounce the series. There might be several reasons for this. In spite of its nationalist discourse, *Valley of the Wolves Ambush* depicts Alevis in a 'positive light' as allies of the state and of the paramilitary protagonist. The series also portrayed various other ethnic and religious communities through different characters, although often negatively, and hence Alevis were not targeted in the same negative way as Kurds, Zazas, Jews or Christians.

In contrast, *Red Apple* was considered to be the 'anti-Alevi' version of *Valley of the Wolves* and Alevis attempted to mobilise a similar reaction against the series as had occurred in the case of the depiction of the 'Kurdish question'. Even though *Red Apple* did not receive as much public attention as *Valley of the Wolves*, the chair of the London Alevi Culture Centre and Cemevi at the time, İsrafil Erbil, protested against the series in a press release, logged an official complaint to the Radio Television Supreme Council and also filed a criminal complaint on the basis that the programmes promoted division and hatred (Emre Cetin 2018a: 91). Erbil argued that the series portrayed Alevis as part of the 'deep state', defaming Alevi youth, Alevism and its values. The complaint was dismissed by the Radio Television Supreme Council and later the prosecution decided not to prosecute the case, yet the series did not last long. Oddly, *Red Apple* did not in the end have any explicit references to Alevis or Alevism and it is difficult to know whether the Alevism theme was dropped because of the complaint or not. One might also assume that as a public broadcaster, TRT might have been reluctant to depict Alevism in order to avoid further controversy. It is interesting to note that despite the proliferation of television drama series in the 2000s via the increase in the number of private channels and the subsequent depiction of politically loaded themes, such as the 'Kurdish question' and religious piety (Emre Cetin 2014), Alevism has not yet made an entrance as a main theme in this medium, even from a nationalist perspective. *Valley of the Wolves Ambush,* which ambitiously touched upon various socio-historical issues in Turkey still stands as a notable exception.

Put in a historical perspective, these incidents demonstrate the expansion of Alevi cultural rights claims towards transnationality. Alevi protests about *Tatort* and *Red Apple* clearly indicate that rights claims in relation to cultural representations take place on a transnational scale. Transnational Alevi communities in Western Europe have been engaging with Turkish media content via satellite since the 1990s and, more recently, via online streaming. The protests against *Red Apple* are evidence that Alevi organisations abroad do not confine themselves to political matters, but also intervene in the Turkish cultural realm. This provides them with further public visibility in Turkey and puts them on the agenda as they interfere in popular matters such as television series, which have been the realm of a hegemonic struggle for different groups (Emre Cetin 2014). These citizenship acts also apply in the case of *Tatort*, where the protests resulted in a further awareness in the German public of the differences among 'Turkish migrants' (Kosnick 2011). The Alevi community's response to *Tatort* highlights how they imagine themselves as part of German society and feel troubled about transporting prejudices and phobias from the Turkish context into Germany. However, the virtual and physical protests that took place in other European countries and Turkey indicate that the binaries of transnationalism are insufficient in addressing the multi-spatiality of these citizenship acts about media. Despite the fact that the series was broadcast to a national audience, the protests about *Tatort* took place in different countries and gathered protesters physically in Germany and in a transversal space online. The *Tatort* protests epitomise transversal citizenship as multi-spatial and as mediated through digital media involving online protests, as well as the use of traditional media in dealing with the colonial gaze towards Alevis (stemming from Turkey and dispersed across different spaces of migration). Transversal citizenship acts have emerged through television and on digital media, while simultaneously taking place on the streets in the form of demonstrations in a number of localities.

Having identified issues of misrepresentation of Alevis and Alevism in the Turkish media and the public reaction of Alevis to them, I would now like to focus on the role of Alevi media in providing a mediascape for citizenship acts. We can distinguish between two aspects of citizenship enactment within Alevi media: 1) Alevi television as citizenship enactment (*media as acts*/citizenship acts in media); and 2) Alevi television as a site through which citizens are invited to act (*media as a site* for citizenship acts/citizenship acts through media). In the following subsections, drawing on interviews I conducted with Alevi television workers and members of the community, and the content of Alevi TV broadcasts, I examine these specific forms of citizenship acts as they emerge in Alevi television.

Media and Alevi Citizenship Acts

Citizenship Acts in Media: Carrying Alevi Culture

As demonstrated in Chapter 2, cultural citizenship is about learning about oneself and others. Alevi television provides substantial knowledge on Alevism and Alevi culture, and enables its viewers to rediscover their own cultural identity. This is particularly important for two reasons: first, the colonial approach towards Alevis has deemed cultural and traditional sources of Alevism, such as *gülbang* and *cem*, as unimportant and irrelevant, thus undermining Alevi history and identity; and secondly, Alevi religious practices in particular have been 'forgotten' as a result of the immense transformation brought about by modernisation and urbanisation in Turkey. As we have seen, many researchers highlight how Alevis' political engagement with Kemalism and later the left has meant the de-religionising of Alevism, eliminating its religious elements and institutions from its identity. Urbanisation has also diluted the physical, face-to-face interactions between ordinary Alevis and their faith leaders, such as *dede*s, thus challenging the lineage-based religious practices of Alevism (Coşan Eke 2021). In this respect, fear has also played a significant role at the generational level, whereby many Alevis have abstained from revealing their Alevi identity in the urban public sphere for fear of discrimination or worse, and as a result failing to pass Alevi knowledge and customs on to the younger generations, in order to protect their children and youth from random and everyday symbolic and physical violence.

Sökefeld (2008b: 272) argues that the Alevi movement has deeply transformed Alevism. *Dede*s and *ocak*s have been replaced by Alevi organisations, the genealogical model by the democratic model, and educated Alevi intellectuals have taken over the role of passing down knowledge and traditions through books, journals and magazines, rather than the traditional oral method of transmission. Therefore, 'Alevism was changed from an oral tradition into a literate discourse' (272). While this is partially true, we need to be beware of positing a purely linear understanding of the transformation of Alevism. For this reason, I argue that Alevi television has actually been reviving Alevism's oral tradition by portraying Alevism 'as a way of life' on the screen and by opening up new channels for cultural citizenship. In his work on Inuit television production, Santo (2004: 382) demonstrates that 'Inuit media production has long served as a site of resistance to these hegemonic incorporating tendencies and has offered alternative means of "schooling" that not only teach Inuit about their culture, but how to practice it'. In a similar vein, Ginsburg (1994: 315) says that Aboriginal media in Australia and social relations built out of it help to develop support for indigenous actions of self-determination. Alevi television draws extensively on community events to make up nearly a third of the weekly schedule. Therefore, television production is enmeshed within everyday practices and events that construct Alevi identity.

Ginsburg (1994: 306) describes this embedded aesthetics as 'a system of evaluation that refuses a separation of textual production and circulation from broader arenas of social relations'.

The cultural reproduction and reconstruction of Alevism on television and the reviving of the oral tradition are not only crucial for the 'cultural future' (Michaels 1987) of the community, but also for their political survival as cultural citizens claiming equal citizenship and recognition. That is to say, without boundary work,[2] without defining what is distinctive about the community, Alevis would not be able to substantiate their rights claims for recognition. The media workers themselves regard Alevi television as a cultural/religious source which disseminates traditional knowledge, the oral transmission of which had been disrupted by migration:

> Urban migration in Turkey resulted in degeneration, not only of Alevism but of many other things. For instance, people are so much busy with work, their finances. There is a sociological dimension to it too. Under such pressure, would there be any room for identity, for Alevism? [. . .] Therefore, Yol TV is a big source of light. It is a carrier of a culture that is diminishing and that is targeted to be destroyed. (Naki, Yol TV)

> For instance, my mum considered herself very ignorant about Alevism. Now whenever I go to her place, Yol TV is on. She keeps talking about things she learned [on Alevism] and asking me questions. I say, 'I didn't know, mum', I also just learned it. I really did not know much about Alevism and it was a real deficit. You fight for Alevism but you are very ignorant about it. Especially for those who grew up in Germany, it is really difficult. Because there is assimilation. You are already assimilated in Turkey, then it becomes more difficult in Germany. I can say that we found out about ourselves through television. (Düzgün, Yol TV)

As Naki's account of his mum and himself demonstrates, learning about Alevism through television is not confined to the younger generations. My interviews with audiences indicate that for first-generation migrants in the UK, Alevi television is a primary source for learning about Alevism. Studies have demonstrated that the break-up of oral tradition and the dissolution of the *ocak* system in which *dede*s passed the knowledge of Alevism to the members of the community have been disrupted by modernisation and urban migration (Coşan-Eke 2021). First-generation Alevi migrants in the UK are also the first generation who have restored their relationship with Alevism through Alevi organisations and Alevi television, while being detached from Alevism's oral tradition. With its ability to enter the domestic sphere, television holds a privileged position as the carrier

---

[2] Boundary work highlights both culture and religion in defining the 'distinctiveness' of the community. In other words, when reflecting on the debate about whether Alevism is a culture or religion, we see an ambiguous identity construction again both as cultural and as religious, albeit mediated through television.

of culture. Hartley (2001, 2007) examines the use of television for learning and contends that it provides general knowledge and teaches us about the day-to-day conduct of public and private affairs, juxtaposing pre-modern and modern modes of address; according to Hartley (2001), cultural citizenship has been taught by television acting as a mass medium. Therefore, what we learn through television is not only general knowledge and the contemporary socio-political agenda but also some form of *civility*, a way of joining political life through our cultural identities. Alevi television enables Alevis to learn about their religion and culture, providing them with a point of reference for making sense of their identity. It also defines Alevi identity as a political entity, as well as being cultural and religious. Learning about one's cultural identity through television paves the way for defining that identity in political terms as well. Using Bhabha's (1990) distinction between the pedagogical and performative temporality of narratives, Alevi television enables the performativity of culture which is excluded from the pedagogies of the nation-state. Equally, though, by means of this performativity, television engenders its own pedagogical temporality in terms of what Alevism is.

At this point, it is worth mentioning that Yol TV and TV10 take a clear stance on not broadcasting *cem* ceremonies, unlike Cem TV. At first, one might think that such a decision stems from seeing television as a mundane, profane medium and the need to respect and protect the boundaries of what is sacred for Alevism. However, both workers at Yol TV and TV10 emphasise that televising *cem* ceremonies comes with the risk of standardisation and homogenisation. They consider that the diversity of Alevism is yet to be unearthed and take up the challenge of depicting it on television by showing the life and events of different Alevi communities on the screen. Such a commitment is expressed more boldly by TV10 as it emphasises Kurdishness through its multilingual programmes (Turkish, Zazaki and Kurdish) and attachment to a Kurdish political agenda:[3]

> When you turn on [Cem TV], you see the *cem* ceremony broadcast. Then viewers think that 'oh this is what the *cem* ought to be'. But this is not the case. When you go Hubyar you see a different *cem*, if you go to Adıyaman, *cem* is different or if you go the Aegean [region], you see a different *cem* [ritual]. (Ali, TV10)

TV10 and its successor Can TV, however, broadcast *semah* and occasionally some parts of the *cem*, reframing it as *dem* or *muhabbet cemi*, an informal community event or gathering rather than a full *cem* ceremony. This is despite, as indicated in my follow-up interviews with Can TV workers, increasing local demand from people who conduct and attend the ceremonies for them to be broadcast. This illustrates how the television workers' attitude towards the *cem* ceremony as a whole

---

[3] Zırh (2012a) mentions that a song competition organised by Yol TV in 2009 paved the way for Zazaki on Alevi television, in which a participant sang a song in Zazaki. Later, the European Federation of Dersim Associations produced a programme about Dersim on Yol TV in Zazaki.

is different from their approach towards particular components of the ceremony and its various rituals, such as candle lighting and *semah*. In this approach, the pedagogies of Alevism on television exclude the showing of complete sacred ceremonies, focusing rather on particular cultural elements, which arguably contributes towards the secularisation of Alevism through fragmenting and reframing it, prioritising its cultural elements over the religious. However, this leads audiences, particularly of the second generation, whose members probably have not attended many *cem* ceremonies before, to turn to Cem TV to see what *cem*s are like and to make comparisons:

> Thursdays they show *cem*s from Istanbul or elsewhere. I like it when they do stuff like that [. . .] We compare. I have only been to a *cem* once in London, so I don't know much. But when I recall them [*cem* on television], I am like 'yeah, they did this'. We always watch it [*cem*] on television. When they perform *semah*, we go like 'they do it like this, we do it like that'. (Ela, 22, undergraduate student)

Most of my interviewees take a different approach to that of the television and do not problematise the broadcasting of *cem* ceremonies as they are really interested in finding out more about Alevism and how different Alevi communities practise the ceremony. The desire to learn about Alevism through television overcomes the tensions between the sacred and the profane and the definition of Alevism as either culture or religion in the eyes of the viewers. For them, having knowledge about Alevism becomes a prerequisite for taking a position on what Alevism is and how to define it. Elsewhere, I have argued that under-represented communities prefer misrepresentation to no representation (Emre Cetin 2015). In this sense, seeing Alevi rituals on television also seems to have a symbolic value for viewers in terms of a validation of their collective identity and self-expression.

As I have discussed in Chapter 3, it is difficult to talk about an Alevi citizenship that advocates only rights for Alevis and, in this respect, Alevi channels are also interested in learning about other communities as well as Alevis. This pedagogical practice can be regarded as a political act where other 'minority' cultures are not considered simply as part of a broad spectrum of 'non-Alevis' but as oppressed or marginalised cultures and communities. For instance, religious minorities such as the Ezidis who were subject to the brutality of the Islamic State of Iraq and Syria (ISIS) and a marginalised community in Turkey have also been producing programmes about their own culture on Yol TV. Other ethno-religious minorities, such as the Assyrian and Greek Orthodox communities in Turkey, were mentioned by my interviewees as groups with whom Yol TV had worked. TV10 (now Can TV) and Yol TV produce programmes that embrace perspectives from a wide spectrum of leftist and Kurdish movements. 'Anti-fascism', 'anti-racism', 'being on the side of the oppressed', 'social peace' and 'equal citizenship' were often mentioned when television workers described their broadcasting values and policy. In this way, Alevi television is not solely interested in Alevis and their culture but has broader political ambitions in giving voice to 'others' in Turkey:

> Our Alevi broadcasting will not save Alevis. Our television must hold a position for making democracy work in Turkey in its fullest sense. [Television] must lead Alevis in this. Strengthening the democratic front would not solely work with Alevis. Of course, the struggle for democracy would have its own forces and institutions. And Alevis would be part of them. We cannot have democracy in Turkey without Kurdish, Turkish, Sunnis and Alevis fighting for it together. (İsmail, Yol TV)

This wider spectrum of interest in learning about others is not confined to simply the culturally or religiously different 'other' because in Alevi TV broadcasting terms 'otherness' is usually presupposed on the basis of oppression. The fact that the majority of Alevis associate themselves with progressive politics and support for the left leads them to have a considerable engagement with the Turkish political agenda, which is also evidenced by the politics of the TUP and later the PP (Ata 2007; Ertan 2017; Massicard 2017). Political talk shows make up almost half of the Alevi television schedules. The fact that Alevi television producers are situated within networks of the left and the Kurdish movement and the politicians' eagerness to appear on Alevi television in order to gain the support of Alevi voters, along with the limited media outlets where left-leaning politics are visible, can be mentioned as other key reasons for high number of political talk shows.

Citizenship Acts through Media: Mobilising the Alevi Audience as Citizens

In 2012 Alevis were alarmed by the harassment and violence that routinely targeted those who did not fast during Ramadan, including the majority of Alevis. In the small town of Sürgü in Malatya, an Alevi family who reported the disturbance caused by the loud noise of the drum played before the *Sahur*, the pre-dawn meal taken prior to the daily fast, was subject to an attempted lynching by a group of Muslims. The unease continued for days and Alevi organisations and Yol TV, in particular, launched a campaign to protect the family. The channel reported on the attack live, calling the family members who were stuck in the house and discussing the attack with members of parliament. Yol TV also provided the telephone number of the Malatya Police Department and other local authorities and encouraged the audience to call them in order to show their support for the family and, importantly, to let the authorities know that Alevis are able to mobilise an international public when an Alevi is in danger. Back then, I was also following the attack on Yol TV in London and called the Malatya police station requesting the security forces take action to protect the family. The officer I talked to sounded frustrated and said, 'Look miss, we do whatever is needed.' Yol TV's campaign mobilised their audience, leading them to take action by making phone calls from the comfort of their own homes as the least they could do and brought the attack onto the mainstream media agenda. The family was saved, although they were unable to continue living in Sürgü because of security risks, and they eventually migrated to the UK with the support of the German and British Alevi Federations.

Previously (Emre Cetin 2018a), I argued that the Sürgü attack exemplifies the role of Alevi television in constructing an Alevi public discourse and reveals the extent to which Alevis are a transnationally connected public. This significant case also demonstrates the power of Alevi television in enabling and facilitating Alevi citizenship acts (through media) with the audience calling the local authorities in Malatya to demand that local forces treat the Sürgü family as equal citizens and to protect them. This is a transversal citizenship act enacted through the media involving a complex set of connections and relations across different national borders, namely a channel broadcasting from Germany reporting an attack in Turkey, mobilising an audience living in different countries in Europe and facilitating the settlement of the family in the UK in order to save their lives. This transversal space was generated by transnational media, enabling an audience to take action thanks to simultaneous reporting. Naki from Yol TV describes the event:

> I was at home casually hanging about and then received a phone called. They said there is a problem in Turkey about a Ramadan drum. I didn't quite get the details. Then I talked to the family and learned that they would be lynched as in Maraş or in Sivas. The excuse is they raised their concern over the drum being played in front of their house [despite it being known that they were not fasting]. I quickly came to the studio. Our television does not have formalities . . . We turned the cameras on, changed the schedule and started the live broadcasting. This is the way we do it, we can go on live now if we want to . . . We started the live [broadcast] and talked to the family. It [the attack] was suddenly on Turkey's agenda [. . .] Members of parliament of CHP [Cumhuriyet Halk Partisi] and HDP [Halkların Demokratik Partisi] went to Sürgü after watching us, we gave the family's contact numbers to them and so on [. . .] All of a sudden, it was on the agenda of all Alevis. What happens next, the parties who get votes from Alevis cannot remain insensible. They have to focus on there, they have to send someone there. So members of parliament went there, it became an issue in the parliament and so on, hence the family was saved. If it wasn't for television, that family could have been [massacred], like in Maraş, or that house could have been burned down, like in Sivas. Even this indicates media is an indispensable and a powerful element. No one can give up on it. (Naki, Yol TV)

As a parallel, Richardson (2020) situates 'bearing witness while black' within a long history of slavery and colonialism, emphasising that the news production of African American activists through smartphones draws heavily on the history of anti-racism. She says that 'in terms of atrocity, witnessing is a form of connective tissue among black people that transcends place' (2020: 12) and this is not specific to the digital era and the affordances of the mobile phone. In this respect, I have discussed the significance of the collective remembering of massacres in the making of Alevi identity (indeed, the rituals and means of commemoration and the collective memory of the community is an interesting topic which deserves the further attention of researchers). Here I would like to argue in relation to the Sürgü attack that Alevi television was utilised as a means of witnessing and was a political act drawing on the collective memory of the Madımak massacre. The Sürgü attack transformed how Alevis use the medium, from a passive form of witnessing (of the Madımak) into an active one, inviting the audience to bear witness and act against the risk of lynching of an Alevi family. They utilised the media to make the Sürgü incident an urgent public issue, drawing on their collective memory of Madımak by inviting non-Alevis such as members of parliament and politicians. It can be argued that without the collective remembering sparked by the images of the massacre in the media, such forms of bearing witness and citizenship acts via the media would not have been possible. That is to say, Alevis have remembered to protect and not to forget (Zelizer 1998) through television. This time, bearing witness through television enabled Alevi citizens to act upon violence and protect community members.

Özkan (2019), who worked at Cem TV for her ethnographic research, tells of a similar incident in Yazgılı (pseudonymised by the author) in which a Kurdish Alevi family was reportedly attacked by the locals during Ramadan. Cem TV covered the attack for four days, bringing it onto the public agenda. However, the narrative about the attack was 'unsettled', oscillating between framing it as an act of religious discrimination and a peculiar and singular incident of banal violence. Özkan (2019) argues that the lack of clear positioning of Cem TV stems from the outlet's ties to the Cem Foundation, which has been actively following a pro-state position for Alevis(m) and also because of the Kurdishness of the family, both of which are difficult to accommodate within the Turkish nationalist perspective of the channel. Yazgılı discussion of Cem TV points to a clear line between citizenship acts through media and mere journalistic reporting of an attack (regardless of whether it is good journalistic practice or not). Rather than highlighting the ethno-religious motivations and calling for protection and political mobilisation in relation to the attack, Cem TV ignored the testimony of the family and their emphasis on their ethnicity, as well as religion, and the family's situating the attack within the broader history of massacres of Alevis. Silencing victims by describing them as unreliable sources operates as a strategy for reframing the attack rather than giving voice to the victims, deeming their experience of violence irrelevant. Nevertheless, despite its pro-Turkish state positioning, Özkan (2019: 319) rightly situates Cem TV within the category of minority media as the channel openly claims to represent Alevis within the otherwise pro-Sunni political context which characterises mainstream media in Turkey and its limitations. In other words, being a pro-state nationalist media outlet is not sufficient for it to be described as mainstream media. But the opposite is also true: being a minority media does not automatically assign Cem TV citizen media status, something which further delineates identity and citizenship as distinct categories.

Mobilising Alevi citizenship through television does not solely involve acts of remembering and bearing witness, as in the Sürgü attack. Television also operates as a way of encouraging Alevi citizens to attend events such as demonstrations and protests. In 2013 the Turkish prime minister, Tayyip Erdoğan, was scheduled to visit Bochum in Germany in order to receive an award for tolerance. The award sparked protest by tens of thousands of people of Turkish origin and, as a result, Erdoğan cancelled his visit. The demonstration was organised by the Alevi Federation Germany. According to some of my interviewees from the Federation who had also been producing programmes for Yol TV, the size of the demonstration was a result of announcements made on Yol TV encouraging people to protest against Erdoğan receiving the prize. My interviewees from Yol TV argued that they had been able to organise the demonstration at very short notice with a high turnout by campaigning on television, which allowed them to explain the importance of this protest to their audience:

> For instance, in Germany we used to start organising demonstrations one month prior to the demo. We used to call people via phone, send them fax messages calling them to the demonstration. Now, we don't need this. We are able to gather 50,000 people in three days through Yol TV. Tayyip [Erdoğan] was going to come here. We learned about it three days before. We said, let's protest against this. We started [protests] in Sivas as fifty people, then we became a hundred, then 1,000, then 3,000. After Yol TV we became 20,000, 100,000 to 150,000. You are able to have better communication with people [thanks to Yol TV]. You can access them directly. (Naki, Yol TV)

No doubt the gathering of masses of people to protest against Erdoğan does not simply stem from the power of Alevi television. The unease caused by authoritarianism in Turkey and the critical mood in the aftermath of Gezi[4] might also have played a significant role in such a mobilisation. This event where Erdoğan cancelled his visit to receive the prize often came up as a theme in my interviews with Yol TV workers when they discussed the significance of Alevi television for the community and their politics. It also demonstrates that the European Alevi Unions Confederation and Alevi Federation Germany were able to use television as an effective tool to influence transnational grassroots Alevi politics and to inform ordinary members, who had not been actively engaged with these organisations, helping them to know more about their activities and support

---

[4] Gezi is a generic name used to describe the spontaneous, massive and nationwide protests in Turkey that occurred in May 2013 and continued for months. It derives its name from the Gezi Park in which the protests first began. Millions are considered to have taken part in these protests, which clearly manifested the social discontent about the JDP's power and the will to pursue a secular lifestyle. The Gezi protests have been framed as an 'Alevi riot' by some pro-government media personalities. Indeed, the overwhelming majority of individuals killed during Gezi were Alevis, as a result of the disproportionate use of violence in Alevi neighbourhoods. See Karakaya-Stump (2014) for a discussion of Gezi and Alevis.

them. In this regard, Alevi television can be seen as a political medium for Alevis in mobilising different citizenship acts, such as protests, so expanding its field of influence to include those not yet active. A similar scenario occurred when the previous head of the European Alevi Unions Confederation, Turgut Öker, was arrested in Turkey in 2019. The Confederation called on the audience to protest against the arrest through Yol TV and initiated a more inclusive collective action, one that included Alevis, with less transnational connectivity. Asker from Yol TV also recalled the *Tatort* protests and said that the station had been very influential in organising the demonstrations and gathering a huge mass of protesters at the time.

These examples indicate that Yol TV draws on already well-established transnational networks linked to the Confederation, unlike TV10, which has not been able to launch influential campaigns, demonstrations or protests. Although TV10 has a close relationship with the DAF, it does not define itself as DAF's media nor does it fully adhere to the political position of the organisation on Alevism. Such a distinction between Yol TV and TV10 demonstrates that citizenship acts through media need further political ties and affiliations beyond viewership.

Transversal citizenship acts through media are also strongly tied to other sites of citizenship acts. For instance, in 2016 both Yol TV and TV10 broadcast protests against the establishment of a refugee camp near the Alevi village of Terolar that included local residents, Alevi leaders, intellectuals and transnational organisations. The camp was designed to accommodate over 25,000 refugees, while the population in nearby villages was stated as around 6,000.[5] The local residents in nearby villages were concerned that the government was settling ex-ISIS militia in the region, leaving Alevis an open target for religious violence, with the eventual aim of displacing them. The protests lasted for more than 90 days and broadcasts from the area were eventually hampered by the security forces, who also attacked protesters. Despite its longevity and the transnational support that it received, the Terolar protests were not able to actively mobilise a large number of community members; later, they faded away after the attempted coup of 2016, which resulted in the closure of Alevi television stations.

Citizenship acts in media can be pursued by media activist themselves, whereas citizenship acts through media require audience engagement beyond media reception. This is not to say that citizenship acts in media do not require a close connection with the audience, nor that they do not have the ability to lead to citizenship acts through media. However, citizenship acts in media indicate the limits of politicisation through media. Alevi television is seeking ways to involve audiences in television production through citizenship journalism; it invites audiences to take part *in* media activism, as well as facilitating activism

---

[5] See https://t24.com.tr/haber/alevi-koylerinde-multeci-kampi-endisesi-isidliler-yerlesirse-can-guven ligimiz-kalmaz,335212; last accessed 21 Janaury 2022.

through the media, as the aforementioned events indicate. While the prospect of implementing citizenship journalism in Alevi broadcasting might not be very promising for a variety of reasons, including Alevis' fear of being identified with Alevi institutions in small towns and villages in Turkey, limited resources and the need for instant access in the age of the digital indicate citizenship journalism as the way forward for Alevi broadcasting. Citizenship journalism might be a way of bridging the gap between citizenship acts in and through media, particularly with the Alevi media's shift to digital.

Alevi citizenship acts in and through media are transversal. They take place across different but connected spaces through media, they simultaneously rely on community organisations and on traditional and digital media, and they raise a voice against historically deep-rooted forms of violence and discrimination which are embedded in the collective memories and imaginaries of the community. The following chapter focuses on these imaginaries to examine how citizenship acts are facilitated by a collective sense of belonging across spatial borders.

5

Transnational Media, Transversal Imaginaries

As it is exemplified by the Sürgü incident, Alevis dispersed across different territories can imagine themselves as a community through the media (Anderson 1983), even when they do not map onto a national community contained within defined national borders. Cohen (1985) argues that community mainly exists in the minds of its members. Alevi media has not only made Alevis visible within national and transnational mediascapes, but has also paved the way for re-imagining Aleviness as an identity across localities and national borders. Alevis imagine themselves as a community that is able to respond to the current politics of Alevi identity in Turkey and abroad, not only in terms of feeling and developing a collective identity but also in terms of citizenship enactment, as discussed in the previous chapter.

This chapter examines how Alevi media enables transversal imaginaries by embedding different spatial levels in their programme planning. It draws on a thematic and critical discourse analyses (Wodak and Meyer 2001) of five randomly chosen episodes from each programme broadcast between 2014 and 2017. These include the following: *Dersim'den Esintiler* ('Breezes from Dersim'), *İngiltere Günlüğü* ('Diary of the UK'), *Seyredelim Alemi* ('Let's Watch the Universe'), *Yola Yansıyanlar* ('Reflections on the Road') and Alevism lesson programmes broadcast on Yol TV; and *Avrupa'dan Yansıyanlar* ('Reflections from Europe'), *Teberik* ('Token') and *Oy Bizim Eller* ('Oh Our Lands') on TV10. The analysis also draws on my interviews with workers of the channels. While gathering my data on the programmes, I was selective in focusing on the community event programmes from Europe (*İngiltere Günlüğü, Yola Yansıyanlar, Avrupa'dan Yansıyanlar*) and local programmes (*Seyredelim Alemi, Teberik, Oy Bizim Eller, Dersim'den Esintiler*) shot in Turkey. This selection is based on identifying the different spatialities depicted in these programmes (local, national and transnational) as themes, which has helped me to distinguish between different levels of imaginary on Alevi television and elaborate on the notion of transversal imaginary that enables transversal citizenship acts through critical discourse analysis. In the following sections, I distinguish between different spatial levels to demonstrate how Alevi media constructs transversal imaginaries.

Ethnography and Archiving through Local Programmes

Despite the fact that Yol TV and TV10 have their main offices in Istanbul and Cologne, they produce programmes such as *Dersim'den Esintiler, Seyredelim Alemi* and *Yola Yansıyanlar* (Yol TV) and *Avrupa'dan Yansıyanlar, Teberik* and *Oy Bizim Eller* (TV10) that focus on different localities encompassing villages in Turkey and small towns where Alevis live in Europe. I argue that Alevi television has undertaken two missions through these local programmes: the first is to act as ethnographers of Alevism by creating a collective archive, taking advantage of the popularity of the medium; and the second is to provide a ground upon which the diversity of Alevism can be known and appreciated by other Alevis following Alevi media. In this way, Alevi media is firmly embedded in a local context while constructing a transversal imaginary.

TV10 produces many programmes in rural Turkey, as well as screening community events from Europe, whereas Yol TV's work in reflecting the localities of Alevis is predominantly confined to Europe. Yol TV documents events which take place in different towns in countries including Germany, France, Sweden, Austria and the UK through programmes such as *Yola Yansıyanlar* and *İngiltere Günlüğü*. These programmes transmit either the entire event without any editing or just cut a few sections without editing the remainder. The events include festivals, concerts, panels, talks, pre- and post-*cem* ceremony gatherings and so on. They also include interviews with Alevi activists or members of the community who attend these events. There have also been programmes which depict the festivals and other Alevi events that take place in small towns and villages in Turkey, such as the Nurhak Festivali (Kahramanmaraş), Sansa Festivali (Erzincan) and the Didim Cemevi Konserleri (Aydın) on Yol TV. Usually, Alevi activists from the European Alevi Unions Confederation attend these events as Yol TV primarily relies on the social network of this organisation. In that sense, Yol TV does not only let the broader Alevi community know about local Alevi events and festivals in Turkey, but also serves as a means to establish and reinforce transnational ties with local communities.

In programmes such as *Teberik* and *Oy Bizim Eller* on TV10, the correspondent visits Alevi villages and interviews the inhabitants about their daily lives and culture. The equivalent of these programmes on Yol TV is *Dersim'den Esintiler*, which focuses particularly on the Dersim region.[1] In *Dersim'den Esintiler*, the

---

[1] Dersim is significant for Alevism for a number of reasons: 1) the Alevi population is denser in the city of Dersim than anywhere else in Turkey; 2) the majority of Alevis are Kurdish and Zaza in Dersim;

correspondent, who is fluent in Zaza and Turkish, interviews residents of different villages, particularly the elderly, in an attempt to uncover the local understandings of Alevism, as well as to depict everyday life in these areas. In these programmes from the villages, the pastoral scenery is often accompanied by Alevi music while the residents engage in different everyday tasks, such as looking after animal stock, making cheese and processing other local food. The programmes also ask the inhabitants about the local issues they face and about their needs and demands. In this way, local issues, such as the provision and access to infrastructure, facilities and resources, the need for modern roads, the mosque building policies of the state in Alevi villages and more particular concerns, such as the establishment of a refugee camp near Terolar, become part of the broader Alevi public agenda. In village programmes shot in Turkey, three main and overlapping themes emerge: 1) nostalgia and a longing for rural life as a source of 'authentic Alevism'; 2) a search to uncover different Alevi rituals and faith; and 3) an emphasis upon diversity within Alevism, in accordance with the fundamental tenet of Alevism that 'The path is one, the practices are a thousand and one' ('*Yol bir, sürek bin bir*').[2]

The depiction of rural life is accompanied by a sense of mourning and a feeling of a loss of religious practice. For instance, in *Oy Bizim Eller* (26 August2014), a villager who worked in building a *cemevi* in the village says while being asked about Alevism:

> Where are the old [times]? We don't have it anymore. Sometimes people from nearby villagers come, sometimes summer timers come. The other day we conducted a *cem* ... [. . .] Because there aren't many people, no community [. . .] In the summer it gets very crowded here. I call out to my fellow villagers, 'come, let's make our villages like in the old days. Let the return begin.'

Here the loss of Alevi rituals is associated with migration and the decline in a rural way of life where revival is seen as possible through the return and re-gathering of the community. The rural life depicted in these village programmes embed Aleviness in this way of life and addresses rural Alevism as 'authentic'. Local bards who have been significant in disseminating Alevi songs and *deyiş* are often part of these programmes. Sometimes the lives of locally well-known, but long-gone, bards, such as Meçhuli and Perişan Ali, are explored, reinforcing the programmes' explorative tone. Ziyaret rituals, such as sacrifice, food apportioning, candle lighting and praying, are particularly focused on and romanticised through the use of the background music, along with the 'anthropological' reporting of the

---

3) Dersim is considered the origin of many *ocaks*; and 4) the 1938 Dersim massacre has recently been integrated into Alevi collective memory as an Alevi massacre. It is also worth noting that recently Dersim has attracted much public and intellectual interest beyond the Alevi movement.

[2] The tenet implies that Alevism is one, but there are different ways of practising Alevi rituals in different regions, as well as ways of practising Alevism differently in different circumstances.

correspondent. Much attention is given to detail and there is detailed questioning about the rituals and a tone of discovery employed in these programmes from the villages. In other words, while documenting the contemporary rural lives of Alevis living in remote places, these village programmes undertake the mission of uncovering an Alevi identity which has been suppressed and disconnected from the viewers. The correspondents' questions, aimed at revealing the 'authenticity' which is assumed to be inherent in the lives being documented, provide these programmes with a sort of 'anthropological mission'. It is a mission to reach the roots of Alevism by talking to the elderly who still hold on to them in their villages and who carry the knowledge of an 'authentic Alevism'. That is why I argue that Alevi television, and these programmes in particular, act as 'ethnographers' who are able to document the lives of different Alevi communities and present them from an 'anthropological' perspective.

The anthropological mission and the documenting of the programme makers is consistent with the media workers' view of the purpose of this type of local programming. These programmes are also seen as a means of giving 'internal recognition' and inclusion as small local communities in villages are said to feel included and made visible through the village programmes. For instance, Ozan from Yol TV argues that rural Alevis feel recognised by and connected to the broader Alevi community through village programmes:

> Thanks to Yol TV we have seen that there are Alevis in the places that we didn't know about. [. . .] You go to the villages [to produce programmes]. You become their guest; you listen to their problems. When Alevis who have been oppressed by the official ideology experience, who have not been able to express themselves, sing their songs [. . .] they build a sense of belonging, they build a connection [through village programmes]. They start to think, yes, we can do it as well.

This is echoed by Haydar at TV10 when he shared a memory about a visit to a village:

> Our live broadcasting vehicle goes into a village in Maraş. A woman starts shouting and ululating and says 'I said they will come, they will come! I told you that they will!' [in Kurdish]. This distinguishes TV10 from others. We went beyond what is popular. There are many people who are able to express themselves well in front of a camera. However, TV10 prioritised those who were never given a chance to talk to the microphone, who were underestimated [. . .] TV10 did this with great care and respect. For instance, a live vehicle departs from Istanbul to a village in Dersim and gives them the microphone.

The anthropological mission assumes a diversity waiting to be discovered and presented both to the community and to the broader public. Workers at TV10 consider including Alevis in rural Turkey in their programmes as a primary goal for making different Alevi communities visible, exploring their way of life and providing them with confidence and pride. This indicates that transversal Alevi imaginary is also a vision, if not a project, shared by workers in Alevi media in terms of making sure that different local communities have their input in defining what the Alevi community is through their visibility in the media. However, the value placed on the recognition of diversity within Alevism and the different interpretations of it do not mean that all forms of Alevism are necessarily accepted as of equal value since these differences also reflect different political approaches within it. Even though my interviewees from both Yol TV and TV10 emphasised that different Alevi communities might have differences in their rituals, quoting the Alevi motto 'The path is one, the practices are one thousand and one', and that these differences must be appreciated, Yol TV has strong reservations about Alevis considering Alevism as 'true Islam', an idea advocated by the Cem Foundation, as discussed in Chapter 1. My interviewees from TV10 emphasise the necessity for diversity within Alevism and do not exclude the Cem Foundation and its media platform, Cem TV, even though they are regarded as complicit with the state in Islamising Alevism. Nevertheless, embracing the Cem Foundation as part of Alevism does not stem from the pluralist attitude towards Alevism of those working at TV10; rather, they are essentialists in the way that they do not exclude any interpretation of Alevism as long as it comes from a section of Alevis. This indicates that transversal imaginary through media is ongoing and dynamic and defined by the politics of boundary-making.

As I shall demonstrate in the following chapters, the audience in the UK draws on Alevi television to learn about Alevism and different Alevi communities living in Turkey and to enact transversal citizenship. The first- and partially second-generation Alevi community in the UK also have strong transnational connections with rural Turkey (Cetin 2013). While village programmes seem to target Alevi migrants in Europe in particular, the reception of these programmes indicates a more complex picture as they also appeal to audiences in Turkey. In fact, both Yol TV and TV10's followers on social media and online streaming live predominantly in Turkey and my conversations with Alevis from Turkey suggest that they too are also interested in these programmes. The majority of Alevis in Turkey migrated to urban areas after 1950s, which to some extent explains their feelings of nostalgia and longing for a rural Alevism (Şentürk 2017).

Appadurai (2019: 562) contends that migration is usually accompanied by a sense of confusion about what has been lost, and therefore about what has to be uncovered and remembered. For those who have been a minority in their homeland, collective memory, remembering and imaginaries are entangled with the collective history of marginalisation, and personal experiences of discrimination and migration. Therefore, while Alevi media uncovers the local histories and way of life of the community through these local programmes, it does not solely build an archive for migrants (Appadurai 2019). The knowledge Alevis have about Alevism has largely been local since different communities were organised into tribes within the *ocak* system and lived in isolation from the broader Alevi community, which had been dispersed across various regions in Turkey. In this sense, the village programmes not only give voice to Alevis from the most disadvantaged backgrounds, but also enable learning about the broader community, crucial for transversal citizenship acts. Travelling across Turkey and visiting many villages,[3] the programme makers enable viewers to consider themselves part of a broader Alevi community, overcoming geographical constraints and local diversity to be part of an Alevi imaginary. Local programmes also serve as a reference point, an archive, a broader map of collective identity reaching beyond transnational connections and building an imagination across different spatialities. As the variety of local programmes indicate, such an imagination does not collapse different spatial levels but incorporates them in the search for a new collective imaginary while carefully maintaining the boundaries between local, national and transnational. In other words, transversal imaginary is only possible thanks to these maintained and co-habiting boundaries between the local, national, transnational and regional, thus embedding local, national and regional conceptions of Alevi identity.

National Coverage and Multilinguality

Including local communities and demonstrating diversity within them in programming is considered a way of building a collective identity by the Alevi media. The emphasis on the local contexts, however, does not diminish the relevance of the national for Alevi media. Both Yol TV and TV10 are committed to following and responding to national political agendas, largely to do with Turkey, through talk shows and news programmes. Their coverage is not exclusively limited to Alevi politics but includes a wide range of issues, such as the Kurdish question, urban transformation, changes to the Turkish constitution, human rights and environmental issues. However, this wide-ranging coverage of political matters does not extend much beyond Turkey to include other countries in which Alevis live. Yol TV has reported news in Turkish from different countries, including the UK, Germany and Austria, but only sporadically. In general, Alevi television is primarily interested in the lives and rights of Alevis and in terms of broader politics those of Turkey rather than of the European countries where Alevis live, even though they are politically active there. For instance, second-generation Alevi migrants in Germany are involved in German politics as union and party members and members of parliament (Sökefeld 2008a; Massicard 2017), with nine out of fourteen members of parliament of

---

[3] Four of the television workers mention the number of visits as around 120. It is not possible to confirm the actual number of visits to different villages in these programmes; however, it is easy to infer that the programmes cover dozens of different villages across Turkey.

Turkish origin being Alevis in 2017. Many Alevis have also been involved in German leftist organisations since the 1970s (Sökefeld 2008a; Massicard 2017). Despite this level of engagement with German national politics, Alevi television does not include any specific programmes on politics in Germany or Europe.

In the UK, Alevis, particularly in London, also engage in national and local politics. They have been elected as councillors in different boroughs in London, such as Hackney and Enfield, and an Alevi member of parliament joined the House of Commons in 2019, as mentioned in Chapter 1. However, their increasing engagement in UK politics has not been reflected in programme content. For instance, *İngiltere Günlüğü* (Yol TV), which was a short-lived programme about the Alevi community in the UK, only had a short section on UK news. The programme covered the local elections in 2014 and interviewed an Alevi councillor candidate for Islington and other politicians, including the Labour Party leader at the time, Jeremy Corbyn. Again, this was only a sporadic, rather than a consistent, attempt to cover the national politics of a different country from Turkey. According to my interviews with the UK correspondents of Alevi channels, a lack of time and a lack of other resources were among the reasons for the lack of coverage of UK politics, even when Alevis were involved. However, the primary reason is the language barrier. The UK correspondents are first-generation migrants who are not fluent in English, which makes it difficult for them to follow contemporary political events in the country. They are also volunteers who mostly give their time according to their availability. The language problem is also an issue for first-generation UK viewers who would probably find it difficult to follow programmes in English. Even where language is not a problem, as is the case with my interviewees in Germany, limited time and resources are also given as among the main reasons for the lack of political coverage. This is in contrast to the engagement with Alevis in Turkey, which seems to be a priority for those who work for Alevi television. For instance, my interviewees say that even though the main office of Yol TV is in Germany the majority of the programmes are oriented towards Turkey.

Yol TV dedicated much of its schedule in 2016 to promoting Alevism lessons, which had recently been introduced into the primary and secondary school curriculum in Germany. These short programmes documented the lessons that took place in different schools, with an explanatory voice-over that invited Alevis to enrol their children in these lessons using the slogan: 'Enrol your children in Alevism lessons to prevent them from joining the enemies of Alevism and to reinforce their Alevi identity.' In this context, 'the enemies of Alevism' refers to fundamentalist Islamist organisations such as ISIS and my interviewees stated that there were some cases of Alevi youth in Germany joining ISIS. No doubt the fear about the rise of radical Islamism also stems from the collective memories of persecution in Turkey. Arguably, the call to sign up to Alevism lessons also serves to distance Alevis from radical Islamism, and therefore rising Islamophobia.[4] Alevism lessons in Germany are not only regarded as a means to introduce Alevi culture to students but also a call to recognise Alevism, which had been invisible in Europe as it was subsumed under a Muslim identity. Further, engaging Alevi youth in these lessons has come to be seen as a means of tackling the disaffection and disengagement of some Alevi youth, both in Germany and the UK, and protecting the next generation from the potential risks that could await them, such as involvement in gangs and drugs, as discussed in Chapter 1 (Jenkins and Cetin 2014, 2018; Cetin 2016, 2017, 2020).

The programmes about Alevism lessons in Germany are sometimes bilingual: the correspondents interview the students and ask their opinion about, and experiences of, the Alevi lessons. It is important to note that the third generation of Alevis in Germany engage with their Alevi identity in schools through the German language rather than Turkish or Kurdish. This is also reinforced by other bilingual programmes (in German and Turkish) on Yol TV aiming to appeal to Alevi youth living in Germany. In this regard, another way of understanding the national context on Alevi media is to examine the languages that are used in the broadcasts.

Both Yol TV and TV10 are committed to multilingual diversity. TV10 aims to provide a balanced mix of Turkish and Kurdish and broadcasts the news in these two languages, as well as in Armenian. The latter can be regarded as a gesture of solidarity with Armenians in Turkey, a practice which implies a parallel between the early 20th-century Armenian Genocide, which took place under the Ottomans in 1915, and the persecution of Alevis.[5] There have also been programmes broadcast in Zazaki and Assyrian where correspondents from TV10 attend events in these communities, while in order to cater for Zaza-speaking Alevis in Turkey, there are discussion programmes in this language as well. TV10's linguistic diversity predominantly reflects languages spoken in Turkey. Yol TV, on the other hand, presents a European linguistic orientation, although it does broadcast some programmes in Kurdish and was the first Alevi channel to introduce programmes in Zazaki. Nevertheless, Yol TV has no priority to increase the amount of broadcasting in Kurdish or Zazaki. This may well reflect the fact that the European Alevi Unions Confederation has been carefully distancing itself from the Kurdish movement in order, as they see it, to protect the political autonomy of Alevis. This marks another point of divergence from TV10, which demonstrates its support for the Kurdish movement by broadcasting in Kurdish.

---

[4] Mandel (1989) notes that Alevis utilise their distance from Sunni Islam in order to gain acceptance from the German public and align themselves with 'Western' values and culture. This argument is partially problematic as Alevis in Turkey also demonstrate a similar attitude in terms of embracing secularism and 'Western' values.
[5] See Çakmak (2019) on the relationship between Armenian and Alevi communities in the 19th century and its perception by Ottoman rule.

It also broadcasts Alevi events put on by the DAF, which is an Alevi organisation with close connections to the Kurdish movement.

Yol TV expects that the number of programmes in Turkish and on Turkey will gradually decrease in the long run as third and subsequent generations are likely to demonstrate significantly less engagement with Turkish politics. This is reflected in the views of Hıdır from Yol TV, one of the founders of the channel, who when talking about the future of Alevi television stated that Alevi television needs to be more Europe-oriented in order to appeal to the younger generation and, more importantly, if it is to survive. From this we can see that the representation of, and the engagement with, different national contexts on Alevi television are dynamic and depend on who the viewers of Alevi media (in terms of age and location in particular) will be. It also demonstrates the changing and complex relationship between the national and transnational as Alevi media negotiates its role in relation to Alevis in Turkey, on the one hand, and those in the diaspora, on the other, who may increasingly see their Alevism as centred elsewhere than Turkey. However, following the closure of oppositional media outlets in Turkey after the failed coup in 2016, Yol TV has taken a clear direction towards being a media outlet for the broader Turkish public within an environment where there is a lack of a multi-voiced media. Employing young journalists and correspondents from Turkey and using social media, including Twitter, Instagram and YouTube, more proactively, Yol TV has gradually re-situated itself as an alternative media for Turkey rather than solely a community media appealing primarily to Alevis. Therefore, the complexities of national politics and challenges to the freedom of the press in Turkey might well have assigned a new role for Alevi media.

Despite their ethnic and linguistic differences and the attempts at Turkish nationalist domination (as argued in Chapter 3), Alevis have maintained their collective identity on the basis of religion. Recent research on Alevi history demonstrates that Alevis were able to sustain their broader networks and collective sense of belonging through the *ocak* system throughout the centuries (Karakaya-Stump 2015, 2021; Yıldırım 2017b). The *ocak* system was able to connect Alevis belonging to the same *ocak* to a certain extent; however, it is difficult to argue that the entire Alevi community was connected on a national scale. Turkish modernity during the Republican era and migration to cities from the 1950s onwards challenged the *ocak* system, and Alevis have mainly been organised around their own or other political parties and village and town associations. Until recently, it was difficult to overcome this local fracturing of the wider Alevi community. The Alevi publications of the 1990s were not widely circulated, although they aimed at addressing 'Alevis as a whole' and Alevi radio of the period was able to reach out only to mainly urban Alevis. Alevi television has changed this as it has enabled Alevis to imagine and situate themselves at a national scale in an unprecedented manner. According to Zeynel from TV10,

> Alevism is no longer a local identity but a national one after TV10. For instance, people wouldn't have told you if they are Alevi when you handed a microphone over to them. Even if they had, they would have done it with fear. Because they used to consider television somewhat official. Then they realised, actually this television is something else, something Alevi. They [Alevis] heard this voice and then emerged a national sense [of Alevism].

İsmail, who has been an activist in the Kurdish movement for years, emphasised that Alevi publications have facilitated the birth of the Alevi movement and television has addressed Alevis as part of a 'national' context, while enabling them to imagine themselves as 'Alevis of Turkey'. According to İsmail, Alevi identity has been able to transcend local borders thanks to television and Alevis have gained further confidence in publicly declaring themselves as Alevis since the media re-drew the boundaries of their collective identity at a national level. Moreover, television has provided them with a space within Turkey's mediascape, rendering them visible within the sphere of cultural production. Even though İsmail did not coin the word 'imagination', what he is referring to is the Alevis' ability to imagine themselves as a community within a national territory thanks to television. However, rather than a homogenised notion of Alevism, both TV10 and Yol TV draw on diverse Alevi practices within different localities in building a national imagination of Alevism. This is how Alevi media embeds the local and national and paves the way for a complex transversal imagination.

From Transnational to Transversal Imaginaries

Distinguishing between 'globalisation' and the 'transnational', Athique (2014: 2) highlights how the transnational is primarily about 'cultural practices that take place across the national boundaries'. Migrant communities and the complexities of their interaction with their home and host countries on the social and cultural levels have created not only a series of social relations but also the production of cultural artefacts. Hence the transnational is particularly about the cultural politics of human geography, which is framed by mobility and interaction across nations. This is not to say that the context of the national has lost its power and impact, but rather that it is contextualised within the transnational construction and exchange of cultural ideas, values and imaginations. As Athique (2014: 3) points out, '[w]e should never underestimate the national in transnational'. Rather than eradicating national sentiments and imaginations, transnational experiences re-construct the national through the lens of these new experiences and imaginations. The fact that programmes on Alevi television primarily focus on Turkish politics indicates that Alevi migrants care for their community members in Turkey and feel a sense of belonging. This is also true for the local context. The transnational indicates the significance of the local, something which is greatly overshadowed by the homogeneous imaginations of the national. It is no coincidence that both channels have programmes on local Alevi communities in Turkey, such as *Teberik* and *Dersim'den Esintiler*, which allow Alevi migrants to rediscover and re-imagine their 'roots' back in rural Turkey. Thus, the transnational experience suggests novel ways of relating the self to a broader understanding of the national and more specific notions of the local. Alevi organisations abroad work to improve the status and well-being of Alevis in the host countries and also to support and enhance the Alevi movement in Turkey. This indicates that the Alevi diaspora holds a transnational understanding of Alevi identity, one which is bound by a desire to see a change in the condition of Alevis. This is also the case for Alevi organisations in Turkey that aim at recruiting members not only in Turkey but in also Europe via local networking and national organisations.

It must be noted, however, that the Alevi transnational imaginary was formed *before* the Alevi media's presence and came about following the Alevi migration to Western Europe from the 1960s onwards. The first significant Alevi transnational mediascape emerged following the mass event of Bin Yılın Türküsü (2000), where more than 100 *bağlama* players played *deyiş* and hundreds of performers performed the *semah* in a stadium, the Kölnarena, in Cologne (Sökefeld 2008a). Sökefeld (2008a: 228) says that Bin Yılın Türküsü turned 'the imagined community of Alevis to a certain degree into a real experience'. Bin Yılın Türküsü was repeated in Istanbul a few months later (Poyraz 2007). The event in Germany was recorded and later the recordings were distributed in Germany and Turkey (Massicard 2017). Video clips of Bin Yılın Türküsü are available on YouTube and two of them had hit more than five million views as at the end of 2021. The event is remarkable in understanding the transnational mediascape for two reasons. First, it was the first public performance on this scale and where Alevi artists and performers met with their counterparts in Germany as well as the audience (Sökefeld 2008a). Secondly, the distribution of the video recordings enabled ordinary Alevis in Turkey to discover this transnational space through a mediated experience. To put it another way, Alevis in Turkey became part of the performance by watching the recordings and being able to imagine themselves as members of the Alevi community across national borders. This transnational mediascape was not capable of being continually sustained until Alevi satellite channels were established in the 2000s. As Georgiou (2007: 24) argues: '[d]iasporic media have initiated and participated in the development of spaces for communication in local and transnational level and, arguably, they have contributed to the emergence of local and transnational public spheres'. Hence, it is important to see that in the case of Alevis, transnational media appeals to both the Alevis living abroad as well as to the community in the home country.

Massicard (2017) and Sökefeld (2008a) say that Alevi activists in Europe have far broader and more active transnational connections than ordinary members of the community. The existence of Alevi media is also a consequence of the existing networks and organisations, which have been active for more than three decades, and of Alevi television in improving transnational networks and constructing transnational imaginations of Alevism, which have arisen from long-established transnational economic, social and cultural networks. In this regard, one can argue that Alevi media not only provides a transnational imagination of Alevi identity but has also democratised the transnational social space by including those who stood at the margins of these networks and those who were not directly involved with transnational connections in Turkey (Emre Cetin 2018a: 94). Relevant here is Georgiou (2013), who proposes 'a three-dimensional mapping of the media that both recognises the different ways in which minorities use them but also the three different ways in which media ecologies become – or could become – more democratic, inclusive and diverse'. These three dimensions (which echo the three sets of relations represented by transnational television outlined above) are: media for seeing the self; media linking 'I' with 'We'; and media linking a big 'We' with a minority 'We' and with 'I'. Although I would argue that these links do not necessarily guarantee more democratic and diverse media ecologies, Alevi television can be seen to establish transnational links which echo the three dimensions described by Georgiou. These are: between the individual and collective understandings of Alevi identity; between the Alevi diaspora and Alevis in Turkey; and finally, between the Alevi diaspora, Alevis in Turkey and broader Turkish society.[6] These complex sets of relations become available thanks to Alevi media, which penetrate into Alevis' everyday lives on a regular basis in different geographies.

Clearly media plays an essential role in how transnational communities imagine themselves. According to Appadurai (1997: 8), imagination can be considered 'a property of collectives', which partly becomes possible because of the collective reading, criticism and pleasure of mass media. Shared media activities allow groups to 'imagine and feel things together' (Appadurai 1997: 8). Mass mediation takes different forms that facilitate interaction 'across national boundaries, and as these audiences themselves start new conversations between those who move and those who stay, we find a growing number of diasporic public spheres' (Appadurai 1997: 22). This imagination forms new conceptions of boundaries, nationalities, moralities and economic prospects that provide a 'staging ground for action, and not only for escape' (Appadurai 1997: 7). As Taylor (2004) argues, social imaginary is not simply a set of ideas but enables the practices of a society.

Alevi media allows Alevis living in Turkey to imagine themselves beyond the boundaries of the Turkish nation-state, connecting them continuously with those living in different countries. Equally, Alevis living abroad can think of themselves beyond their dual citizenship and of Aleviness as existing across national

---

[6] We can only talk about limited connections between the Alevi transnational community and the host communities, except those established through the local programmes, such as *Al-Canlar* (broadcast in Berlin), since Alevi television mainly broadcasts programmes in Turkish and Kurdish.

boundaries. Adverts, talk shows, news and documentaries all draw the boundaries of the Alevi public sphere as they address Alevis of different geographies and define their identity in its economic, cultural and political aspects on a transversal level across the local, national and transnational. In other words, Alevi media facilitates regular contact with other Alevis living in different countries, primarily from the comfort of their own living room. This also enhances the local understanding of community and bonding, which before had only been available through face-to-face contact. Different local interpretations and practices of Alevism are recognised through documentaries or talk shows about different Alevi groups. While Alevi television suggests a common understanding of Alevism by drawing the borders of Alevism for its audience, it also lets the audience acknowledge nuances of difference between different Alevi groups.

Moreover, the fact that Alevis are a minority both in Turkey and abroad introduces further complexities. An implication of being a minority in the home and host countries is the construction of an Alevi identity as a hybrid entity that includes the problems, concerns and practices of Alevis at the local and national level both in Turkey as well as in the countries in which Alevis reside. Elsewhere (Emre Cetin 2020a), I have provided a critique of the presumptive binaries of home/host and sending/receiving countries in studies of media and migration. While trying to tackle this 'methodological nationalism' (Wimmer and Schiller 2003), drawing on transnational binaries can lead to a similar methodological trap of disregarding intersectionality and ethnic, religious and other forms of diversity within transnational contexts. Taking the social situatedness of audiences and the complexities of global media flow into account, Athique (2016) argues that we should approach the transnational as a spectrum. He contends that we need to deal with the methodological challenge of unstacking 'the Russian doll of transnational spectrum in an illustrative fashion' (Athique 2016: 185). Focusing on Cem TV and Yol TV, in another study I examined different conceptions of transnational imaginary stretching across different national and regional boundaries (Emre Cetin 2018a). Cem TV's transnational imaginary draws the boundaries of Alevism incorporating the Balkans and a geographically vague notion of Muslim countries consistent with the Cem Foundation's understanding of Alevism as a branch of Islam. Yol TV, as I also indicate in this book, embeds European national contexts as well as a broader identity of Europeanness into Alevi social imaginary. Therefore, the case of Alevi media demonstrates that regional spatialities which cannot be explained solely through the notion of transnational spectrum also do matter.

As the case cited in the introduction to this chapter indicates, the fact that Yol TV tried to mobilise Alevis abroad in order to save the lives of an Alevi family in the Turkish village of Sürgü shows the strong connection between Alevis living abroad and Alevis in Turkey. This transversal imaginary connects Alevis abroad to their counterparts in Turkey and gives them a sense of responsibility towards others, leading them to raise their voice against the symbolic and physical violence towards Alevis in Turkey. This is despite the 'decisive difference between Alevi identity in Turkey and in the diaspora . . . [and] the fact that Alevis in Turkey have to live with an at least latent threat of discrimination and even violence' (Sökefeld 2002: 90). The fact that Alevis in the diaspora still consider themselves to be a part of their community in their homeland empowers Alevis in Turkey, something that is aided by the explicit projection of Alevism through television, which also serves as a way of dealing with common prejudices about Alevis. According to Stevenson (2003: 336), '[c]ultural versions of citizenship need to ask who is silenced, marginalised, stereotyped and rendered invisible'. Alevi television keeps these questions about Alevis and other communities on the agenda, challenging in particular the hegemonic concepts of Turkish citizenship which were discussed in Chapter 3.

Alevis constantly make cultural rights claims through Alevi television. To employ Isin and Ruppert's (2020: 9) framework, this is the figure of the citizen as an embodied subject of experience who acts through media to make rights claims. As discussed in Chapter 3, cultural rights claims are not limited to Turkey but also include Germany, the UK, Austria and other European countries, and these claims are shaped by different national contexts. Alevi television embraces these differences and makes the transnational case for the broader Alevi community. As mentioned earlier in this chapter, local lives, problems and the politics of Alevis living across Europe and Turkey are also represented. In other words, contemporary Alevi citizenship is diverse and transversal imaginations facilitated through Alevi media reinforce this diversity. However, the limit of this diversity is defined by the political orientations of these channels as described in Chapter 1, by their resources, by Turkish politics and by the transnational Alevi communities. Therefore, the transversal imaginaries constructed by Alevi media are not homogeneous and stable and do not represent various localities and national contexts equally, amalgamating them proportionately. Rather, it is a dynamic entity which is shaped by the complexities of transnational politics and Alevi citizenship.

Alevi broadcasting demonstrates that the social imaginary engendered by media does not eliminate the spatialities of the local, national, transnational or regional. On the contrary, it reinforces a dynamic relationship between them. As argued by Appadurai (1997), a transnational imagination is only possible through the transnational flow of people, goods and ideas; whatever flows on this transnational scale is initially located in local, national and regional contexts. In this regard, I distinguish between different levels of imagination, local, national, transnational and regional, which are not mutually exclusive but interdependent. I put forward the concept of transversal imaginary for an understanding of the dynamic relationship between different spatial levels of the local, national, transnational and beyond. Drawing on my understanding of cultural citizenship as transversal, I argue that transversal imaginary transverses 'the national within transnational' (Athique 2014: 3) and engenders a trans-border sense of belonging and space. Transversal imaginary allows us to recognise the co-presence of the local, national, transnational and beyond, and unpack the complex relationship between them. Transversal imaginary also overcomes the bifocal undertones of transnationality (as sending and receiving, departure and arrival, home and host) and allows room for thinking beyond the nation-state framework that acknowledges the complexities of migration. It enables us to address the embeddedness of different spaces as a whole, while acknowledging the autonomy of each spatial level.

Arguably, the transversal imaginary can better apply to communities that are minorities both in sending and receiving countries, such as Alevis, Ezidis and Assyrians, as their sense of belonging to their community has not been overtaken by national identities. Transversal imaginary is also a useful concept in understanding how imaginaries emerge in a spatially embedded way through digital technologies. Therefore, it may well explicate the dynamics of digital diasporas (Brinkerhoff 2009; Everett 2009; Gajjala 2019; Sobande 2020) and digital citizenship acts (Isin and Ruppert 2020) since the technological affordances of the digital cross-cut these different levels of the local, national, transnational and regional in a more complex way than ever before. Alevi media production takes places within this transnational space as a transversal practice: the stations have representatives in different European countries who report and produce programmes on a regular basis and recently have been looking at ways to encourage citizen journalism, which may be able to facilitate a balanced local coverage from Turkey in particular.[7] That is to say, transversal imaginary is mainly possible through this complex transnational network of production and reception and a broader vision as to who constitutes the Alevi community, including the local, national, transnational and regional situatedness of its members. In the following chapter, focusing on the viewers of Alevi media, I examine the transversal imaginaries of the viewers.

---

[7] Key actors in Alevi television can be considered privileged in terms of being active parties in the Alevi transnational networks. Nevertheless, their prospects for citizen journalism indicate a will to democratise the media production and create channels through which media activism can be dispersed towards ordinary members of the community, while they also hope to share the burden of laborious television production with limited resources.

6

Alevi Viewership and Transversal Imaginaries

Transversal imaginaries are constructed through the media; however, a mere focus on media content, representations and the perspectives of the media producer is not sufficient for understanding viewers' imaginaries and their citizenship acts through media. In the case of Alevis, the engagement with Alevi media is defined and sustained by a sense of belonging to a community and by communal ties. Therefore, transversal imaginaries need to be understood through their embeddedness in the history of the community and their collective memories and personal experiences of oppression and discrimination. Alevi viewers follow Alevi media to learn about their culture, history and the contemporary agenda of the community, and regard their media as an alternative source to help find out more about contemporary Turkish politics. Therefore, this chapter focuses on the viewers' interpretation of their identity, their engagement with Alevi media and the multi-spatial references they use in making sense of their identity, belonging, media engagement and citizenship acts.

In this chapter, I first examine the extent to which Alevi viewers draw on their personal experiences in discussing their engagement with Alevi media and the collective memories of oppression and persecution. I then focus on how viewers learn about Alevism through media, given the lack of reliable sources and the change in Alevi institutions, such as the *ocak*s, which disrupted the passing down of knowledge of Alevism. I argue that exploring Alevism through media serves as a ground upon which citizenship can be enacted because learning about, and therefore situating, oneself and others is a necessary condition for transversal citizenship. Finally, I investigate how transversal imaginaries are constructed with reference to media and distinguish between how different notions of localities emerge in the accounts of the first and second generations.

Personal Stories, Collective Histories

Akdemir (2016: 183), who conducted ethnographic research on Alevis in the UK, mentions that the participants provided only a brief account of their migration due to the sensitivity of the issue as some of them had arrived in the UK by illegal means. My experience has been the opposite since the overwhelming majority of my interviewees have elaborated on their life in Turkey, the reasons for their migration, their journey, and their arrival and settlement in the UK. Actually, their migration stories have been a means for them to situate themselves within a collective history of Alevism as they often linked their past to massacres, discrimination and poverty. My insider position as a Kurdish Alevi, and my local knowledge regarding the towns, villages, personalities, lifestyles, tribes and lineages quickly engendered trust and the participants easily opened up about their past and background. Second-generation participants often provided a detailed account of their childhood and how they found out they were 'migrants'. This has enabled me to address the continuities and divergences between the first- and second-generation's understanding of Alevism and their engagement with Alevi, Turkish mainstream, UK and other media content.

Poverty is stated as a key reason for migration. Cetin's (2013) study of suicides among the second-generation Kurdish Alevi community in London highlights economic reasons as encouraging migration to the UK, where the experience of poverty and financial difficulties is related to the socio-cultural marginalisation of Alevis in Turkey. Therefore, poverty must be understood in relation to the social positioning of Alevis as mainly working class or poor urban and rural dwellers. My interviewees understand this relation between their socio-economic position in Turkey and its causes and their hopes for an economically more secure life after migration:

> The reason why we came here was economic ... Economic reasons and other oppressions ... (Hüseyin, 62, male, retired)

> The first reason was poverty. Maybe it was political more than economic ... We lived under difficult circumstances there [Turkey]. Being Alevi, being Kurdish come on top. How to put it? ... It was a crime, a stigma ... If you have the label of Kurdish, Alevi, then you are a different citizen. A second-class citizen. (İbrahim, 54, male, coffee-shop owner)

> The reason was to make a living ... Aleviness ... There was oppression. (Hasan, male, 58, retired)

> When you are stripped off all your rights, what is the point of living there [in Turkey]? (Naki, male, 57, unemployed)

The correlation that my interviewees assume between their economic position and ethno-religious identity leads them to value their financial and their children's educational achievements in the UK. They often portray their settlement in the UK in a positive light in terms of economic advancement, as well as in terms of individual freedom, recognition of their community and their ability to organise in Alevi organisations. Cetin's (2013) and Akdemir's (2016) findings also confirm that any discrimination and harassment that Alevis suffer in the UK are seen as individual instances rather than resulting from state policies against Alevis.

Almost all of the first-generation participants situated their background and stories of migration within the context of Alevi history. In these narratives, Alevi history constitutes a combination of uprisings and massacres from the 13th century onwards. Influential religious leaders and bards of the time, such as Hallac-ı Mansur, Nesimi, Baba İshak, Baba İlyas, Hacı Bektaş-ı Veli and Pir Sultan Abdal, are often mentioned in the discussion of different topics, including what Alevism is, why Alevis need their own media, and the persecution and emancipation of the community. As Mustafa, who describes himself a Turcoman Alevi and member of 'the '68 generation',[1] explains:

> From Baba İshak, Baba İlyas, Çelebis, Celali uprisings to Atatürk[2] ... I know Atatürk well and I like him very much. Some of us don't. They like him at the core, but they don't know him much. We came since Kerbela ... We need to develop ourselves. We need to have radios, television stations, organisations ... (Mustafa, male, 67, retired)

These narratives also serve as a background for understanding their views on media, and Alevi television more specifically. According to my interviews, Alevis argue that they are entitled to their own media because Alevism has been under continuous and systematic attack for centuries. Alevi television is one of the means of ensuring that Alevis gain equal status with others. Sakine, who has been a political activist since she arrived in the UK as an asylum seeker and was very active in the London Alevi Cultural Centre and Cemevi, and later in the Federation for ten years, summarises this clearly when she says that 'television is a weapon of struggle for the community'.

As the previous quotation illustrates, the experience of discrimination also enables the interviewees to situate their private lives as Alevi individuals within the collective history of Alevis and the history of persecution. While discussing first-hand experience of discrimination, the first-generation participants, in

---

[1] The '68 generation in Turkey is the counterpart of the youth movements worldwide at the end of the 1960s. Despite the common emphasis on sexual freedom, women's liberation and anti-militarism in the worldwide movements, the '68 generation in Turkey was more aligned with socialist ideology, inspired either by Mao-Zedong or V. I. Lenin and also influenced by the armed struggle by Che Guevara. In Mannheimian (1998) terms, politically active, leftist members of this generation are to be thought of as a generation unit, rather than a generation. Members of this generation unit were mostly organised under legal and illegal organisations, the latter mostly akin to armed struggle. This struggle ended in the military memorandum of 1971 and most of these young people suffered from legal sanctions.
[2] The founder of Turkish Republic. See Küçük (2007) and Kehl-Bodrogi (2003) for the significance of Atatürk for some Alevis.

particular, interpret their personal experiences in relation to a collective history of persecution and violence. For male interviewees, first-hand experiences of discrimination often took place when they were in the military during conscription (also see Cetin 2013) or at school or work, whereas for female interviewees, it took place locally in small towns and came from neighbours or strangers, who would often harass them because of their clothing or because their hair was not covered.

As I discussed in Chapter 4, massacres also serve as a key reference point for an Alevi collective memory and the formation of Alevi identity. Any form of discrimination, bullying or harassment revives the memory of massacres in individual's accounts:

> They mob you even if you become a teacher or a governor. They don't let you be. I worked in factory in Maraş for a while. They [my colleagues] kept nagging me 'why don't you pray [*namaz*]? Why, is it a bad thing?' and I didn't. They eventually fired me. Maybe I would have been killed if I happened to be at Maraş during the events [massacre]. (Hasan, male, 70, retired)

> We haven't been able to call ourselves Alevi. All the nearby villages knew that we are Alevi, though. We didn't have anything significant until Maraş [massacre]. Then there was violence in Elbistan. For instance, my dad was walking with his *kirve*,[3] who is a Sunni guy. They ask our *kirve*, 'why are you walking with him? Alevis tear the Koran . . .'. (Mehmet, male, 59, chef)

During the interviews, massacres were often mentioned either by specifically naming their place and date or by a more general reference to 'massacres'. The historiography of violence differed from one interviewee to another and there was no singular or coherent narrative of persecution which applied to every viewer. This is not surprising as Alevis do not gain knowledge of massacres through formal education and there is no established canon of Alevi history to be transmitted as studies in this area are still emerging and are not yet consumed by the wider community. Nevertheless, the Dersim (1938), Maraş (1978) and Madımak (1993) massacres were often mentioned and served as a framework for situating personal experiences of symbolic and physical violence and discrimination in terms of these attacks.

Personal narratives of state violence experienced following the 1980 military coup and during the 1990s following the intense armed conflict between the Turkish military and Kurdish guerrillas of the PKK were also significant for the participants:

---

[3] A *kirve* is the godfather of the circumscribed male. Kirveness is a form of kinship which has been particularly significant among Kurdish Alevis. For instance, in some Alevi communities, kirveness prohibits endogamy and obviates blood feuds. Arguably, particularly in places where Alevis live with Sunnis, such a kinship with Sunnis serves as a means of security for Alevis.

> If we stayed in the village during the Kenan Evren[4] period [following the coup] ... They took a lot of people from villages and many became paralysed [because of torture]. We did not go back to the village out of fear during that time. They've done a lot to Alevis. Many lost their kidneys [because of torture]. Many were also struggling financially back then. Look, it is a good thing that we are abroad now. (Mustafa, male, 67, retired)

> The emancipation of Alevis, Kurdish, Armenian, other minorities in Turkey ... Alevi belief requires that we align with the oppressed. The pressures over Kurds, their oppression is ongoing. We've seen that women and children were massacred because of their language, their culture. Altogether, with such people, with labourers, we need to unite with those who have been oppressed. (Hüseyin, male, 62, retired)

In a similar vein, the Armenian Genocide of 1915 has been used as an example to explain the policies and mechanisms employed by the state for othering and then executing members of different communities. For the majority of my interviewees, discrimination and violence against Alevis has a long and intermingled history with the politics of ethnicity, religion and the left in Turkey. As discussed in Chapter 3, Alevi struggle for recognition and claims for the right to be different has led to a demand for equal citizenship and this demand is made on behalf of other oppressed communities as well as Alevis.

It is important to emphasise that none of my participants regard Alevis as powerless victims[5] within the narratives of violence and discrimination, regardless of their engagement with the Alevi movement as active members or affiliates. On the contrary, the majority of them regard the Alevi history of violence as a common experience shared with other oppressed communities which leads them to redefine Alevism as a political identity and agency:

> When Gazi happened ... I remember leaving my three-year-old daughter in order to go to the protests. Albeit no one else around me was willing to go, including people from our village, I was so keen to attend. (Nuray, female, 47, housewife)

Nuray, who has been actively engaged with the London Alevi Cultural Centre and Cemevi in Wood Green, and later with the Federation, for more than eight years, thinks that acting against oppression does not necessarily relate to her privileged position of being settled in the UK or the Alevi movements' ability to organise abroad. Instead, it is more about individual willingness and motivation and living one's identity. She emphasised that fear and assimilationist policies were the main reasons why the other people from her village did not attend the Gazi protests, rather than a sense of victimhood. Instead, the emphasis upon the massacres and

---

[4] Kenan Evren was the leader of the National Security Council which staged the military coup on 12 September 1980. He was later tried and sentenced to life imprisonment, but died in 2015 before the Supreme Court gave its final verdict.
[5] See Dressler (2021) for a critique of discourses on victimisation.

violence more broadly serves as evidence of the oppression of the community. As discussed in Chapter 4, bearing witness and remembering the massacres of the past is also a reminder of the need for protection from them in the present and the future.

Exploring Alevism through Media

From the viewers' perspective, Alevi television has been regarded as essential in achieving two main goals: making Alevis visible and getting their voices heard; and reviving Alevi culture, religion and history. In this sense, Alevi television has been given the mission of representing and exploring Alevism. Enforced silence on Alevism and the inability to identify oneself as Alevi beyond the boundaries of the community is a recurrent theme in the interviews. The majority of the first-generation migrants migrated from Turkey at the end of the 1980s, just before the Alevi movement took its transnational turn and began to exert its significant influence upon Turkey. Therefore, the first generation's past experiences took place at a period where a public declaration of being an Alevi would more likely result in physical harm. However, this does not mean that Alevis are now comfortably able to call themselves Alevi in public. At best, an Alevi's public self-identification with Alevism is regarded as 'divisive' and 'sectarian', and could easily lead to discrimination, hate crime or physical violence in Turkey. Therefore, public recognition through television of Alevism matters for many of my interviewees:

> At least people heard about Alevism [thanks to television]. Alevism did not even have a name . . . Have we been able to tell that we are Alevis while going to school? (Dilek, 57, female, retired)

> You weren't able to call yourself as Alevi in small towns. But now I want to tell everyone who I am. (Hasan, male, 70, retired)

> There was no such thing before, everything was hidden. At least we see it on television. *Cems* and so on . . . All was in secret. We see it now on television. It is good. Alevis develop themselves, they know that they are Alevi, they know themselves. We didn't know ourselves, who we are . . . Out of fear . . . We knew it but we couldn't say it. (Zeynep, female, 56, housewife)

The presence of Alevi television is a way of coming out of the closet, so to speak, for the viewers, and validates their identity at the public level. While media defines the communal boundaries, it also seeks the attention and recognition of others. According to Zeynep, knowing oneself as Alevi can no longer be sustained within communal boundaries but requires the acknowledgement of outsiders and the acceptance of Alevi identity. Alevi television enables this without putting individual Alevis on the spot. The burden of representation (Tagg 1988) is taken from the shoulders of the individual or particular Alevi communities and is passed onto Alevi television, which does not objectify them with an external gaze:

> The reason why Alevis have television is that they haven't been able to express themselves or they haven't been able to express themselves as they like. Alevism has been discussed by others, defined by others. Hence Alevis established these channels to express themselves, to define themselves. (Hasret, 36, male, waiter)

Examining Alevi broadcasting in the 1990s Open Channel in Germany, Kosnick (2007: 108) argues that Alevis mainly aimed to challenge stereotypes, correct the negative images of Alevism that Sunni Muslims and the German majority might have, and mobilise the sympathetic interest of the public. Even though my interviews with television workers did not confirm the persistence of this concern, some viewers seem to adhere to the goal of fixing the problematics of the external gaze through making oneself visible on television. Here one can identify the parallel between the distrust of Sunni Muslims and mainstream Turkish television in depicting Alevism. Alevi protest at the series *Red Apple*, as discussed in Chapter 4, before it was broadcast can also be regarded as an outcome of this distrust. Arguably, with Alevi television the external gaze is not actively invited to recognise Alevis, as it would by Al-Canlar and other local diaspora broadcasting experiences, which aimed at changing the dominant Sunni Muslim perspective. The external gaze towards the community is rather expected to be able to see and acknowledge Alevi existence in a more subtle but determined way, one aimed at a long-term change. Such determination could be inferred from my interviews with television workers who seemed to remain calm following the closure of their stations and have sought different ways of being on screen again. In other words, neither Alevi televisions nor the viewers expect recognition to be easy or smooth. They regard it as a long process in the struggle for recognition.

It must be noted that the viewers' expectations from Alevi television are not confined to the politics of representation. The severing of the traditional ties between *ocak*s, *dede*s and *talip*s, which also embedded a way of living Alevism, created a sense of loss – in Sökefeld's (2002a) words, a 'collective amnesia'. As argued in Chapter 4, Alevi television attempts to fill this gap by bringing the diversity of Alevi communities and events to the screen. As confirmation of this mission, viewers also refer to television as a source of Alevi knowledge and rituals:

> I watch Alevi channels and I really like them. They are really good for the Alevi community. It is really good that we don't lose our tradition. I gained a lot from them. I learned a lot. Yes, we are Alevis but nobody taught us anything [about Alevism]. We learned things [about Alevism] from television. (Arif, male, 53, off-licence owner)

> For instance, TV10 was trying to keep our culture alive. They were passing our culture to new generations. (Abidin, male, 56, coffee-shop owner)

The desire to know and learn about Alevism also indicates a shift in Alevis' views as to what Alevism is. Here Alevism is regarded as external to the community, something to be learned and grasped and then applied, rather than a way of living.

This view also emerges in the viewers' approach to Alevi television. The viewers think that Alevis have lost a lot of knowledge about Alevism and its tenets due to oppression; Alevi media provides viewers with sources, more importantly oral and visual sources, through which they can make sense of Alevism and other Alevi communities:

> For instance, TV10 has been able to go to every region in Turkey. They have been able to broadcast from different regions. They did very good programmes both visually and research-wise. (Sakine, female, 47, housewife)

According to Arif, Abidin, Sakine and others, television not only exposes local knowledge and the practices of Alevism, it also reveals them through research. As argued in Chapter 5, Alevi television has equipped itself with an anthropological mission to discover different Alevi communities and broaden their viewers' conceptions about Alevism, based on first-hand experience. It enables Alevis to imagine themselves as part of a broader entity and that knowledge and communities are out there to be discovered. Through television, Alevis feel themselves to be part of a community whose boundaries are yet to be drawn and which are continuously expanding. In this sense, Alevi media are also given the mission of discovery and exposure which is shared, or maybe even foreseen, by the television workers, as demonstrated in Chapter 5.

The trust invested in Alevi television to pass on Alevi knowledge is striking. With few exceptions, none of my interviewees questioned the reliability of Alevi television in producing knowledge on Alevism. Being an insider media organisation seems to be sufficient in establishing trust between media and viewers. Despite their political distance from Cem TV, for instance, some of the viewers seem to take *cem* ceremonies broadcast on this channel at face value. Interestingly, the second-generation viewers share this perspective with the first-generation:

> Cem TV, Yol TV, I would watch these as well because my dad did. And some others too. Because I feel like they are the most reliable sources to listen to. (Damla, female, 23, accountant)

Despite their distance from Turkish media, the second-generation also engages with Alevi media with a curiosity and interest in Alevism. In other words, gaining knowledge is a key motivation for the second-generation viewers to watch Alevi television as well. For this reason, Alevi media has a sense of reliability by being an insider's voice, which also demonstrates that community boundaries matter for making sense of media content, particularly for minorities. It also indicates an essentialist notion of Alevism that the viewers might have about Alevi media – that if it is Alevi, it is trustworthy.

One can argue that the reliability attributed to television stems from 'media power' and a trust in media elites who have resources and the socio-cultural capital that ordinary viewers might lack (Ball-Rokeach 1998; Uslaner 1998; Portes 2000;

Livingstone and Markham 2008). This might be partially true. However, the participants' critical perceptions of mainstream Turkish media challenges the notion of media power as respectable. While television is regarded as a reliable source of knowledge on Alevism, mainstream Turkish channels are not deemed trustworthy for gaining an understanding of Turkish society and engaging with the Turkish political agenda. Elsewhere, I argue that Turkish television is the main source for learning about Turkish culture for the second-generation Kurdish Alevis in London and refer to this as 'mediatised culturalisation' (Emre Cetin 2020a). Even though Turkish television is not regarded as a reliable source, second-generation interviewees draw on television series and news to make sense of mainstream culture in Turkey, which they would otherwise have no experience of. Alevi television is also a reliable source for making sense of Turkish politics for the majority of my interviewees:

> They pass you what happened in the country [Turkey] on a reliable basis. The lickspittle media [mainstream Turkish media] is a lie machine. You can't find the right way just watching them. No way . . . (Abidin, male, 56, coffee-shop owner)

> Yol TV was giving news of the oppressed. It was clarifying who was oppressed and who the oppressors were. And these did not please the state, that's why they closed it. [. . .] Our television did nothing wrong. (Hasan, male, 70, retired)

I conducted more than half of my interviews in the aftermath of the state of emergency after the attempted coup of 2016, which resulted in a monovocal media environment reinforced by the authoritarian measure of closures. IMC TV and Hayat TV, which were left-leaning alternative channels that were also shut down, are often mentioned as other sources of reliable news and opinion. For the majority of my interviewees, Halk TV remains the only option for following the Turkish political agenda. Alevis' interest in left-leaning media, such as IMC and Hayat, is in alignment with their preference for positioning themselves in solidarity with other 'democratic forces' of Turkey, such as the left or the Kurdish movement, and seeing their emancipation through alliances with them. It also indicates the boundaries of Alevi cultural citizenship, which does not confine itself solely to Alevi identity and politics but more broadly embraces the Turkish political agenda.

Transversal Imaginaries

In this section, I examine the Alevi viewers' transversal imaginaries which embed different layers of the local, national, transnational and regional. As argued in Chapter 5, a transversal imaginary helps us to distinguish between these different layers, while also enabling us to address the relationship between them without being limited by the binaries of the home and host countries, or countries of arrival and departure. Also, the Alevi Revival has been mainly understood in terms of temporality, a sort of historical break, which created an emerging unexpected interest in and engagement with Alevism. The spatial dimension of the revival has been examined through a particular focus on transnational social spaces, mainly between Germany and Turkey (Sökefeld 2008a). However, Zırh (2008) emphasises that the Alevi Revival is a multi-sited phenomenon that includes different localities. For my interviewees, village life and past experiences, and first- and second-hand knowledge of it, appear to be prominent in constructing their transversal imaginaries. The village holds a significant value for interviewees, even though not everyone visits their village regularly:

> I feel homesick all the time. Missing the homeland . . . Today I am 70 years old. I visit Turkey and the places of my childhood are different. (Hasan, male, 70, retired)

Talking about the village is a way of locally and culturally situating themselves for many of my interviewees. For instance, Abidin, who emphasised that the closure of Alevi television is an issue for Turkish democracy, enthusiastically showed me the pictures of his village during the interview. Some interviewees also asked me where I was from and commented on Dersim, which is predominantly populated by Kurdish Alevis, and the villages they visited there and made comparisons between them. Village and regional associations established by Kurdish Alevis are widespread and well attended in London. While drawing the boundaries of different Alevi communities based on place of origin, they also play a significant role in shaping UK Alevi politics and the Federation. They sometimes make decisions about whom to vote for during *cemevi* or Federation elections, making the associations' members act as a block vote. They also choose not to hold funerals at the *cemevis* to challenge the *cemevi*'s authority if they are not happy with the actions of the community leaders or activists. Sustained and re-constructed ties through village and regional organisations in London which are also closely connected with the Federation indicate the complexities of transversal imaginaries and translocality. For my interviewees, the rural life of the past is also regarded as the source of 'authentic identity', 'true Alevism' or 'traditional Alevism', which are deemed to be fading or already lost. This partially explains the fascination with the village programmes on Alevi television and the channels' policy of giving voice to rural Alevis (as demonstrated in Chapter 5). For the viewers, village programmes serve as a way of connecting with 'original' sources, capturing a vanishing lifestyle.

Villages also serve as a temporal reference point through which the continuity of a sense of belonging and community ties can be sustained. One viewer, Gülizar, started her interview by telling her childhood story of the Maraş massacre. Her statement is very important as we still have only limited knowledge about the massacre and such knowledge is produced thanks to some witness and survivor accounts. Furthermore, her account also reveals the embeddedness of temporality and spatiality in the conception of the village as homeland and Alevis' inability to regard themselves as 'Turkish citizens':

My dad was in Maraş during the events [massacre]; then we went to Germany. We returned back to Turkey; then we came here. We weren't granted settlement in Germany. [. . .] I was little [at the time of the Maraş massacre]. My [great] uncle's house was burned down. He was shot, his wife was shot. My dad's uncle was killed. My dad was held captive. It was really painful. I would never wish it to happen again. Even now, when I visit Maraş I feel eery. You don't feel comfortable. You feel weird – I don't know. I went there after 32 years. I didn't feel like I missed it there. There was nothing. Because you have flashbacks . . . Yes, maybe I don't fully remember everything but I felt sour. It felt so difficult. Yes, I have uncles there but I felt sour – I don't know. Next time I went, we visited the *cemevi*. I didn't feel . . . I don't know if it was me or else. My parents don't go to Maraş unless they have to. After the Maraş [massacre], many left the town. My dad went to Germany. Then we had to leave three or four years after him. They [the locals] turned to be our enemy, I don't know how. The elderly would know better . . . We haven't been able to talk about this in the family because my parents would feel so sad. My dad would remember his uncle. My aunt-in-law was shot. [The bullet] hit her through her stomach and came out of her back. And this was done by her neighbour. Other relatives also died. It's so painful, the Maraş events . . . My granddad had a gun; that's why they didn't come close to us. The military came as well . . . It's really difficult to go through those days. I don't know. Then we moved to another city. But you're a nomad there because you don't live in your hometown. You are not comfortable [there] – you don't have a village or anything. You don't have your roots. You don't even have space to bury your dead. Our lot is being buried here and there. We don't have a place. They sold it at the time – our granddads sold it. They've sold it and came to Maraş. They haven't thought like, maybe our children would come and visit, maybe we have funerals . . . What can you do now? Nothing . . . Some of us die in Europe and remain there and some of us in Turkey, in a random place. Our funerals are lost, their places are lost. (Gülizar, female, 48, housewife)

As her parents were forced to migrate from Maraş following the massacre, for Gülizar migration is strongly associated with a sense of the loss of homeland. Home also means a place where one can be buried and can return to where one belongs. The lack of a space to be buried in Maraş dominates her account of migration. Zırh (2012b: 1759) states that 'providing proper customary funerals constitute a strong motivation for organizing in the context of migration' and Alevi organisations employ television broadcasting, among other sources, such as booklets and journals, in their endeavour to revive Alevi mortuary services. Gülizar has been an active member of the Federation by organising events and undertaking different responsibilities within the organisation. Her sensibility about death and funeral confirms Zırh's point about the significance of funerals and how they facilitate recruitment to Alevi organisations, so that one's body would not be abandoned. This is also discussed by other interviewees, such as Hüseyin (male, 62, retired): '[W]e live as an Alevi when we are alive but we are buried like Sunni when we die.'

In this regard, community ties are sustained through funerals and places of burials. Aleviness transcends the boundaries of life and death: one is Alevi even after death. Gülizar's concern about the loss of a space in a graveyard and the dispersal of family members' dead bodies across different places is not only a concern about where bodies are buried, but also a way of mourning. Displacement following the Maraş massacre also has a temporal dimension. It not only indicates the loss of home but the loss of immediate ties to the past and present, and even to an 'eternal future' symbolised by death. In this sense, locality, the village in particular, is not only a spatial address, a place of origin, but is also a temporal 'home' for one's communal identity, sustaining connections with one's ancestors and their past and future.

Where interviewees come from also defines who they are. In other words, locality is a key definer of Kurdish Aleviness. Rather than referring to their country of origin, my interviewees prefer to detail the region and village they come from, as well as their tribe. Ali, who has been engaged with Alevi and village organisations for 20 years, says that:

> We all came here as Alevi Kırmanci. Some call it Kurdish... Villages of Gürün, villages of Elbistan... We all belong to same tribe, Sinemilli. People came here and engaged with different political factions, Kurdish, socialist, atheist... But it is clear where we all came from. (Ali, male, 47, business owner)

As discussed in Chapter 1, Kurdish Aleviness is an ethno-religious identity (Aydın 2018; Cetin, Jenkins and Aydın 2020) and Aleviness is strongly tied to tribes and tribalism, particularly in the case of Kurds (Gezik 2012, 2018). The sense of community, which is defined by ethno-religiosity, is now sustained through these local and contemporaneous transnational connections. Some of my interviewees mentioned that they have relatives and family members abroad, in European countries in particular:

> We are seven siblings. Four of us are here, one is in Sweden, one is in Canada, one is in Turkey. (Ali, male, 47, business owner)

> I have three siblings in Germany, one brother in Turkey. (Abidin, male, 56, coffee-shop owner)

Akdemir (2016: 89) also notes that many of the participants in her research had connections, particularly with Germany, while some preferred the UK over Germany as the final destination. Having relatives and family members across different European countries is a powerful dynamic that reinforces the transversal imaginaries in my interviewees' accounts. Transnational ties with family members, relatives and acquaintances living in different European countries demonstrate how transversal imaginaries constructed by Alevi media correspond well to the lived experiences of their viewers.

While for the first-generation Alevi, identity and their local origin stand out in defining who they are as a person, the second-generation interviewees fluctuate between different identities and conceptions of citizenship. Unlike the first generation, who associate their Britishness with passive forms of citizenship, such as holding a passport, paying taxes or having access to the National Health Service, all of my second-generation interviewees' sense of belonging and citizenship are situational as they describe themselves as Alevi, Kurdish or British depending on who is asking and under what circumstances. A designation of Britishness is always accompanied by some sort of origin, either as Alevi or Kurdish or both.

> British comes after Kurdish Alevi. I don't think I ever said to myself, 'yeah, I'm British'. I say, 'I'm born and raised here'. But when they ask me, 'I'm Kurdish Alevi'. I do say, 'I am British'; it is always my nationality I say is British. My ethnicity always is Kurdish Alevi. It just depends what they are asking me. There is a difference, yeah. (Damla, female, 23, accountant)

> If somebody asks me, [I would say] I am Alevi. To be honest, I would say it but I don't know much about it. Like I can't explain it to anybody. Alevism is this, Alevism is that . . . But this is where I see myself as. Alevi community is so huge. They are not all so . . . Yes, they are everywhere but only a minority are putting their voice out. They are visible but people overlook. (Ela, female, 22, undergraduate student)

While talking about her visits to Turkey, which includes visiting her grandparents in their village, family members in Istanbul and holiday destinations such as Antalya and Bodrum, 29-year-old Sevil says that she feels she is:

> an outsider, as a complete outsider. I don't feel like a foreigner there in the same way that I don't feel like a foreigner in here. But an outsider. . . . (Sevil, female, 29, political adviser)

Göner (2017a) argues that Kurdish Alevis are constructed as outsiders within the Turkish nationalist imagination and this position is adopted by the community members themselves who have not been able to associate themselves with the 'ideal citizenship' of the Turkish Republic. Interestingly, this perspective applies to the second-generation interviewees despite the fact that their experience in Turkey is limited to short visits:

> I can't really openly say I am Kurdish; I am Alevi in Turkey. Kurds have always been humiliated; Alevis' houses were demolished. Lots of things happened. People probably are still in fear [in Turkey] but when we were there . . . For instance, when we were there NMP [Nationalist Movement Party][6] had a demonstration . . . Shall we speak in Turkish or in English? . . . We didn't know what to do. We know what to do here when there is a demonstration but you feel a bit lost in Turkey as there are

---

[6] The Nationalist Movement Party and its youth and paramilitary organisations are considered to have initiated and/or escalated violence during the Alevi massacres of the 1970s. See Sinclair-Webb (2003) and Çakmak (2020).

> always things happening. Well, as I said, we had to walk through the crowd to get to our hotel. We were really afraid. We stayed silent. We thought to get a taxi but even if we did, the traffic wasn't moving. We spoke quietly amongst ourselves. We spoke English. I think we pretended to be English. We didn't know how to act. (Özlem, female, 23, undergraduate student)

Özlem and her three other cousins feel safer pretending to be English in the face of a nationalist demonstration in Turkey, given that it would be difficult to infer their identity from their looks. In this account, an ordinary tourist's visit to a seaside town becomes a challenge for the second-generation. Akın, whose parents migrated to the UK when he was four, also tells how he quickly becomes friends with Kurdish waiters in the luxurious hotels where he stays and this makes him feel settled. Despite having no first-hand life experience of Turkey, the second-generation carry a strong sense of being outsiders, which is probably reinforced further by migration to the UK as they do not know how to protect themselves in risky environments in Turkey.

Alevi television is able to facilitate generational affinities among Alevis living in different places by being a common cultural reference point. It enables younger generations to make sense of and connect with the Alevi cultural identity of previous generations:

> My parents watch it because it's their channel, their people's channel. The talks there or the music they play, it's the music they would sing. It's what they want to watch. They want to watch their own people. I don't know what it is but maybe just to see their own people. My mum, she loves it. For instance, my mum says that my granddad used to attend *cem*s. They have an *ocak*. Always *cem* . . . My grandad used to go to *cem* every week and my mum saw him going. They also watch Alevi TV. When I go to my granddad's, they also watch the same channels. It is not a habit, I think. It is the thing that they grew up with. When I go at my granddad's, I watch Cem TV and Yol TV. I think it is mainly kind of influence as well. If you see them watching it, you want to watch it as well. They even get the pleasure of seeing their own people there. They enjoy watching their own [culture], for instance . . . When they did music videos, we had someone from our village playing. I often see him on TV. When I see him, I would love it. He is on TV, I even watched it yesterday. It is nice. (Damla, female, 23, accountant)

Damla's statement is important in terms of addressing the significance of affect in engaging with Alevi television, which indicates that struggle for recognition is also about the politics of affect. Seeing one's identity and culture on television is not solely about making oneself visible or getting the message across or fighting against prejudice. It is also about the pleasures of consuming cultural artefacts and feeling a sense of validation by seeing oneself on screen.

The sense of validation created by the community constructed through television is addressed as a source of pleasure. Listening to Alevi songs, *deyiş* and *gülbang* is also mentioned by Abidin, İmam, İbrahim and others as a source of pleasure and a way of living one's identity through television. As mentioned in Chapter 1, Alevi radio stations were very influential during the 1990s in Turkey and Alevi music served almost as an implicit signifier of Aleviness and an accepted, 'risk free', form of cultural expression, unlike Kurdish music, which had led to fines being imposed by the Radio Television Supreme Council on the radio stations that played them. Examining how the Kurdish audience engage with Turkish nationalist fictional programmes, I (Emre Cetin 2015) found out that the viewers prefer misrepresentation to being invisible and think that it is better to be depicted as 'villain guerrillas' than not to be represented at all. No doubt, everyday cultural signifiers such as clothing and music are able to facilitate viewing pleasures stemming from cultural identities. More importantly, however, the ability to consume the same cultural content in a village in Turkey and in London or elsewhere is able to generate transversal imaginaries that cut across different spatialities. By showing *dedes* visiting their *talips* based in a village as well as in London, Alevi television, I argue, introduces a similar sense of connectivity and continuity among community members across familial relationships and beyond. Damla identifies a generational continuity between herself, her mother and grandfather in relating to Alevi rituals and practices, in both face-to-face (*cems*) and mediated (television) forms. It is also important to note that the local has an exceptional space in the transversal imaginary. To put it plainly, transversal imaginaries are mainly sustained through local ties and connections which are strongly situated within the national and transnational.

Significantly, despite occasionally visiting their parents' villages, the second-generation's conception of the local has nothing to do with village or small towns in Turkey, which are mainly places of departure for their parents. When asked about local programmes on television, they mentioned a show broadcast on a mainstream Turkish channel which is available on Turksat and aimed at Turkish migrants living in Europe:

> I have actually been on them. I've actually been on *Londra Mahallesi* ['Neighbourhood of London']. It was on 2012. I was working at a solicitor's firm; I was a training solicitor. It was broadcast on the day when my grandparents came here to visit us from village in Turkey. We watched it together at my uncle's. It's even on YouTube now. (Akın, male, 35, solicitor)

> There is this programme, *Londra Mahallesi*, I watch it every once in a while. They repeat it at night. If I see it, I watch it, but I wouldn't specifically go and say 'let me watch Londra Mahallesi'. I do like to see what is going on, what they do talk about. I find it quite entertaining actually. Maybe because it is on Turkish TV, it attracts my attention. I'm like, 'London's on Turkish TV, we see these people.' I feel some sort of affinity. That's why I watch it. (Ela, female, 22, undergraduate student)

Transversal imaginaries are constructed differently for the first and second generation, based on their transnational ties and conceptions of locality. While the village or area defined by tribal ties are more significant for the first generation, the second-generation viewers tend to relate to London or to even more specific areas of the city, such as Enfield or Hackney. Instead, villages and localities in Turkey are experienced through affinity and social relations carried on in London rather than relating to physical space. In other words, villages are still lived by the first generation through their social life with other village members in the UK and though their regular visits to the villages in Turkey, whereas villages are mainly 'experienced' by the second generation through social circles in the UK as they rarely visit villages. The first generation's past and sense of belonging to Kurdish Aleviness through village life is carried on in Alevi television through village programmes, which are rarely consumed by the second-generation viewers. This indicates the divergences in imaginary of different generations and re-addresses transversal imaginary as translocal.

So far, I have demonstrated the extent to which transversal citizenship draws on ethno-religious identity formation. However, transversal imaginaries and acts of citizenship have not been sustainable because of the unstable political climate in Turkey. They have been disrupted due to the closure of television channels following the attempted coup in 2016. In the following chapter, I focus on the closure of Alevi media and discuss its implications for transversal citizenship.

7

Communicative Ethnocide and Transversal Citizenship

Three Alevi television stations, Cem TV, TV10 and Yol TV, were on air before the attempted coup of July 2016. But following it, TV10 was closed down in September 2016 by decree, under the government's state of emergency, and Yol TV's broadcasting was suspended in December 2016 by the Radio and Television Supreme Council on the grounds of insulting the president, praising terrorist organisations and broadcasting without a Turkish licence. Cem TV remained in operation and is based in Turkey. However, given that each TV channel represents different political orientations within the Alevi community and that the Turkish government approaches each one differently, we cannot examine authoritarian approaches towards media simply by resorting to the use of umbrella terms such as the silencing or freedom of media. Although such terms are useful in addressing the broader structures of state oppression, they overshadow the governmentality, the nuanced approach that the state adopts in silencing the spectrum of alternative voices.

For this reason, the closure of Alevi television stations in Turkey needs to be situated within the history of the Alevi community and the Turkish state's policies towards Alevis in order to see the nuances of silencing and oppression. While these policies have been part of a broader blow to media freedom in Turkey, I argue that the closure of Alevi channels is an attempt at the communicative ethnocide of the transnational Alevi community by silencing the multiple voices within that community, weakening its transnational connections, and damaging the multi-spatiality between the local, national, and transnational, and therefore the transversal imaginary that was fundamentally supported by Alevi television. By looking at Alevi television and comparing it with Kurdish media, my aim is to demonstrate that ethnocide as a form of cultural annihilation also has serious consequences in terms of media communications and transversal citizenship. In this chapter, I start by providing a theoretical framework for ethnocide by drawing on Appadurai (2006), Clastres (2010) and Yalçınkaya (2014). I then introduce the concept of communicative ethnocide and discuss its relevance for understanding challenges towards transversal citizenship.[1]

Ethnocide: The Cultural Annihilation of a Community

'Genocide' is a legal term which refers to the destruction of a community by the persecution of its members. Although the term is primarily used in reference to the persecution of the Jewish community by the Nazis during the Second World War, this was not the first act of genocide and many communities were intentionally destroyed before this time, including the Armenians in Turkey during the First World War (Akcam 2013). Lemkin (cited in Clavero 2008), who coined the term genocide, has suggested that the term ethnocide can also be used as a synonym; in legal studies, ethnocide often refers to cultural genocide and the cultural destruction of indigenous cultures (Clavero 2008). In the 1970s, it was particularly used in relation to indigenous cultures in the Americas (Barabas and Bartholeme 1973; Lizot 1976; Escobar 1989; Venkateswar 2004), although later the concept was used to explain the cultural destruction of different communities living in different countries (Lamarchand 1994; Clarke 2001; Williams 2002; Casula 2015). A report by the UN on the genocide of indigenous populations refers to ethnocide as follows:

> In cases where such [state] measures can be described as acts committed for the deliberate purpose of eliminating the culture of a group by systematically destructive and obstructive action, they could be deemed to constitute clear cases of ethnocide or *cultural genocide*. (Cited in Clavero 2008: 99)

Ethnocide can be regarded as a cultural weapon that aims to destroy the culture of a community with or without killing its members. While genocide, according to Clastres (2010), aims to annihilate the body as the marker of race, ethnocide annihilates the mind; it is, he argues, 'the systematic destruction of ways of living and thinking of people from those who lead this venture of destruction' (103). Although Clastres makes a comparison between genocide and ethnocide, he does not equate one with the other and acknowledges that the destruction of bodies is worse than the destruction of a culture, but only on the grounds that 'less barbarity is better than more barbarity' (103). Williams's definition of the 'culture as ordinary' (2002) allows us to reflect on the everyday dimensions of ethnocide, where we can see how it interrupts, transforms and distorts the everyday practices of an ethnic community, including its symbols and rituals, which provide it with its particular characteristics. Ethnocide can take different forms, such as suggesting the adoption of alternative rituals to those specific to the community, or forcibly replacing them with different practices, or the destruction of culturally

---

[1] For an earlier version of this chapter, see Emre Cetin (2018b).

significant spaces where everyday practices and encounters take place, and so on. Hence ethnocide can be thought of as a programme which attacks the culture of communities on a day-to-day basis.

Essential to both genocide and ethnocide is the concept of the 'Other' since in both cases the Other means difference and this difference has to be dealt with. For this reason, in making sense of ethnocide, it is useful to compare it to genocide's vision of the Other. While the genocidal mind sees Others as evil and wants to eliminate them, the ethnocidal mind wishes to transform them by eliminating the difference and making the Others identical to itself. Whereas the genocidal mind sees a hierarchy of races, with its own superior to Others, the ethnocidal mind presupposes a hierarchy of cultures (Clastres 2010). In this sense, ethnocide involves a cultural war against the Other, with the aim of diminishing the characteristics of what makes the Other different and foreseeing an eventual assimilation of the Other into the mainstream, thus 'reducing the Other to the same' by 'the dissolution of the multiple into one' (Clastres 2010: 108).

For Clastres (2010) it is a universal fact that all cultures are ethnocentric, but being ethnocentric does not necessarily entail that a culture is ethnocidal. For this to occur particular tools and opportunities are required and these are afforded through the formation of the state. For Clastres, the state is a requirement and precondition for ethnocide:

> All state organizations are ethnocidal, ethnocide is the normal mode of existence of the State. There is thus a certain universality to ethnocide, in that it is the characteristic not only of a vague, indeterminate 'white world,' but of a whole ensemble of societies which are societies with a State. (111)

Simply put, the systematic cultural elimination of the Other requires the state's organised and institutionalised power. Violence is seen as inherent in the existence of the state and the need to engage in systematic violence both leads to and requires the organisational capacity of the state. It is important to emphasise this interconnection in order to understand the complexity of ethnocide as a cultural form of violence. While Clastres sees ethnocide as an inherent characteristic of state societies and considers ethnocide as a tool that can be used by every state, he also recognises the potential for resistance by the Other in such societies. For Clastres, 'the ability of resistance of the oppressed minority' means that ethnocide is not an inescapable fate for the Other (103). Whether the Other is able to resist ethnocide or not depends on the community's history and the way that the community is organised. One needs to look at the community's capacity as well as the state's approach in a given historical context in order to understand the extent of ethnocide.

According to Yalçınkaya (2014), the Turkish state's approach towards Alevis must be seen as a form of ethnocide, even though Alevis themselves have tended to view it rather as assimilation. Yalçınkaya (2014: 23) argues that the state's policies towards Alevis is an attempt at getting them to comply with the state's definition of the ideal citizen, and for this reason ethnocide is a more accurate concept to understand the state's approach towards Alevis. Unlike assimilation, which aims at destroying Alevi as an identity, along with Alevi cultural practices so that culturally Alevis become indistinguishable from the Sunni Muslim majority, the Turkish state is concerned with redefining Alevis and their culture to produce a political identity commensurate with that of the ideal Turkish citizen. Yalçınkaya adopts a Foucauldian approach which sees ethnocide as a creative activity that creates an identity, while transforming it according to the desires of the state. The state's ethnocidal policies does not aim at destroying Alevis per se. Instead, it seeks to destroy the community's internal order and its power of self-regulation (Yalçınkaya 2014: 32); what lies at the core of this ethnocidal project is the religious practices of Alevis. The state wants to transform Alevi identity through displacing, re-designing and re-conceptualising Alevi rites and rituals (Yalçınkaya 2014). The discussion of whether the *cemevi* is a place of worship and whether the *cem* itself is a religious ceremony exemplifies this approach. The state resists recognising the *cemevi* and the *cem* as essentially and distinctively religious and instead attempts to redefine them as 'culturally deviant' practices. In order to examine the ethnocide of Alevis, Yalçınkaya (2014) focuses particularly on the period in which the JDP government launched various projects involving Alevis, such as the Muharrem Fast Breaking, the Alevi Opening and the Mosque-Cemevi project. At the Muharrem Fast Breaking in 2008, Alevi faith leaders, *dede*s, were invited to break their Muharrem fasts according to Islamic conventions and at some official meetings such as the Alevi Workshops in 2009 the *dede*s were treated as though they were *tariqa* leaders, that is, leaders of an Islamic school of Sufism or sects (Ecevitoğlu and Yalçınkaya 2013; Borovalı and Boyraz 2015; Lord 2017).

Yalçınkaya (2014: 32–5) describes the particular methods through which ethnocide operates. These are: 1) displacement of the community; 2) destroying its locality and geography (also see Göner 2017a; Orhan 2019); 3) destroying the memory of the community; and 4 the displacement of the community's performances. Following the massacres[2] of Koçgiri (1921) and Dersim (1938) and the pogroms of Çorum, Malatya, and Sivas during the 1970s, Alevi communities were forcibly displaced and re-settled or had to leave their villages and neighbourhoods in order to avoid the escalating violence. Yalçınkaya expands the displacement to include housing policies and the gentrification of

---

[2] Scholars use different concepts for understanding the Dersim massacre. Göner (2017a) calls it genocide since the massacre constituted the systematic extermination of local people who had been targeted on the basis of their ethnic, religious and community ties, including remaining small Armenian communities following the Armenian Genocide of 1915 in the region. Bruinessen (1994) prefers 'ethnocide' as the extermination was based on a selective approach sparing some tribes, and did not target the entire local community of the region (also see Keiser 2003). Alevi organisations such as the Alevi Federation Germany and DAF acknowledge the Dersim massacre as genocide.

urban areas, where Alevi neighbourhoods were pushed out towards the margins of cities. The second method targets human-made or natural places that are deemed sacred by the community, such as specific locations of pilgrimage, rivers or hills. Building a dam on the Munzur river in Dersim, which is considered sacred by the local Alevis, exemplifies this method. Destroying localities is also about destroying the collective memory of the community as these places are also spaces of remembering and commemoration and of reproducing the myths that construct the collective identity and sense of belonging. In a similar vein, the management of the Hacı Bektaş Lodge and the festival organisation by the state in the 1990s is another example of this triple function of destroying the locality, collective memory and displacing the performances by scripting, spectacularising and de-sacralising them as staged performances. Replacing sacred fire with a candleholder, opening and closing the *cem* ceremony with *namaz* and running a *cem* ceremony for Ramadan are other ways of displacing *cem* performance (Yalçınkaya 2014: 35).

I would, however, like to introduce a fifth method of ethnocide: destroying the communicative means of the community, and it is this which I refer to as 'communicative ethnocide'. As discussed in this section, the Turkish state's perspective towards Alevis is highly influenced by its genocidal and assimilationist policies against Armenians and Kurds (Ateş 2011; Dressler 2013, 2021). Ateş (2011: 21) argues that Alevi persecutions in the Republican period stemmed from the threat felt by the state as a result of Alevi rights claims. Persecution has been a systematic bio-political method employed by the state and executed either by armed forces, as in Koçgiri and Dersim, or by paramilitary support, as in the massacres of Çorum, Malatya and Sivas (Yalçınkaya 2020). While ethnocide is the cultural counterpart of this approach, communicative ethnocide is the specific method which targets communication among the members of the community and their ability to feel part of it via media and communications. The following section unpacks this concept by focusing on Alevi media and comparing it with Kurdish television, which has also been systematically targeted by the communicative ethnocide policies of the state towards the Kurdish community.

Communicative Ethnocide: Destroying the Communicative Means of a Community

As 'the suppression of cultural differences as deemed inferior or bad' (Clastres 2010: 108), ethnocidal violence can target the locality, memory, performances and the communicative capacity of the community. Thus, communicative ethnocide is not an isolated process but is part of the ethnocidal project undertaken on a particular community. Its aim is to destroy the communicative means and capacity of that community in order to interrupt and eventually annihilate its cultural formation. Communicative ethnocide can take place through various means and media, including cultural events, social gatherings, press, television and social media. While each means of communicative ethnocide deserves to be investigated in depth, here I would like to focus on the communicative ethnocide that takes place in the context of television broadcasting, which then has further implications for the uses of digital media (discussed in Chapter 8).

As with ethnocide more broadly, communicative ethnocide requires the power of the state because currently states are the main actors regulating communication policies via, for example, television licences, channel allocations and infrastructural regulations. Furthermore, states are the primary actors which hold particular agendas and policies concerning minorities (Brubaker 1996). Taken together, therefore, communicative ethnocide can be seen as a planned and regulated action of the state. It can take both a passive form, where the state, for example, sets up legal barriers to the operation of ethnic media, and an active form, such as imposing a ban on broadcasting in particular languages, or interrupting and censoring broadcasting. In both cases, the aim is to hinder or eliminate: 1) the interaction between the members of the community; 2) the members' ability to stimulate and guide their social imaginary as to what constitutes their community; 3) the multivocality within the community; and 4) the cultural self-reproduction of the community through media. Therefore, it has significant implications in terms of identity politics, minority rights and the way collective identities that are under- or misrepresented in the media express themselves and enact their rights claims in and though media.

Communicative ethnocide has a number of consequences for ethnic communities in four main domains: representation, language, space and citizenship acts. For those communities that are under- or misrepresented in the mainstream media, ethnic media provides opportunities to raise their own voice (Bailey *et al.* 2007; Matsaganis *et al.* 2011; Karim and Al-Rawi 2018), something which communicative ethnocide seeks to eliminate by silencing such communities by demolishing the potential for a multivocal media ecology. Ethnic media is also crucial for the linguistic survival of many communities as it serves as a means to revive dying languages and to popularise them among community members. Communicative ethnocide diminishes this opportunity as well as interrupting the transfer of native languages to the new generation. It also has serious consequences in terms of the spatiality of community identity in the digital era, where members of the same community in different localities can connect not only through television but also social media. Especially for those minorities that are usually dispersed through different locations, that is, stateless or migrant communities, communicative ethnocide means the interruption of self-imaginaries which are constructed and sustained mainly through media. Finally, ethnic and community media is able to engage and mobilise communities in an active way so that community members can become involved in everyday politics and rights movements as well as community politics (Bailey *et al.* 2007;

Matsaganis *et al.* 2011; Karim and Al-Rawi 2018). Communicative ethnocide diminishes this potential for citizenship acts by destroying the community's own public sphere.

The contemporary situation of Alevi television exemplifies these features of communicative ethnocide where Alevi culture is being silenced in the media as part of the broader ethnocide policy of the state. At this point I shall examine the communicative ethnocide of Alevi television through three distinct but related dimensions: infrastructural; audience; and transversal.

Infrastructural Dimension

Along with eleven channels, most of which were Kurdish channels, TV10 was closed down under the state of emergency in September 2016, which also meant that all its equipment and infrastructure were confiscated to be sold to third parties. An appeal by TV10 to resume broadcasting was later rejected by the State of Emergency Commission. However, TV10 has operated online, albeit with limited resources and a reduced programme schedule, which has resulted in a loss of a wide section of its audience who do not have internet access. Yol TV's blackout also took place in late 2016 under the state of emergency; however, the way it was silenced was different, but like TV10 it is also available online as well as on IPTV, which has also resulted in a loss of audience, as will be discussed more in detail in Chapter 8.

It is important to understand that communicative ethnocide is not necessarily totalitarian in the sense that the state recognises and responds differently to the differences, even nuances, contained within ethnic identities. The Turkish state's varied approach to different Alevi television stations can be seen to be a result of this nuanced approach. For instance, TV10, which is regarded as the voice of Kurdish Alevis, has been subject to harsher measures, such as the confiscation of tools and equipment and the arrest of journalists working for the channel, whereas Yol TV was closed down due to the Radio and Television Supreme Council's decision. Since the first Alevi TV station, TV Avrupa, started broadcasting, Alevi television has explored a variety of ways of representing Alevism and the Alevi identity, from broadcasting video clips of Alevi music to producing programmes on Alevi religion. Until recently, different Alevi television channels could be clearly differentiated in terms of their political orientations as an extension of the differences within the Alevi movement and the effect that these orientations have had on programming content in relation to Alevism itself. Thus, as well as reflecting different political orientations within the Alevi community, Cem TV, TV10 and Yol TV also adopt different definitions of Alevism. Within this variety of representations of Alevism, the state has a particular 'preferred Alevism', which clearly situates it within Islam. This preferred Alevism has been voiced by Cem TV. For many of my interviewees, the Cem Foundation and Cem TV are a state project which works to assimilate Alevis into the Turkish–Islam synthesis.[3] This accounts for the fact that while TV10 and Yol TV, which do not promulgate this 'preferred' definition, have been subject to different forms of communicative ethnocide, Cem TV has remained untouched and is on air. As Clastres (2010) and Yalçınkaya (2014) argue, ethnocide does not aim to annihilate ethnic identity, as is the case with genocide, but aims to make the Other resemble the Same – the more similar it is to the Same (in this case Turkish–Sunni–Muslim), the better. This is the role that Cem TV assumes in its representation of Alevism, one that approximates Aleviness (Other) to Sunni Islam and Turkishness (Same). In many ways, it is similar to the Kurdish TV station TRT Kurdi, which was established by the Turkish state to fulfil the requirements of the European Union, and which can be thought as serving the same mission and representing the 'preferred Kurdishness'.[4]

The fact that Alevi channels with different political orientations have been subject to varying measures is itself indicative of the complexity involved in understanding how communicative ethnocide works and how it needs to be distinguished from cruder forms of censorship. While both these other forms and communicative ethnocide are violations by the state, the latter works by targeting a community and obstructing its communicative means in order to destroy the community's cultural formation. Hence, I argue that the closure of TV10 and Yol TV cannot simply be seen as attacks on freedom of speech or media but are deeply rooted within the state's ethnocidal policy against Alevis and must be regarded as a specific part of Alevi ethnocide.

Audience Dimension

While it is more common to interfere in the content, production and regulation of ethnic television through the means of censorship and control, communicative ethnocide can also encompass the audience. For instance, in the case of Kurdish television, the viewership act itself can be regarded as an ethnic manifestation and communicative ethnocide has set its sights on viewership practices. The satellite dishes on top of the roofs of Kurdish homes were distinguishable with the change

---

[3] The Turkish–Islam synthesis can be regarded as the founding principle of the Turkish Republic, where the ideal citizenship is described around the composition of Turkishness and Muslimness. However, the term Turkish–Islam synthesis became a more systematic ideological programme in the 1980s and was proactively reinforced by the state (Güvenç et al. 1991).

[4] Smets (2016: 742) mentions that TRT 6's editors are journalists who were recruited from amongst the Gülenists before the coup and at a time when the Gülenists were supported by the government. This also indicates the state's approach to the communicative ethnocide of the Kurds, which is one of Islamising them through the means of a religious organisation – in other words, reassembling the Other (Kurdish) as the Same (Turkish) through the use of the common ground of religion (Islam). It is no coincidence that TRT 6 has been more attractive to those Kurds who are more religious and for whom their Muslim identity matters (Arsan 2014).

of satellites from Eutelsat to Intelsat and, because of this, the Turkish authorities were able to detect who was watching Med TV – the dishes acted as flags of identity. This resulted in

> the smashing of satellite dishes, the intimidation of viewers, dish vendors, dish installers, and coffee-houses; a more effective form of repression is cutting off electricity from villages and small towns during prime-time hours when MED-TV is on the air. (Hassanpour 1998: 61)

This has not happened to viewers of Alevi television as it is not possible to detect who they are by simple surveillance techniques, as was the case with the Kurds. However, the closing of television channels and limiting them mainly to online communication has necessarily had an effect on the audience. My interviews with viewers in the UK reiterate the urge for visibility and the feeling of loss on a collective level following the closures. Nuray, who has been active in the Federation in the last ten years, says that Alevi channels have been a meeting point for the community:

> I used to watch Yol TV a lot. I really liked the programmes there. They were really important, TV10 and Yol TV, because they were depicting Alevis. We weren't mentioned in the news in any other channels, even in the case of important matters, maybe just in a line or two . . . Our channels made Alevis meet. Their closure is such a loss for our community. (Nuray, female, 47, housewife)

The interviews conducted with those who work for Alevi television suggest that the closure of the channels has been a challenge, especially for those Alevis who live in remote and rural areas. Rural Alevis find it much more difficult to represent themselves and to get their voices heard in media and politics. In this sense, Alevi television holds a symbolic significance for Alevis who live in remote places, particularly where there is a Sunni Muslim majority. At the same time, one can argue that the closure of oppositional television stations in the aftermath of the attempted coup has also pushed urban Alevis to rely more on Alevi television in order to receive information other than that provided by government-supported media organisations. My informal discussions with Alevis living in Ankara and Istanbul, especially with those who do not or cannot use social media, suggest that they have found it difficult to access reliable news sources after the closure of oppositional television channels, including Alevi media. In this way, communicative ethnocide is more destructive during periods of authoritarianism and increasing censorship where communities require more information about the political agenda in order to protect and defend themselves and sustain their community ties.

Transversal Dimension

The experience of Kurdish broadcasting in Europe, starting with Med TV and followed by Medya TV and Roj TV, illustrates an active form of communicative ethnocide which has strong parallels with the fate of Alevi television broadcasting. Originally dispersed into four states, Iraq, Iran, Syria and Turkey, the Kurds are currently a large community, of which there are an estimated 14 million in Turkey and 850,000 in Western Europe.[5] While the Kurdish movement dates back to the late Ottoman period, the struggle gained considerable momentum in 1978 with the formation of the PKK and their policy of armed opposition to the Turkish state and call for independence, and later for autonomy and cultural rights. Kurdish television broadcasting in the Turkish context has been very much framed by this armed conflict and political struggle, as well as international crises in the region. It makes an interesting case study of a medium for an ethnic group which does not have a state yet is aiming to build a national identity through television in a transnational context (Hassanpour 1998, 2003; Sinclair and Smets 2014; Keleş 2015; Smets 2016).

Med TV started its broadcasts from the UK in 1995 with a licence from the Independent Television Commission (ITC) granted for ten years. However, as a result of diplomatic pressure from the Turkish state, less than four years later, in March 1999, its licence was revoked by the ITC (Sinclair and Smets 2014: 324) with accusations that the channel supported 'terrorism' and broadcast 'hate propaganda' (Hassanpour 1998, 2003). This was followed by raids on the studios of Med TV, arrests of the television staff and the seizure of its computers and hardware from its offices in Belgium, Germany and the UK, after which it began its broadcasts via the French-based Eutelsat, until France Telecom refused to renew its licence (Hassanpour 1998, 2003). Following a similar pattern to the political parties established by the Kurdish movement, which were continuously closed down and re-opened under different names, Med TV was re-established again as Medya TV in France in 1999, from which it broadcast until 2004, when the 'Conseil Superieur de l'Audiovisuel [...] the French licensing authority, found that Medya TV was merely a successor channel to Med TV and revoked its broadcasting licence' (Sinclair and Smets 2014: 325). Following Medya TV's closure, Roj TV, which was primarily based in Denmark, replaced the channel. Sinclair and Smets (2014) provide a detailed account of how Roj TV led to another international crisis, this time between Denmark and Turkey, involving various parties, such as Eutelsat and Reporters Without Borders, in a long judicial process. In the event, the Danish court ruled against a ban on Roj TV or on Nuce TV, the latter having been designed as a replacement in the event of Roj TV's closure. Recently, the Kurdish television landscape has expanded to include various local, national and transnational channels as well as thematic broadcasting such as news and children's television. However, the state of emergency has given an opportunity for the Turkish government to silence Kurdish media by arresting

---

[5] See http://www.institutkurde.org/en/kurdorama/; last accessed 19 November 2021.

Kurdish journalists, closing down news agencies and blacking out television channels such as Jiyan, Mezopotamya and Denge.

The presence of Med TV and the studios, offices and production facilities of its successor stations in different European countries, such as the UK, Belgium, Germany, Sweden and Russia, reinforced the identity of Euro-Kurdishness, which as Soğuk (2008: 185) notes is cultivated through such a sense of aterritoriality and borderlessness. Despite its Euro-Kurdish identity, Kurdish broadcasting from Europe has been subjected to a transnational form of communicative ethnocide in which various countries have been involved in the Turkish state's attempt to silence Kurdish television. In Sinclair and Smets's (2014: 320) words, '[n]ever before in the history of European television broadcasting has there been a case in which the European Union [. . .] countries have aggressively fought to fine, censure and close down television channels broadcasting from within the EU'. This aggression by these EU countries has been stoked by international initiatives arising from the Turkish state. As Hassanpour (1998: 53) comments, '[a]mong the Middle Eastern countries, Turkey is the first and the only one to use its full state power to silence MED-TV', and in order to implement its communicative ethnocide, the state has used different methods. Within Turkey, it has 'unleashed its coercive forces to prevent the reception of the airwaves within Turkey, whereas in Europe, it used diplomatic power, espionage, jamming, and various forms of intimidation to stop the emission of television signals' (Hassanpour 1998: 53).

Even though the Turkish state has attempted to intervene in Alevi politics in European countries with, for example, its attempt to change the curriculum for Alevi lessons taught in Germany (as communicated in an interview with a member of the Alevi Federation Germany), there has been no direct interference by the Turkish state in the broadcasting by Alevi television channels in Europe, unlike the situation with Kurdish television. However, the threat of possible action in the future and the measures taken against Alevi television in Turkey means that communicative ethnocide challenges the transversal imaginary of the Alevi community. Naki from Yol TV explains the extent to which Yol TV serves as a means of connectivity for Alevis living in different countries:

> Because this television does not belong to individuals, firstly the German Federation of Alevi Unions then other European countries [the members of the Alevi Unions living in European countries] had to watch it. In such a position, it means, say you live in Cologne, then you are able to watch what Alevis in Sweden do. You could watch what Alevis in Denmark do. Before that, Alevis had to meet together once a year or every six months and they would explain the situation in the UK, Sweden, Denmark and so on. But thanks to this system which has started a year ago, those in the UK were able to follow activities in Duisburg. (Naki, Yol TV)

This is not only the case with Yol TV, which is run by the European Confederation of Alevi Unions. As well as having a studio in Germany, TV10 also serves as a medium for the transnational connectivity of the Alevi community in Turkey and

Europe. As emphasised in earlier chapters, both channels have specific programmes which are produced in and about different localities in Turkey and Europe, giving voice to the Alevi communities living in these various local contexts. As most of the channels have been based in Europe and have appealed to Alevis in Turkey as well as Europe, Alevi television has made a significant contribution towards the transnational experience of Alevis. As my interviews with television workers in Germany and Alevi audiences in the UK suggest, Alevi television has reflected and re-constructed the Alevi public sphere as they have culturally bonded Alevis living in different countries and localities, have helped Alevi organisations to expand transnationally and have enabled the Alevi community to gain confidence in being more explicit about their identity. Mustafa emphasised the ability to stay in tune with the community events in the UK even when he was in Turkey:

> Reflecting our own essence, sharing our faith and values with public, let them know, coordinating the news between us . . . There was a disconnection between Europe and Turkey [Alevi communities] and it wasn't this much when we had Yol TV. They are watching it in Turkey too. For instance, when I was in Turkey during the summer, they used to broadcast our festivals here and other things. I was able to follow it through Yol TV. Also TV10. . . . I used to watch them both. Unfortunately, now we are prevented. (Mustafa, male, 67, retired)

As mentioned by Mustafa, Alevi television has been informative about contemporary events and debates within the community by following and screening their events. Loss of such connection re-shapes transversal imaginaries as Alevis have lost the effortless everyday following of geographically dispersed communities through television. Hence the closure of Alevi channels and the challenge of retaining their audience have had significant transnational consequences for the community. This has interrupted the circulation of information in different localities and hindered the involvement of European Alevis in Turkish politics and the interconnectedness of Alevis in Turkey and in Europe. In this regard, it is not the communicative ethnocide of only those Alevis in Turkey but also the transnational Alevi community, which is connected on a day-to-day basis through satellite television.

A keen activist from the Federation, Sakine, shared an anecdote which indicates the broader implications of the closure as television also forms connections with other affinity communities, such as the Ehl-i Hakk,[6] who are a marginalised ethno-religious community mainly based in Iran:

> It was back in 2011 or 2012 . . . We attended the Çorum memorial [in Çorum] followed by the Sivas [Madımak in Sivas] memorial, which then concludes with a *cem* ceremony in Hacı Bektaş on the 4th of July . . . This has been done repeatedly in the last four years. It was the first time that I attended, if I'm not wrong. In

---

[6] For the similarities between Ehl-i Hakk and Alevis, see Omarkhali and Kreyenbroek (2021).

> Pir Sultan's village [in Sivas] ... We visited there every year and stayed there for a couple of days. While chatting in the village centre ... In Topuzlu ... There is a local place called Topuzlu where Pir Sultan used to attend *cem*s or maybe hiding from the authorities or seeing people. A place in a woodland which has a *cemevi*, a soup kitchen and so on ... They said, 'we have visitors from Iran staying in Topuzlu, Ehl-i Hakk from Iran came'. If I remember it right, two buses full of people [Ehl-i Hakk] were there. We went there and introduced ourselves. They said, 'we know you, we know who you are'. They know all about the festival [Alevi Festival in London] and other things about here. We were really surprised. Then they said 'Yol TV, Yol TV' with a little bit of Turkish [that they speak]. This is invaluable. A *can* [Alevi] from Iran, from your culture, from your belief, knows about what is happening here [in the UK]. How many Alevis live in the UK, what they do, what their achievements are ... Or us [know about Alevis in] Canada, Austria, Europe, Turkey ... (Sakine, female, 47, housewife)

Notably, Sakine's account demonstrates that there are connections beyond Europe stretching to Iran and Canada.[7] My interviewees in Alevi television also mentioned their attempts to connect to migrant communities in North and South America.

Both Kurdish and Alevi television broadcasting in the Turkish context demonstrates communicative ethnocide does not necessarily have only a national dimension, despite the fact that it is implemented by the nation-state. Instead, in the era of satellite and digital technologies, communicative ethnocide can and does take place in a transnational context where various national and international actors are involved, as has been the case with Med TV and its successor television stations.

Communicative ethnocide does not take place in a vacuum; instead, it should be seen as part of a broader project of ethnocide. Even though it has been implemented within the specific conditions of the period after the attempted coup of 2016, during which the JDP government has aimed to re-establish its authority over different factions of the opposition, the closure of TV10 and Yol TV must be regarded as part of the pre-existing ethnocide policy of the Turkish state, for whom satellite broadcasting is regarded as a further challenge to its broader national policies and its project of constructing the 'ideal citizen'. At the same time, satellite broadcasting has proved an opportunity for migrant communities such as Alevis to reaffirm existing identities while constructing an imagined transversal one within a transnational public sphere and to pursue their political ambitions. But satellite technology does not guarantee a realm which is free from state interventions, as Kurdish and Alevi television demonstrate, even though Alevi television, through the use of online broadcasting technology, has managed to circumvent these interventions, although with a more limited size of audience.

---

[7] See Erol (2012) for the Alevi community in Toronto.

Despite mobilising Alevi audiences for different Alevi causes and enabling transversal citizenship acts through media, as discussed in Chapter 5, Alevi television channels have not been able to make their closure a public issue. TV10 has regularly organised demonstrations in Istanbul in order to protest at the closure and to demand the release of the television workers who have been held under arrest between 2017 and 2019. However, the attendance at the demonstrations has been limited to dozens at best. On the other hand, Yol TV has not launched a public campaign and politicised the issue for the community. To put it more clearly, Alevi transversal citizenship acts through television have not been used to fight against communicative ethnocide. There might be several underlying reasons for this. First and foremost, the closure resulted in a disruption in the relationship with the viewers. Hence, the disruption has also meant that it has lost its influence on the community to make the case against television closure a visible issue. Secondly, the government intervention has been part of a set of broader measures in controlling and censoring public debates. Therefore, public campaigns in Turkey have been more difficult to organise and support, particularly for communities such as Alevis and Kurds. Thirdly, the closures did not specifically target Alevis but put them in the same box as many oppositional and controversial parties of Turkish society, such as Gülenists. Limited resources have also been a problem in campaigning against closures, especially given the difficulties Alevis face in simply trying to survive. Lastly, Alevis might not have considered media and their right to express themselves as priorities in an uncertain political context.

Nevertheless, Alevi citizenship acts on television against communicative ethnocide have occurred in the form of media activism and resistance against the closures (Emre Cetin 2020b). The attempt by Yol TV to promote IPTV technology amongst the members of the European Alevi community can be regarded as an example of this resistance. The need to promote new types of digital communication technology for Alevis in Turkey, as well as audiences abroad, presents a challenge for Alevi broadcasting and its resistance against communicative ethnocide. While technological advances do not necessarily guarantee the creation of a freer public sphere for communities such as Alevis, they can provide short-term, and possibly even longer-term, opportunities for survival in the face of a communicative ethnocide directed by the state. The Alevi case demonstrates that the opportunities for resistance against communicative ethnocide are very much bounded by the community's transnational capabilities, including community organisations, the political mobilisation of its members and the community's infrastructural media investments.

In Chapter 8, I discuss the resistance strategies of Alevi broadcasting in detail and how the new period of online streaming has changed their relationship with the viewers. Back in 2017–18, when I conducted most of my interviews with television workers and the members of the community, the repercussions of the closure had not been felt as strongly as when writing this book in 2022.

My follow-up interviews and observations on social media indicate that the transversal citizenship has been challenged by the geographical re-focusing of the channels and digital divides among Alevi viewers. In the next chapter, I examine how the closure of Alevi television accelerated the shift to digital media, and social media in particular, and how it distorted the transversal imaginary by dividing it across different audience groups and geographies through a compulsory shift to digital communications.

8

Limits of Transversal Citizenship

The closure of Alevi television has created new ways of broadcasting and engagement with viewers and pushed Alevi media production almost out of the televisual zone. Despite the ubiquity of digital technologies and their availability, presumably in places other than where television could penetrate, the Alevi media's rapid and compulsory shift from television to digital media has not been straightforward. This chapter focuses on how Alevi media adapted to the digital media environment, which has been transformed by the authoritarian policies of the Turkish government (Yanardağoğlu 2021), and the extent to which this transformation has limited transversal citizenship.

The Alevi media's presence, both in zones of television and digital media, reinforces an approach to media ecology where traditional and digital forms of media co-habit and where such co-habitation is strongly defined by the users' collective identity and their access and uses of media. The following section examines the extent to which online broadcasting and a reliance on social media has resulted in viewer fragmentation and the marginalisation of different viewer demographics due to the digital divide. This is followed by a focus on how different resistance strategies employed by Alevi media have been rendered insufficient because of structural issues and technological impediments that have divided Alevi broadcasting along the lines of geography and ethnicity. The final section focuses on viewers and their distance from Alevi media, which limits the enactment of transversal citizenship through media.

Digital Avenues: Fragmentation and Marginalisation

Following the closure of Alevi television stations, online streaming became key for Alevi broadcasting. The stations heavily relied on their websites to stream programmes and started using social media more efficiently though live streaming, posting short videos edited from the programmes on Facebook and YouTube, and posting content on Instagram. Can TV has around 70,000 followers on Facebook, while Yol TV has nearly 250,000 on the platform and just over

140,000 followers on Instagram, as of December 2021. My follow-up interviews with Haydar from Can TV and the statistics that he generously shared with me confirms that Facebook is the main 'social media channel' through which the station is followed, while Yol TV also posts on YouTube and Instagram proactively. Neither of the channels are offered by most leading IPTV providers in Turkey, but they are mainly followed by European Alevis using this technology. The channels' statistics on their Facebook accounts, IPTV data and their anecdotal evidence about their interactions with viewers indicate that viewership has been divided across technologies, particularly in line with geography and locations. While viewers in Turkey mainly follow these channels though social media, viewers in Europe continue to engage with Alevi media predominantly through IPTV and satellite. For instance, 63.4 per cent of followers of Can TV are from Turkey, followed by 15.1 per cent from Germany, 4 per cent from France and 3 per cent from the UK, as of December 2021.

Both Yol TV's inability to reach out to the east of Turkey, which is predominantly populated by Kurds, and Can TV's subscription to Hotbird, which is mainly used by a Kurdish audience, demonstrate that Alevi media has been de facto divided along the lines of ethnicity as a result of the closure. Yol TV has also been able to appeal to non-Alevi audience through their social media content as a result of the oppressive media environment in Turkey, where only a handful alternative media outlets have remained. For instance, İsmail from Yol TV says that

> writers and academics in Turkey, even the opposite side [mainstream media] use and circulate our content. Recently, our news video on the Boğaziçi University protests[1] hit 40 million views. [...] We have a microphone almost everywhere. Today what we call mainstream such as CNN and so on ... We have achieved having a microphone where they are.

Hence, communicative ethnocide has distorted the 'imagined community' through media in the broader sense by redefining Yol TV as an alternative news media rather than a community media and by pushing Can TV towards an ethnic enclave based on Kurdishness (Squires 2006; Florini 2019).

Transversal citizenship has been possible thanks to complex transnational networks situated within different spaces. While it is relatively easy to maintain those networks and enhance decentred and multi-spatial connectivity online, as the data from the channels' social media accounts and the interviews suggest, digital media has not been a completely open space due to the digital divide among Alevis. In the Turkish context, rural Alevis and those living in cities other than the metropolises such Ankara, Istanbul and Izmir remain on the margins of

---

[1] The Boğaziçi University protests started following President Erdoğan's appointment of Melih Bulu as vice-chancellor in 2021. Academic staff and students protested at the top-down move by the president against the democratic culture of the university and at Bulu's lack of academic integrity and his political affiliation with JDP. Later Bulu was replaced by another appointed vice-chancellor, Naci İnci.

digital engagement with and through Alevi media content. This also means that the transversal imaginaries are more oriented towards and shaped by Europe and urban Turkey because of online streaming.

Transversal citizenship must also be considered in terms of how viewer demographics are likely to affected by the digital divides following Alevi media's shift to digital.[2] While there is no data to confirm this, arguably being on air via satellite means that the Alevi media has been consumed in households where the engagement of women and children is more likely on a household level. The social media data, however, suggests that three-quarters of the followers of Can TV are men. Women might still be viewing the channels via Hotbird or IPTV, but such a gender disparity might signal a broader digital divide among Alevis in terms of their gender identity. Earlier Hopkins (2009) argued that migrant Alevi women were active users of the internet. It is also very likely that Alevi women are interested in other engagements than those with Alevi media online. Viewer demographics are likely to be changed on the basis of age as well. For instance, Can TV's Facebook statistics indicate that 21 per cent of followers are aged between 35 and 44, whereas those aged between 25 and 34 constitute 18 per cent and those aged between 45 and 54 17 per cent. Arguably social media has enabled Alevi media to reach out more successfully to a slightly younger audience demographics. These figures suggest both gender and age appear to be key axes of digital divides among Alevi users in terms of engaging with Alevi media content via Yol TV's and Can TV's social media accounts.

The last two years following the outbreak of the Covid-19 pandemic have introduced further complexities in terms of online streaming and sustaining the satellite audience in the digital sphere. Inviting guests from different countries to talk shows through streaming and other applications, such as Skype, has been widely employed and is now a well-established practice, one that significantly reduces planning time and relevant travel and accommodation costs for the channels. Talk shows have gained further prominence with the lack of community event programmes and village programmes as a result of lockdowns and various travel restrictions at the transnational level. The Federation and community centres in the UK have also begun online streaming through social media in order to make up for the lack of community events. It could be argued that Alevi organisations have gained more autonomy over mediatising their own events after the closure that resulted from Covid-19 restrictions. For instance, in 2020 the Alevi Festival in London, which used to take place in Stoke Newington, and recently on the Federation site in Enfield, was broadcast on YouTube and Facebook. Similarly, in December 2021, the Tenth Alevi Festival was streamed on YouTube; the transmission, which lasted more than seven hours, was viewed by

---

[2] See Sökefeld (2002b) for early research on Alevi websites.

more than 16,000 viewers. The Federation turned one of its rooms at its Enfield site into a studio in order to keep in touch with the community and keep Alevism on the agenda in response to the lack of face-to-face contact during the pandemic.

The Covid-19 period also saw an upsurge of individual streaming by organisations, as well as private individuals such as academics and *dede*s, on the topic of Alevism. However, my observations suggest that these programmes were also repetitive in terms of inviting the same speakers or dealing with similar topics and the viewer numbers for such programmes rarely hit the hundreds. I am doubtful, therefore, whether such an upsurge translates into any rise in interest or increase in the diversity of topics, themes and voices. On the one hand, the closure of the channels, followed by the pandemic a few years later, fragmented the community media production. The lack of face-to-face interaction also led Alevi television to focus on broader issues at the expense of allowing time for an Alevi agenda. Haydar mentioned that the debates within the community hardly took place as the community events were solely online. Although this comment is specific to the Covid-19 lockdowns periods, it signals a broader issue affecting online streaming, which severs the organic ties between community members. The shared physical space has been a key for television broadcasting in reinforcing existing ties and connections between television producers and the community members attending events. However, on the other hand, one can argue that this peculiar period enabled ordinary community members to produce online content which might later be articulated within Alevi media production. Therefore, the diversity of voices might further be incorporated into community media through the work of self-trained content users, enabling Alevi media to exploit the democratic potentials of digital media and communications.

My observations of the social media accounts of Can TV and Yol TV and follow-up interviews with channel workers suggest that digital media has not been a free space for the dissemination of Alevi media content. The channels have had to deal with various issues of hate speech, death threats, suspension of pages, hacking and trolling. Haydar mentioned that they have not been able to employ YouTube as much as they were hoping because Can TV videos were constantly removed from YouTube because of JDP trolling[3] and the complaints logged by them:

> Our social media has been very vibrant, followed by 20,000 people. In the last year, this number has dropped dramatically. The main reason [behind this] is the restrictions imposed by the platforms. Some of them are due to technical reasons [such as copyright issues[4]], but the majority of them are based on the complaints

---

[3] A common idiom used to describe the owners of the Twitter accounts which provoke, manipulate or simply tweet in support of the policies of the JDP.
[4] The high copyright costs for music videos streamed on YouTube is also mentioned as an issue by both of the stations as YouTube stretch their budget and prevent the circulation of Alevi music production through their media.

about our content. [. . .] For instance, they [trolls] have got Can TV's page removed from YouTube. Facebook also denied access to our users. We have managed to reinstate it after some correspondence [with Facebook]. However, the exchange of emails takes time and in the meantime, you lose followers and the trust of followers. This is a major thing. (Haydar, TV10)

Haydar considered this as indirect censorship as the recent regulations require social media platforms to comply with the government through their country representatives. In Haydar's words, 'although these look like global platforms, we are now imprisoned in Turkey after these regulations'. Yol TV was also impacted by hackers on YouTube:

Our YouTube page has been stolen by the hackers. They sold it to the Far East. YouTube is very problematic. It is a pain to reach them and receive a reply. For four months we have emailed them every single day. We also sent them official letters five times. Eventually we got our YouTube channel back. Our videos were all deleted. But we also lost some advert income. (Baki, Yol TV)

Both of these accounts suggest that Alevi media is still under attack from partisan trolls and hackers, despite being removed from the Turkish satellite Turksat. Another instance was noted by Can TV about how a Facebook customer services operator in Turkey changed their attitude from kindness to silence and cut communications after they found out what kind of a page Can TV's was. Media workers reportedly received formulaic death threats where the same message was sent from multiple users to many of the workers. Issues stemming from social media regulation in Turkey and self-regulation of platforms, YouTube and Facebook in particular, illustrate that digital media is not a space free from censorship. No doubt, social media censorship might not be as systematic as the closure of channels, nor would it particularly reflect the respective platforms' policies towards minority communities, but that such difficulties are present and visible on social media and the constant efforts of putting the pages back highlight a contingent form of censorship which arises within the Turkish national context of media freedom more broadly and the cultural hatred and phobia towards the community more specifically. In terms of digital platforms, these incidents illustrate that the 'global standards' of self-regulation are insufficient to address local issues of online hate, trolling and hacking.

This complex relationship encourages re-thinking the relationship between different forms of media at a collective level. People engage with different media simultaneously. Television audiences are also users of social media and, despite the ubiquity of digital media, marginal communities in particular significantly engage with traditional media. Madianou and Miller (2012: 170) argue that 'polymedia is an emerging environment of communicative technologies within which each individual medium is defined in relational terms in the context of all other media'. Access, affordability and literacy serve as preconditions for polymedia; therefore, they describe it as an aspiration rather than the norm. Also, polymedia focuses on interpersonal relationships and the extent to which the relationality of media and the different textual genres produced by them are grasped to be at individuals' disposal and within their moral positioning. In this respect, media ecology (Postman 1992, 2000; Ito *et al.* 2010) is also a useful concept for understanding people's relationship with various forms of media, one that enables us to address media as environments. Early uses of the concept suggested a humanistic approach in thinking of the relationship between humans and media, carrying with it some techno-determinist undertones since media was considered mainly as technology (see Postman 1992, 2000). Ito *et al.* (2010) later developed a nuanced understanding of media ecology, taking into account the complexities of structural conditions and the infrastructures of place and technologies, while examining young people's uses of media in everyday life. Media ecology is also promising in understanding how complex media systems work in relation to one another and how they transform and are transformed by economic, social and cultural structures and technical infrastructures. It allows us to distinguish between different forms of media and to understand why people do or do not accommodate various media into their daily lives. However, both concepts, polymedia and media ecology, mainly emphasise the diversity within the digital. In this regard, I propose focusing on the co-existence of traditional and digital forms of media, while analysing different contexts in the Global South or minorities in the Global North. Media ecology might still be a useful concept for understanding these contexts as long as we take digital divides into account, as indicated by the case of Alevis. The case of Alevi media indicates that we need to think of traditional and digital media as co-habiting within the same media environment. In particular, this is crucial for the marginalised communities, whose resources are relatively limited.

Furthermore, such multiple ways of engagement not only occur on a personal or individual level but take place within a collective context, as the Alevi case and others demonstrate. That is to say, switching between different media or the simultaneous uses of various media is not only a matter of individual preference or affordance, but also about collective imaginary, a sense of belonging and the will to engage with others of a similar background or identity. Florini (2019: 183) demonstrates that Black digital networks emerge across different platforms, in a 'transplatform technological space in which the collection of people operate' and they arise from the long-standing history of Black cultural production. Even though engagement with digital media often takes place on an individual level through mobile devices, the notion of the collective also strongly defines another level of engagement. That is to say, imagined communities are still a relevant topic of research on digital diasporas (Gajjala 2019; Bernal 2020; Ponzanesi 2020; Sobande 2020).

It is also important to explore why communities and individuals turn to different media for different needs and uses, and how they overcome particular limitations of access or censorship. For instance, recently the monovocal media environment pushed many users to draw on social media and digital platforms to access reliable news sources in Turkey. The Arab Spring (Howard and Hussain 2013; Bebawi and Bossio 2014; Mohamed and El-Dosouky 2021) and Gezi protests not only indicate that people turn to digital media to protest but also use it as a first-hand news source in times of crises (Yesil 2016; Tufekci 2018). However, as indicated by their social media data, Alevi media's compulsory shift to the digital is yet to 'train' those viewers who did not on the whole rely on digital media to engage with Alevi politics as users. If it had, it would have been possible to talk about transversal citizenship acts solely in digital media. Arguably, transversal citizenship will be enacted in and through digital media in the future as more Alevis participate in online spaces of community media production.

Limits of Transversal Citizenship Acts in Media

Communicative ethnocide is not a one-way stream, so to speak. Communities which are targeted can also resist ethnocide through different methods and means. These include the use of different media such as broadcasting online, finding more creative ways of engaging in media activism, such as encouraging citizen journalism, and transferring their human resources to different media organisations or using them for different media productions (Emre Cetin 2020b). The experience of Alevi television epitomises the resistance against communicative ethnocide. Both TV10 and Yol TV did not regard their closure as an end but looked for alternative ways to continue broadcasting, as well as seeking out temporary solutions in order to survive conditions under the Turkish state of emergency. Ali from TV10 explains how they are planning new documentary projects, some with the help and sponsorship of the community, despite the fact that their equipment was confiscated:

> We signed contracts with some of our friends [previous workers] after the closure of TV10. We are trying to produce some programmes that we were unable to do when TV10 was on air. As a preparation, as a transition to a new television, there is a crew of five to six people in Turkey. They are working on documentaries on Alevi *ocak*s, significant Alevi women in history, such as Ana Fatma and Elif Ana. They co-produce and work as separate groups simultaneously. We were unable to do these while on air, even if we wanted to because responding to the daily agenda and the daily routine of the channel did not allow us. (Ali, TV10)

In this case, the production of documentaries also operates as a mean of resistance, one which can help the previous workers of the channel remain engaged and used for researching and producing more about Alevi culture. This also serves as a way of existing during the period of political chaos as the future of media freedom in Turkey does not seem very promising and TV10's future, in particular, remains uncertain due to legal complications arising from the decree laws passed under the state of emergency. However, the channel has not been able to realise any of these documentary projects due to financial difficulties and further restrictions during the state of emergency, even though a few of them have undergone some initial preparation and research process.

The fact that TV10 was based both in Germany and Turkey has, according to Hasan, also helped a great deal in ensuring the survival of the channel. Although they have had no access to the technical infrastructure in Turkey, they have been able to broadcast online thanks to their equipment in Germany and, in this regard, transnationalism has helped Alevi television to survive and has worked against the attempts at communicative ethnocide. There have also been demonstrations in Istanbul every Saturday, with the attendance of various Alevi organisations protesting against the closure of TV10. As the legal procedure has become more complicated because of decrees and the state of emergency, TV10 decided not to wait for the court's verdict in order to continue broadcasting. Later in 2018, TV10 was relaunched under a new name, Can TV. Can TV has ended signing up with the Hotbird satellite, which covers Turkey but requires different satellite settings from Turksat. This means Can TV is not de facto available to the viewers in Turkey, unless they are determined to watch it by constantly switching between different satellites. My follow-up interviews with TV10/Can TV workers suggest that the channel draws on an existing Kurdish viewership that was using Hotbird already:

> Actually, we have been relying on an already established Hotbird viewership. For instance, if there are ten channels available there, one of them is us. Both for Europe and Turkey. We are watched in Turkey on Hotbird thanks to the potential of Kurdish [media viewership]. When we go to the [Kurdish] region, we see observe this. In the villages, for instance. But if you go to the Aegean region [in the west of Turkey], we no longer exist there. We are only able to reach to the Kurdish population in Aegean [Turkey]. Maybe half of that population . . . This means that [with Hotbird] we are only able to reach half of our potential audience [in Turkey]. (Haydar, TV10/Can TV)

Thus, Can TV has unwillingly been confined within Europe and has mainly been available to Kurdish Alevis via Hotbird in Turkey as a result of the closures.

Yol TV has also employed various strategies to retain its audience during the blackout. It broadcasts online and has tried to encourage its viewers to move to the IPTV system where viewers can watch Yol TV on their television through the use of a special device fitted to it. Yol TV benefits from events organised by the European Alevi Unions Confederation, which are used to inform the community about this new system and at which the IPTV boxes are available for sale. During the Alevi Festival in London in 2018, IPTV boxes were on sale in the festival venue. However, the Yol TV table did not receive many visitors. This could be either because many Alevi viewers in the UK were already using the technology or because they were not willing to give up on their satellite-watching habits and invest in another technology.

Interestingly, for Yol TV the geographical reach is the opposite of Can TV. My follow-up interviews suggest that Yol TV finds it difficult to reach viewers in the east of Turkey, which has a dense Kurdish population. İsmail from Yol TV mentioned that they are unable to establish a presence in the Kurdish region, even though there is a substantial, keen audience. The economic constraints, such as the cost of internet connections, prevents viewers from following the channel on social media. My early interviews with, for example, İsmail, Naki and Ekber from Yol TV explain how the channel sought a long-term solution to the disruption caused by the instabilities of Turkish politics and pressures from the Turkish state. These included changing the satellite through which Yol TV is broadcast, as well as using terrestrial broadcasting. Both of the solutions suggest a Europe-centred vision which anticipates the future of Yol TV in the European broadcasting market. İsmail, who was one of the founders of the Federation in Germany and produced programmes for Yol TV, says that:

> When we restart broadcasting, we need to dedicate 30 to 40 per cent of the programmes to Europe. We just aim at Turkey, transforming Turkish democracy for the better. But we live here. I have been living in this country [Germany] for forty years now. My children grew up here, went to university here. I have now grandchildren here. They go to school in this country and they are impacted by the life conditions here. Our television must contribute towards their lives. Also, our doctrines [of Alevism] are aligned with Europe. Our doctrine, our faith, our lifestyle is not in conflict with Christianity. (İsmail, Yol TV)

Despite such a European vision, one shared by other co-workers at Yol TV, the channel still remains focused on Turkey and has developed their team based in Istanbul by employing young journalists and media professionals who had been working for alternative media before the coup attempt. As a community television, Yol TV has already been on the spectrum of alternative media in Turkey (Atton 2001; Downing, 2001; Rodriguez, 2001, 2011; Couldry and Curran 2003; Waltz, 2005; Rennie 2006; Bailey et al., 2007, Coyer et al., 2007; Kenix, 2011; Lievrouw, 2011). However, with the silencing of alternative media more broadly during the state of emergency and the following period, Yol TV has re-situated itself as an alternative news and opinion source for different oppositional groups amongst the Turkish public. Previously Yol TV produced programmes in collaboration with the *Birgün* newspaper in Turkey and the We Will Stop Femicide Platform, a network against male violence towards women in Turkey. They also invited journalists and media producers from other closed channels, such as IMC TV and Hayat TV, to their programmes as a gesture of solidarity. Hence, despite the prospects of the process of 'Europeanisation' by the channel workers, Yol TV has ended up being a reliable news outlet for counter-publics in Turkey (Fraser 1990).

The state of emergency and the following period of increasing authoritarianism has also rendered the production of village programmes in Turkey more difficult. The media workers noted various instances where they were prevented from filming or even entering villages by public and law enforcement officials. Broadcasting from Terolar (discussed in Chapter 4) is an example of a situation where media production from the village was disrupted. The curtailing of village programmes has implications for embedding localities into transversal imaginary. To put it bluntly, the compulsory shift towards digital media, followed by the Covid-19 pandemic, has been a blow for transversal citizenship as locality and the diversity of the Alevi community are difficult to embed in transversal imaginary. This demonstrates that transversal imaginaries require the materiality of 'being there' and the physical space and presence are at the heart of the construction of a collective imaginary.

All these demonstrate that communicative ethnocide is a challenge for transversal citizenship, one which cannot simply be overcome through various resistance practices. First, the closures have resulted in a loss of audience, particularly those who cannot afford the internet connection or IPTV technology. Secondly, producing local programmes, particularly those focusing on rural Alevis, has been more difficult as the unofficial use of 'law enforcement' has taken place in villages and the countryside. Thirdly, the connectivity and imaginary, which include different spatial levels and have been sustained through satellite transmission, have been disrupted as each channel is mainly available in different regions in Turkey and requires IPTV or social media use, particularly in Europe. That is to say, transversal citizenship is enabled through a shared media content by and on the community. Simultaneous uses of multiple technologies of online broadcasting and satellite lead to fragmentation and the elimination of disadvantaged groups, such as rural and elderly viewers. There are also internal dynamics within the audience community which distance viewers from Alevi media, despite their enthusiasm for media content by and for Alevis. In the next section, I examine how such distances hinder the political mobilisation of viewers and indicate the limits of transversal citizenship acts through media.

Limits of Transversal Citizenship Acts through Media: Critical Distances

In Chapter 6, I mentioned that Alevi television has not been able to facilitate Alevi citizenship acts that protest at the closure of television stations. The audience's critical approach is noteworthy in terms of making sense of Alevi viewers' engagement and disengagement with Alevi media. Nevertheless, it is not possible to situate these critical perspectives completely as contesting (Hall 1973) since these viewers emphasise that they watch and appreciate the very existence of Alevi television. Despite this overall positive attitude, they also develop what I call 'critical distances' towards programme content and broadcasting. In order to understand why Alevi citizenship is not enacted in response to the closure of the channels and to make sense of the limits of transversal citizenship acts through media, I argue that we need to examine such viewer accounts. This section will examine critical audience perspectives which have been prominent among my interviewees.

Lack of Professionalism

The Alevi audience sets high expectations for Alevi television both in terms of the style of programmes and the variety of content. A lack of professionalism was identified as a problem by some of my interviewees. Under-prepared television presenters, technical glitches and a predominant reliance on community resources are mentioned as the main sources of discontent.

> I really like them [Alevi channels] but they have many deficiencies. Their broadcasting is so plain. I think this is about lack of money. For a good journalist, for a good columnist you need money. They are not able to invite them. Probably it is costly too . . . (İmam, male, 47, writer)

> I know all the representatives of Yol TV in the UK. They are sincerely committed but are uneducated. This job must be done by those who are knowledgeable. Unfortunately, it is not. And this is not very productive. (Hüseyin, male, 63, retired)

Apparently, Alevi viewers do not think that alternative channels are exempt from providing viewers with high-quality content and this criterion applies to Alevi television. This is also about the community's self-expectation of doing better and representing Alevis in different cultural realms with pride.

> You know diaspora . . . Armenian diaspora, Jewish diaspora . . . And we exist all over Europe. We established the Secretariat [in the UK parliament]. We need to be politically and economically strong. In order for them to make themselves known in the world. We have a very nice belief system. Why don't we make it known, we announce . . . Why aren't we powerful in the US? If we are powerful in the UK, we should be as such in the US too. We are not heard in the US at all. (Mustafa, male, 67, retired)

A lack of professionalism is a point of difference between Alevi viewers' expectations and those of television producers. When I asked about what they could do differently in hindsight or what were the weaknesses of Alevi broadcasting, none of the television producers identified 'professionalism' as an issue. In fact, they do not evaluate themselves against such a benchmark, one which is reinforced by the mainstream media, but they think that an 'amateur spirit' is crucial for creating a sincere and close relationship with viewers, as well as with Alevism. For instance, Hıdır from TV10, who has been producing and presenting village programmes, highlighted professional standards as a problem. He criticised some of his colleagues whom he expected to have definite work hours and to adhere to professional work standards.

Programme Diversity and Repetition

As demonstrated in Chapter 6, the majority of my interviewees appreciate the content on Alevism and Alevi culture; nevertheless, they would also like to see Alevi broadcasting offer a variety of programmes on different topics. They were critical about non-selective content; this content reflects the weaknesses of the community and poses an obstacle to improvement. Those programmes which depicted community events without proper editing or contained interviews with those attending the community events were widely criticised in particular:

> They play music all the time and they play bad music. I really like music and am aware of the meaning of music for Alevis. But they are playing bad music. They have the ambiance of fifth grade '*türkü bar*'[5] or *pavyon*[6] ... (Hasret, male, 36, waiter)

> They play *deyiş* on television but they don't give the background, don't mention the name of the poet [. . .] We think we listen to folk songs but it is like *arabesk*.[7] (Dilber, female, 50, administrator)

While few of the participants criticised Yol TV for being the voice of the chair of the Federation in Germany, some criticisms were directed towards TV10 in terms of their close engagement with the Kurdish movement. For instance, İmam, who produced a few programmes for Yol TV and has been a political activist in a different faction of Kurdish movement than the PKK, said that 'TV10 is not really an Alevi channel. I see it as the channel of the Kurdish movement which aims at appealing to Kurdish Alevis so that they are not lost to the Alevi movement.' Such perspectives are important, even though they do not echo the dominant themes in my interviews since they remind us that neither the Alevi movement nor the perspectives of Alevi individuals are uniform and that such diversity often poses a challenge for the Alevi media in terms of its ability to be embraced by a wider audience. Interestingly, none of the television producers mentioned the goal of reaching more Alevi viewers and widening their scope to embrace different Alevi communities. This is striking as it indicates that Alevi broadcasters regard the political lines of division among the Alevi community as deeply ingrained and consider them as a given. Neither Yol TV nor Can TV prioritise appealing to Alevi viewers, for instance, that are close to the Cem Foundation; instead, they are more

---

[5] *Türkü bar* can be thought of as a traditional pub serving alcohol and offering live Turkish folk music; it is usually furnished in a traditional folk style and preferred by leftists and folk-music lovers.

[6] A *pavyon* is a specific kind of entertainment venue in Turkey, one usually preferred by men. A *pavyon* is open until late at night and offers popular live music and employs hostesses who accompany the clients during the night and occasionally serve as sex workers.

[7] A Turkish popular song genre influenced by Egyptian music, *arabesk* has long been excluded from public broadcasting since it has been associated with a lower-class cultural habitus and cultural degeneration, even a contamination of Turkishness and Turkish modernity with oriental influence. See Stokes (1992).

interested in facilitating transversal connections among Alevis living in remote villages and Alevis belonging to different Alevi organisations in Turkey and abroad.

A Closed Window

Alevi television can be regarded as a form of a mediated public statement about what Alevism is and that Alevis exist. In this regard, it serves a public function, a way of taking Alevis out of their enclaves and highlighting them as a (counter-)public. This is the dual aspect of community broadcasting: addressing the community as an entity in itself, while at the same time engaging with the broader public sphere. That is why Alevi broadcasting constantly negotiates the boundaries of the community by including different topics which are not necessarily about Alevis. However, some of the interviewees feel a tension with regard to boundary-making through television. They deem Alevi television to be 'a closed window', one that does not invite non-Alevis to look through.

As argued in Chapter 3, Alevi citizenship is not confined to demands about Alevi rights but is situated within the broader context of Turkish politics in terms of the rights to equality and diversity. Such a perspective also sets the criteria for Alevi media, which is expected to engage with the broader Turkish public. Alevi broadcasting dedicates a great deal of its programming to talk shows on Turkish politics; however, the target audience of these programmes are still Alevis. Some of my interviewees would like to see Alevi broadcasting appeal to a non-Alevi audience:

> Television is really important to disseminate the Alevi perspective. But my understanding of television is a bit different. I would love to see a variety of programmes. When you talk about television, it shouldn't be all about Alevism. Alevism must be among all other things. It can be like a news channel. A non-Alevi should be able to find something about themselves. It shouldn't be a channel only broadcasting for Alevis. (Servet, male, 57, unemployed)

This can be interpreted as a need for self-validation through social recognition by members of the public that goes beyond the legal rights obtained from the state. Alevis want to be seen and heard but not only on the topics which have direct relevance to them but also concerning other issues about Turkish democracy. In other words, Servet's perspective on Alevi broadcasting expands Alevi citizenship towards other citizenship acts initiated by other groups and communities. Here I must emphasise that Yol TV has been partially able to fulfil the expectation of addressing non-Alevi audiences after their closure and has responded to the audience demands about professionalism. Short videos on YouTube, which include street interviews with ordinary people on a variety of topics, and short news items specifically produced for social media dissemination through Instagram and other platforms, exemplify this.

Significance of Political Alignment and the Distance from the Turkish State: Cem TV

As discussed previously, Cem TV remained on air following the coup attempt and thereafter. We might expect that Alevi viewers might turn to Cem TV in the face of the limited media and communication opportunities. However, such an orientation towards Cem TV has not been seen. On the contrary, there is a strong negative attitude towards the channel among some of my participants. This suggest that political differences that challenge the essential notions of Alevi identity still matter in the times of crisis:

> I don't want anything like Cem TV [for the community]. But I would self-sacrifice (*canım kurban*) for Yol TV, İmece, TV10 ... Because they want to hear what you have to say. Cem TV is an assimilated television. Is it not? (Turabi, male, 47, shop owner)

> I see Cem TV as TRT. You cannot distinguish it from Havuz Medyası;[8] it is in touch with them. It doesn't appeal to us, nor does it reflect values of Alevism. There are only *deyiş* and songs [on Cem TV]; other than that. it is empty. I don't see it as healthy. They are aligned with the mainstream media. (Hüseyin, male, 62, retired)

The views of Turabi and Hüseyin align Yol TV and TV10 with other alternative television stations in Turkey, whereas Cem TV is considered to be part of the mainstream spectrum. This denotes that the viewers do not deem ethno-religious identity a sufficient point of reference for their media engagement but look for a shared political vision. In other words, they think of alternative media outlets closer to themselves than Cem TV and, therefore, contest the essentialist notions of Alevism.

The critical approach towards Cem TV also serves as a way of boundary-making through media engagement as a proactive refusal to watch the channel is also a way of distancing oneself from a particular form of Alevism, one which is considered to be 'state-sponsored':

> My lot [parents] would generally watch Yol TV and TV10 ... They wouldn't watch Cem TV. I sometimes look at what they do. I don't see Cem TV as Alevi television. I also don't consider the Cem Foundation as an Alevi organisation. They are a clique in the state. (Hasret, male, 36, waiter)

> Cem TV is under state guidance. They are positioned according to the state's demands. For instance, during Gezi while people were struggling on the streets or while our Cans were killed by the police, I remember it very well, despite having many resources, they were broadcasting cheese adverts. So you can't feel

---

[8] The term can be translated as 'pool media' and refers to pro-government media outlets. It stems from the leaked phone calls in 2014 which revealed that some business people were forced to create a financial 'pool' by the government through which mainstream media organisations could be purchased (https://turkey.mom-rsf.org/en/context/history/; lasat accessed 22 December 2021).

> like it is your television, that it is like you ... Because there is a struggle, there is an unfairness. You know we are like always in solidarity with the oppressed and are against the oppressors ... Cem TV is always there but is there under the state guidance. (Sakine, female, 47, housewife)

As demonstrated in Chapter 3, Alevis make their rights claims mainly by addressing the Turkish state; therefore, the community media's approach to and distance from the state matter in terms of defining their political position. For the viewers who regard Cem TV as propagating the state's approach towards Alevis(m), the channel's proximity to the Turkish state is also an issue. Therefore, transversal citizenship requires a particular positionality against the Turkish state, which is not automatically granted to any Alevi media outlet.

Unlike the viewers, Alevi television workers implied their distance from Cem TV rather subtly.

They under-emphasised the implicit competition and disapproval of each other's broadcasting and their different political stance during the interviews. My ongoing informal dialogue with them, however, suggests that they are as critical as the Alevi viewers towards Cem TV and their rather respectful distance stems from deeper political divides. This means that Cem TV is not where viewers of Yol TV or TV10 turned to during these stations' closure and Cem TV is not regarded useful for enacting transversal citizenship. The views of Alevi audience and media workers suggest that having one's own community media is not sufficient. In the case of Alevis, transversal citizenship requires a political alignment and a more broadly shared perspective both on Alevism and Turkish politics.

Communicative ethnocide has had a detrimental effect upon enacting transversal citizenship in media as media workers have mainly focused on surviving and carving out an established space in digital media. The viewers' distance from the community media, stemming from political differences, high expectations of having diverse content and professional standards in Alevi media, also limited the enactment of transversal citizenship through media. The Alevi media's enforced shift to digital media and communications has challenged the extra-territorial connectivity of the community through media since transversal citizenship has not been able to fully exploit the democratising potential of digital media as a result of digital divides. Nevertheless, multiple voices emerging in digital media have potentials to create a more inclusive and participatory media ecology for the Alevi media.

9

Transversal Citizenship in a Complex Media Environment

Alevis have been claiming equal citizenship for decades regardless of the specific differences between their rights claims and their political differences. However, insufficient attention has been paid to this fact by researchers, who often frame the Alevi movement in terms of 'identity politics', cutting its connections to the state and political power. While the Alevi movement grew dramatically in Turkey and abroad following the Madımak massacre of 1993, its right claims were shaped by the leftist politics of the 1970s and by the Turkish state's policies of oppression and ethnocide (Yalçınkaya 2005, 2014). Isin's (2008, 2009, 2012, 2013) theory of citizenship enactment offers a useful framework for understanding the events, sites and scales of Alevis' rights claims which cut across various spatial contexts. Transversal citizenship, therefore, crystallises the different scale of these rights claims, including the local, national, transnational and regional, which are mediated through Alevi media and can be regarded as a particular form of citizenship enactment that involves media (site) and different forms of activism on and through media (event).

Transversal citizenship consists of two key aspects: imaginaries and citizenship acts. Ponzanesi (2019: 551) contends that migration is 'not only about loss of memory and identity but also about the possibility to construct new imaginaries, new archives, and new narratives'. Alevis have constructed a transversal imaginary through their media and are exploring the construction of new narratives about their identity, their past, their local knowledge and their way of life. This has been made possible because of the complex transnational networks embedding different spatial levels. Transversal imaginaries can be considered a prerequisite for citizenship acts where community members are able to imagine themselves extra-territorially while making their rights claims in local, national, transnational and regional contexts. In other words, transversal citizenship acts are enabled through the construction of transversal imaginaries by the Alevi media, which embed local, national, transnational and regional spaces into self-imaginaries of the community. Alevis were organised under the *ocak* system for centuries, where local ties between *pir*s and *talip*s were crucial in the making of Alevism. The Alevi media enables different Alevi communities to re-connect with their local origins while making rural Alevis visible through village programmes. It also articulates the contemporary localities of transnational communities, such as towns and cities in Europe, within the Alevi imaginary through broadcasting events and festivals. This is how a complex and patchy transversal imaginary constructed through Alevi media enables the incorporation of the extra-territorial geography that is occupied by various Alevi communities.

Transversal citizenship is enacted in and through community media. Transversal citizenship enacted in media mainly refers to learning about an oppressed and marginalised self-identity. As I have argued, cultural citizenship is about learning about oneself and others. Alevi emigration to urban areas has made it difficult for Alevis to maintain their ethno-religious ties with their *pir*s and fellow *talip*s as they no longer experience the relative freedom that they had in their villages in terms of practising their religious rituals. The decline in the passing of their religion through oral communication due to the oppression in cities where Alevi identity is exposed and the difficulty of maintaining ties with the *ocak* system have led Alevis to 'collective amnesia' (Sökefeld 2002a). The 1990s publication boom on Alevism partially addressed the need to know more about Alevism by the community members and engendered a particular public discourse on Alevism (Vorhoff 1998; Yıldırım 2017a). Also, Alevi radio production (Özkan 2022) disseminated Alevi music and paved the way for a wider Alevi music market, giving voice to local and new bards, as well as enabling a cultural space for old musical forms of *gülbang* and *deyiş* to be experienced by Alevis in towns and cities. Alevi television, on the other hand, has been a key and everyday source for learning about and remembering Alevi rituals, as well as local differences and diversity within the community, enabling viewers to make sense of their identity.

While defining the contemporary boundaries of the community, television has also helped viewers to discover their history and learn about the rituals, myths and cosmology of Alevism through programmes with contributions from writers, community leaders and *pir*s. I have argued that such boundary-making, as performed by the Alevi media, is crucial for Alevi citizenship as, without Alevis being able to define who they are, they would not be able to make their rights claims. Therefore, media workers and community leaders appearing on the media constantly engage with this boundary work as key actors of citizenship acts in media. As Tanikella (2009: 170) states, 'media producers are important agents in the production of diasporic communities because they reflect locally constructed identities back to the target communities and also represent these identities in the public sphere'. In the case of Alevis, such an influence expands towards the broader community as the Alevi media operate in Turkey as well as Germany.

Citizenship acts through media refer to the taking of collective action through media about matters concerning the community and they are deeply embedded in the collective memories of persecution and individual and personal experiences of oppression. Protests against the misrepresentation of Alevism in the well-known television series *Tatort*, Alevi broadcasting and their campaigning against the violence shown towards a family during Ramadan in a small town in Malatya, Turkey, bringing Alevis living in different European countries together, exemplify citizenship acts through media. Such citizenship acts require the viewer's active engagement with community media, which is carried beyond the contexts of reception by means of demonstrations, protests and phone calls. Citizenship acts through media also indicate that the power of community media lies beyond the symbolic realm and is able to lead to a significant change in terms of cultural politics in transnational contexts and in protecting the members of the community against physical violence.

Transversal citizenship draws on personal stories of oppression and discrimination, which are often situated within the collective history of Alevis. In other words, while engaging with community media, individual Alevi viewers remember and relate to their personal experiences of what Alevism is and how they are discriminated against by the state or by non-Alevi individuals. The way Alevi viewers situate their personal experiences within the collective history of Alevism can be regarded as a political force that mobilises Alevi individuals through media (as well as through other means). Interestingly, Özkan (2022: 287) notes that this is also the case for Alevi viewers in Turkey, where 'Alevi audiences' responses to televised Alevism were informed by their everyday experiences of discrimination and fear'. While such politics of affect engage Alevi viewers with their media, Alevis also turn to television in 'filling the gaps of knowledge' about Alevism. Alevi viewers refer to their community media to explore Alevism, learn about rituals and history, make sense of the diversity within the community and learn about marginalised others. The Alevi media's construction of transversal imaginaries corresponds to the transversal imaginaries of the viewers, which primarily refer to local, national and transnational contexts in which they situate themselves (to varying degrees depending on the viewer's positionality). To put it succinctly, the transversal imaginaries constructed by the media do not remain solely in the realm of media but have a sociological basis in terms of the transnational social space (Faist *et al.* 2013) that Alevi viewers are part of.

Transversal citizenship has its own limits, stemming from what I have called communicative ethnocide, as well as digital divides and the viewer's distance from community media. It is important to note that the main political differences among the community are also reflected in the Alevi media, both in terms of their approach to Alevism and Turkish politics and in terms of their viewership profile. Hence, transversal citizenship requires a shared political perspective and cultural understanding of what Alevism is. The shared political perspectives emerge prior to media engagement, yet are sustained and reinforced through it. Therefore, transversal citizenship is not about challenging existing differences among community members along the lines of politics but about maintaining them. While both Yol TV and Can TV appeal to similar viewer profiles in terms of their political orientation, Cem TV holds a very different position. This explains why Alevi viewers did not turn to Cem TV, even though it is another Alevi television, after the closure of Yol TV and TV10, demonstrating that as well as requiring an ethno-religious collective identity, transversal citizenship also requires the political alignment of community members. This is crucial in terms of indicating the 'political character' of transversal citizenship, even though at first sight it mainly seems to be about ethno-religious identity. In this way, the concept enables us to see the transitivity of ethno-religious and political identities, and highlights the problems stemming from reducing one to the other. Aleviness is an ethno-religious identity; however, it is not possible to detach it from politics in its contemporary form, as illustrated by transversal citizenship.

Transversal citizenship also has its limits in terms of the viewers' critical distance from the Alevi media, which stems from their expectations of professionalism and better media content, and which opens up ways of engagement with non-Alevi viewers. That is to say, Alevi viewers aspire to respectability and recognition from non-Alevis through their community media. Arguably, this is partially achieved by Yol TV, which is deemed to be an alternative news source for the broader Turkish public following the consequences of the increasing authoritarianism and closure of various alternative media outlets in Turkey. Recently, Özkan (2022) identified a similar attitude among Alevi viewers in Turkey, who see televised Alevism as a way of confronting discrimination and providing them with public visibility.

The exclusion of Alevi television from Turksat, and hence from the Turkish mediascape, has facilitated its rapid shift to online streaming and social media. However, rather than maintaining their existing viewer body or being able to reach out to a broader audience through digital media, the Alevi media has lost its ability to address the community in Turkey and Europe as a whole. Satellite television's ability to call viewers as part of a broader community on a daily basis at the household level has not been transferred to the digital realm due to the digital divide among the community. For example, despite the fact that Alevi women are likely to engage with digital media more broadly, they make up only one-third of the viewers of the Alevi media online. Similarly, the younger and older viewer demographic is lost due to both the digital divide and the different habits of user engagement online. This has also hindered the media's ability to embed different localities in online streaming to the same degree as satellite. Yol TV finds it difficult to address viewers located in the east of Turkey, whereas Can TV is mainly confined to the Kurdish-populated regions. In addition, both of the channels mainly reach out to urban Alevis in Istanbul, Ankara and Izmir. This has two main consequences for the Alevi media: weakened connections with rural locales in Turkey, and an ethnic division in terms of reaching out to Kurdish and Turkish viewers simultaneously. Therefore, while digital media has enabled Alevi media to survive the constraints of national politics and communicative ethnocide, it has fragmented the Alevi audience.

The future of Alevi transversal citizenship is likely to be defined by Turkish politics, as well as by digital technologies or the politics of transnationalism. This can be foreseen by the fact that the media workers and viewers are now focused on the Turkish national elections likely to take place in 2023 in the hope that the elections will bring an end to the JDP government and the power of President Erdoğan. No matter how transformative the election might be, such a short-term vision indicates the fragility of transversal citizenship and indicates that Alevis deem the survival of their media in any form as sufficient in terms of the politics of representation. It also illustrates that national politics do matter in terms of enabling or hindering local engagement and for the maintenance of the extra-territorial space and boundaries of Alevism on a symbolic level through media.

In this book, I have demonstrated that transversal citizenship is mediated through community media and requires an understanding of different forms of media as co-habiting. This is for two main reasons. First, traditional forms of media are still significant for marginalised communities and their mediated connections because of digital divides. Punathambekar and Scannell (2013) note the need for studying the television of the Global South, particularly in India and Middle East, and that what television means today and how is thought about has changed greatly. We need a critical approach towards celebratory accounts of the digital media as enabling participation and engagement, particularly if we think on a collective level. Secondly, television as a medium has still a particular ability to penetrate into the everyday lives of the audience and address them as a community in a similar way to Anderson's (1983) idea of nation-building. It is important to recognise that diaspora identity-construction and boundary-making in digital media is about social imaginaries rather than being a collection of engagements of the individual members of diasporic communities. Therefore, transversal citizenship highlights this continuity and co-presence, which is also likely to be the case for the next decade. This point is particularly important if, for instance, we are to defend public broadcasting against the aggressive business model of subscription on-demand online streaming services (Iosifidis 2020). In other words, to see technological advancement as inevitable and irreversible should not blind us to acknowledging the need of communities for traditional forms of connection and engagement. How to respond to this problem at the level of public policy in media and communications is yet to be addressed by governments and by funding and regulatory bodies.

Transversal citizenship requires the lens of decoloniality not only in examining different forms of citizenship beyond the Global North but also in situating citizenship acts at the community level. This would help us to see how particular cultural histories pave the way in shaping and hindering citizenship acts in and through media. By situating Alevi acts of citizenship in and through media within Alevi history and the Alevis' struggle for recognition, I have illustrated that Alevis have produced their particular forms of engagement with media in the shape of citizenship acts. In examining how these citizenship acts have been hindered by the Turkish state, I have suggested the usefulness of employing the concept of communicative ethnocide which has been part of a historical and systematic programme targeting the community's capacity, sources and other material bases in order to prevent their engagement with media. I have also demonstrated the relevance of this concept for an understanding of other communities and their media, such as the Kurdish media.

From a similar perspective, I would like to discuss the broader context within which transversal citizenship can be a useful conceptual tool for understanding different communities and the ways in which they connect through different forms of media. I would like to begin by reminding the reader of Athique's plea not to underestimate the importance of the national within the transnational, nor to underestimate the local within the national, transnational and regional. Transversal citizenship enables us to address the complex relationship between these different levels and to see them as interrelated. The concept enables us to overcome the limitations of thinking within binaries and methodological nationalism (Wimmer and Schiller 2003) that are presumed within the transnational. Wimmer and Schiller (2003: 599) have suggested that '[go]ing beyond methodological nationalism requires analytical tools and concepts not colored by the self-evidence of a world ordered into nation'. The Alevi case demonstrates that focusing on community media necessitates lenses that cannot be used fully while only focusing on transnational social spaces (Faist *et al.* 2013). We also need to think beyond two (or more) national contexts if we are to better examine community media production and consumption. Both Shankland (2010) and Zırh (2017b) demonstrate that Alevi geography and their transnational connections require an extra-territorial perspective which can see beyond national borders while not underestimating their significance. This is also the case for stateless communities, such as the Ehl-i Hakk and Ezidis, particularly the latter which is dispersed across different countries while still maintaining a strong sense of community across borders (Omarkhali 2014; Omarkhali and Kreyenbroek 2022). For those communities such as Alevis, for whom locality is a key marker and maker of identity (given the *ocak* system), addressing how they imagine and relate back to different locales and how this is incorporated into the broader community identity through media is key to understanding their transversal imaginaries and citizenship acts.

Taking cultural specificities into account in media studies is a way to adopt a decolonial perspective. The coloniality that underpins the notion of universalism can be challenged by local knowledges and histories. While theories on media and democracy are deemed as all-encompassing and as universal and relevant for understanding the Anglo-European context, research on community, ethnic or diaspora media are treated as 'case studies' and are mainly regarded as valuable in understanding a culturally specific context in a given period of history. We need to acknowledge that such an epistemological prioritisation comes with a risk of what Anibal Quijano criticises as the 'Totality' (of modernity/rationality), which subsumes 'silenced histories, repressed subjectivities and subalternatized knowledges' (Mignolo 2007: 451). We need to be careful in using umbrella theories or concepts such as media freedom and in assessing the value of theory and concepts in terms of their supposed applicability to broader cases and contexts. Delinking allows us to identify the nuances that stem from local histories and knowledges and enables us to situate them within the broader project of pluriversality (Mignolo 2007, 2021; Mbembe 2016).

The silencing of Alevi media is not simply a matter of media freedom; rather, it is part of the longer history of the silencing and persecution of the community, regardless of the Turkish state's measures against other groups (which again should be examined with reference to their own histories and relationships with political power). Concepts of transversal citizenship and communicative ethnocide should be considered as attempts at what Mignolo (2007, 2021) calls epistemic delinking. This book has endeavoured to question Eurocentric hierarchies of epistemology and has proposed a focus on cultural specificity as a way of challenging colonial legacies in media studies. We need to pursue this perspective further and look at different communities and their engagement with media through a decolonial lens if we are to contribute to the production of critical knowledge.

References

Açıkel, F. and Ateş, K. (2005), 'Ambivalent Citizens: Alevi Identity as "the Authentic Self" and "the Stigmatised Other" of Turkish Nationalism' (London School of Public Policy Seminar, University College London).
Açıkel, F. and Ateş, K. (2011), 'Ambivalent Citizens', *European Societies*, 13(5): 713–33. DOI 10.1080/14616696.2011.597868
Adorján, I. (2004), 'Mum söndürme' iftirasının kökeni ve tarihsel süreçte gelişimiyle ilgili bir değerlendirme', in İ. Engin and H. Engin, (eds.), *Alevilik* (Istanbul, Kitap), 123–36.
Akcam, T. (2013), *The Young Turks' Crime against Humanity: The Armenian Genocide and Ethnic Cleansing in the Ottoman Empire* (Princeton, NJ, and Oxford, Oxford University Press).
Akdemir, A. (2015), 'Alevis and the JDP: From Cautious or Neutral Relations to Open Conflict', *Eurasian Journal of Anthropology*, 5(2): 63–77.
Akdemir, A. (2016), *Alevis in Britain: Emerging Identities in a Transnational Social Space* (PhD thesis, University of Essex).
Akdemir, A. (2017), 'Boundary-making and the Alevi Community in Britain', in T. Issa (ed.), *Alevis in Europe: Voices of Migration, Culture and Identity* (London, Routledge), 173–88.
Akkaya, G. (2013), *Sır içinde sır olanlar: Alevi Kadınlar* (Istanbul, Kalkedon).
Akpınar, A. (2016), 'II. Abdülhamid Dönemi Devlet Zihniyetinin Alevi Algısı', in Y. Çakmak, and İ. Gürtaş, (eds.), *Kızılbaşlık, Alevilik Bektaşilik: Tarih, Kimlik, İnanç, Ritüel* (Istanbul, İletişim), 215–26.
Algan, E. (2003), 'Privatization of Media in Turkey and the Question of Media Hegemony in the Era of Globalization', in L. Artz and Y. R. Kamalipour (eds.), *The Globalization of Corporate Media Hegemony* (New York, SUNY Press), 169–92.
Anderson, B. (1983), *Imagined Communities: Reflections on the Origins and Spread of Nationalism* (London: Verso).
Appadurai, A. (1997), *Modernity at Large: Cultural Dimensions of Globalisation* (Minneapolis, University of Minnesota Press).
Appadurai, A. (2006), *Fear of Small Numbers* (Durham, NC, and London, Duke University Press).

Appadurai, A. (2019), 'Traumatic Exit, Identity Narratives, and the Ethics of Hospitality', *Television & New Media*, 20(6): 558–65. DOI 10.1177/ 1527476419857678

Apter, A. (2016), 'Beyond Négritude, Black Cultural Citizenship and the Arab Question in FESTAC 77', *Journal of African Cultural Studies*, 28(3): 313–26. DOI 10.1080/13696815.2015.1113126

Arsan, E. (2014), *Türkiye Kürtlerinde TRT Şeş algısı: Anadilde Yayıncılık Üzerine Bir Araştırma* (Istanbul, Bilgi University).

Ata, K. (2007), *Alevilerin İlk Siyasal Denemesi: (Türkiye) Birlik Partisi (1966-1980)* (Istanbul, Kelime).

Ateş, K. (2011), *Yurttaşlığın Kıyısında Aleviler: 'Öz Türkler' ve 'Heretik Ötekiler'* (Ankara, Phoenix).

Athique, A. (2014), 'Transnational Audiences, Geocultural Approaches', *Continuum: Journal of Media & Cultural Studies*, 28: 4–17.

Athique, A. (2016), *Transnational Audiences: Media Reception on a Global Scale* (London, Wiley).

Atton, C. (2001), *Alternative Media* (London, Sage).

Aydın, B. (2020), 'Self-reflections on Migration and Exile', in K. Smets, K. Leurs, M. Georgiou, S. Witteborn and R. Gajjala (eds.), *The Sage Handbook of Media and Migration* (London, Sage), 615–19.

Aydın, S. (2018), 'The Emergence of Alevism as an Ethno-religious Identity', *National Identities*, 20(1): 9–29. DOI 10.1080/14608944.2016.1244521

Bailey, O. G., Cammaertz, B. and Carpentier, N. (2007), *Understanding Alternative Media* (London, Sage).

Bailey, O. G., Georgiou, M. and Harindranath, R. (2007), *Transnational Lives and the Media: Re-imagining Diaspora* (London, Palgrave Macmillan).

Ball-Rockeach, S. J. (1998), 'A Theory of Media Power and Theory of Media Use: Different Stories, Questions, and Ways of Thinking', *Mass Communication and Society*, 1(1–2): 5–40.

Banaji, S. and Buckingham, D. (2013), *The Civic Web: Young People, the Internet, and Civic Participation* (Boston, MA, MIT Press).

Barabas, A. and Bartholeme, M. (1973), *Hydraulic Development and Ethnocide: The Mazatec and Chinantec People of Oaxaca, Mexico* (Copenhagen, International Work Group for Indigenous Affairs).

Bardakçı, M., Freyberg-Inan, A., Giesel, C. and Leisse, O. (2017), 'The Alevi, the AKP Government and the Alevi Initiative', in *Religious Minorities in Turkey: Alevi, Armenians and Syriac and the Struggle to Desecuritize Religious Freedom* (London, Palgrave Macmillan), 97–127.

Bebawi, S. and Bossio, D. (2014), *Social Media and the Politics of Reportage: The 'Arab Spring'* (London, Palgrave Macmillan).

Bernal, V. (2020), 'African Digital Diasporas: Technologies, Tactics, and Trends, Introduction', *African Diaspora*, 12(1–2): 1–10. DOI 10.1163/18725465-bja10007

Bhabha, H. (1990), *Nation and Narration* (London, Routledge).
Bhambra, G. K. (2014), *Connected Sociologies* (London, Bloomsbury).
Borovalı, M. and Boyraz, C. (2015), 'The Alevi Workshops: An Opening Without an Outcome?', *Turkish Studies*, 16(2): 145–60. DOI 10.1080/1468 3849.2015.1043279
Boulianne, S. and Theocharis, Y. (2020), 'Young People, Digital Media, and Engagement: A Meta-Analysis of Research', *Social Science Computer Review*, 38(2): 111–27. DOI 10.1177/0894439318814190
Boyraz, C. (2019), 'The Alevi Question and the Limits of Citizenship in Turkey', *British Journal of Middle Eastern Studies*, 46(5): 767–80. DOI 10.1080/13530194.2019.1634396
Bozkurt, F. (1998), 'State–Community Relations in Restructuring of Alevism', in T. Olsson, E. Özdalga and C. Raudvere (eds.), *Alevi Identity* (Istanbul, Swedish Research Institute in Istanbul), 85–96.
Brinkerhoff, J. (2009), *Digital Diasporas: Identity and Transnational Engagement* (Cambridge, Cambridge University Press).
Brubaker, R. (1996), *Nationalism Reframed: Nationhood and the National Question in the New Europe* (Cambridge, Cambridge University Press).
Bruinessen, M. V. (1991), *Agha, Shaikh and State: The Social and Political Structures of Kurdistan* (London, Zed Books).
Bruinessen, M. V. (1994), 'Genocide in Kurdistan? The Suppression of the Dersim Rebellion in Turkey (1937–38) and the Chemical War against the Iraqi Kurds (1988)', in G. J. Andreopoulos (ed.), *Genocide: Conceptual and Historical Dimensions* (Philadelphia, University of Pennsylvania Press), 141–70.
Bruinessen, M. V. (2016), 'Alevi Kürtlerin Etnik Kimliği Üzerine Tartışma, "Aslını İnkar Eden Haramzadedir!"', in *Kürtlük, Türklük, Alevilik: Etnik ve Dinsel Kimlik Mücadeleleri* (Istanbul, İletişim), 87–114.
Çakmak, Y. (2019), *Sultanın Kızılbaşları: II. Abdülhamid Dönemi Alevi Algısı ve Siyaseti* (Istanbul, İletişim).
Çakmak, Y. (2021), 'Nur Baba'dan Bektaşi Kız'a Edebiyatta Bektaşî ve Kızılbaş/ Alevîlere Yönelik Olumsuz Algı (1913–1945)', *Folklor Edebiyat*, 27(1): 245–63.
Çalışkan, E. (2020), *Burdened Recognition: Alevis within the Politico-legal Frameworks of Turkey, the United Kingdom and the European Court of Human Rights* (PhD thesis, Queen Mary College).
Calzada, I. (2020), 'Technological Sovereignty: Protecting Citizens' Digital Rights in the AI-Driven and Post-GDPR Algorithmic and City-Regional European Realm', *Regions eZine*. DOI 10.1080/13673882.2018.00001038
Calzada, I. (2022), *Emerging Digital Citizenship Regimes: Postpandemic Technopolitical Democracies* (Bingley, Emerald Publishing Limited).
Çamuroğlu, R. (2008), *Değişen Koşullarda Alevilik* (Istanbul, Kapı).
Carmi, E., Yates, S. J., Lockley, E. and Pawluczuk, A. (2020), 'Data Citizenship:

Rethinking Data Literacy in the Age of Disinformation, Misinformation, and Malinformation', *Internet Policy Review*, 9(2): 1–22. DOI 10.14763/2020.2.1481

Casula, P. (2015), 'Between "Ethnocide" and "Genocide": Violence and Otherness in the Coverage of the Afghanistan and Chechnya Wars', *Nationalities Papers*, 43(5): 700–18. DOI 10.1080/00905992.2015.1048673

Çavdar, O. (2020), *Sivas Katliamı: Yas ve Bellek* (Istanbul, İletişim).

Çelik, B. (2020), 'Turkey's Communicative Authoritarianism', *Global Media and Communication*, 16(1): 102–20. DOI 10.1177/1742766519899123

Cetin, U. (2013), *Anomic Disaffection: A Sociological Study of Youth Suicide within the Alevi Kurdish Community in London* (PhD Thesis, University of Essex).

Cetin, U. (2016), 'Durkheim, Ethnography and Suicide: Researching Young Male Suicide in the Transnational London Alevi-Kurdish community', *Ethnography*, 17(2): 250–77. DOI 10.1177/1466138115586583

Cetin, U. (2017), 'Cosmopolitanism and the Relevance of "Zombie Concepts": The case of Anomic Suicide amongst Alevi Kurd Youth', *British Journal of Sociology*, 68(2): 145–66. DOI 10.1111/1468-4446.12234

Cetin, U. (2020), 'Unregulated Desires: Anomie, the "Rainbow Underclass" and Second-Generation Alevi Kurdish Gangs in London', *Kurdish Studies*, 8(1): 185–208.

Cetin, U., Jenkins, C. and Aydin, S. (2020), 'Editorial: Alevi Kurds: History, Politics and Identity', *Kurdish Studies*, 8(1): 1–6. DOI 10.33182/ks.v8i1.558

Chouliaraki, L. and Georgiou, M. (2017), 'Hospitability: The Communicative Architecture of Humanitarian Securitization at Europe's Borders', *Journal of Communication*, 67(2): 159–80.

Chouliaraki, L. and Georgiou, M. (2022), *The Digital Border: Migration, Technology, Power* (New York, New York University Press).

Clarke, G. (2001), 'From Ethnocide to Ethnodevelopment? Ethnic Minorities and Indigenous Peoples in Southeast Asia', *Third World Quarterly*, 22(3): 413–36. DOI 10.1080/01436590120061688

Clastres, P. (2010), *Archeology of Violence* (Los Angeles, Semiotext(e)).

Clavero, B. (2008), *Genocide or Ethnocide, 1933–2007: How to Make, Unmake, and Remake Law with Words* (Milan, Giuffre Editore).

Cohen, A. P. (1985), *The Symbolic Construction of Community* (London, Routledge).

Coşan Eke, D. (2014), 'Transnational Communities: Alevi Immigrants in Europe', *Journal of Alevism-Bektashism Studies*, 10: 167–94.

Coşan Eke, D. (2017), 'The Resurgence of Alevism in a Transnational Context', in T. Issa (ed.), *Alevis in Europe: Voices of Migration, Culture and Identity* (London, Routledge), 145–56.

Coşan Eke, D. (2021), *The Changing Leadership Roles of Dedes in the Alevi Movement* (Bielefeld, Transcript).

Couldry, N. and Curran, J. (2003), *Contesting Media Power: Alternative Media in a*

Networked World: Alternative Media in a Networked World (London, Rowman & Littlefield).

Cupples, J. and Glynn, K. (2013), 'Postdevelopment Television? Cultural Citizenship and the Mediation of Africa in Contemporary TV Drama', *Annals of the Association of American Geographers*, 103(4): 1003–21. DOI 10.1080/00045608.2011.653741

Delanty, G. (2002), *Citizenship in a Global Age: Society, Culture, Politics* (Buckingham, Open University Press).

Delanty, G. (2003), 'Citizenship as a Learning Process: Disciplinary Citizenship versus Cultural Citizenship', *International Journal of Lifelong Education*, 22(6): 597–605.

Deniz, D. (2012), *Yol/Re: Dersim İnanç Sembolizmi* (Istanbul, İletişim).

Diminescu, D. (2008), 'The Connected Migrant: An Epistemological Manifesto', *Social Science Information*, 47(4): 565–79.

Diminescu, D. and Loveluck, B. (2014), 'Traces of Dispersion: Online Media and Diasporic Identities', *Crossings: Journal of Migration & Culture*, 5(1): 23–39. DOI 10.1386/cjmc.5.1.23_1

Downing, J. D. (2001), *Radical Media: Rebellious Communication and Social Movements* (Thousand Oaks, CA, Sage).

Dressler, M. (2008), 'Religio-Secular Metamorphoses: The Re-making of Turkish Alevism', *Journal of the American Academy of Religion*, 76 (2): 280–311.

Dressler, M. (2011), 'Making Religion through Secularist Legal Discourse: The Case of Turkish Alevism', in M. Dressler and A. S. Mandair (eds.), *Secularism and Religion-Making* (Oxford, Oxford University Press), 187–208.

Dressler, M. (2013), *Writing Religion: The Making of Turkish Alevi Islam* (Oxford, Oxford University Press).

Dressler, M. (2014), '"Our Alevi and Kurdish Brothers": Some Remarks on Nationalism and Minority Politics in Turkey', in K. Omarkhali (ed.), *Religious Minorities in Kurdistan: Beyond Mainstream* (Wiesbaden, Harrassowitz Verlag), 139–57.

Dressler, M. (2021), 'Physical and Epistemic Violence against Alevis in Modern Turkey', in S. H. Astourian and R. H. Kévorkian (eds.), *Collective and State Violence in Turkey: The Construction of a National Identity from Empire to Nation-State* (Oxford, Berghahn), 347–71.

Dutta, M. J. (2020), 'Whiteness, Internationalization, and Erasure: Decolonizing Futures from the Global South', *Communication and Critical/Cultural Studies*, 17(2): 228–35.

Dwyer, S. C. and Buckle, J. L. (2009), 'The Space Between: On Being an Insider-Outsider in Qualitative Research', *International Journal of Qualitative Methods*, 8: 54–63. DOI 10.1177/160940690900800105

Ecevitoğlu, P. and Yalçınkaya, A. (2013), *Aleviler 'Artik Burada' Oturmuyor!* (Ankara, Dipnot).

Emre Cetin, K. B. (2014), 'The "Politicization" of Turkish Television Dramas', *International Journal of Communication*, 8: 2462–83.

Emre Cetin, K. B. (2015), *The Paramilitary Hero on Turkish Television: A Case Study on Valley of the Wolves* (Newcastle upon Tyne, Cambridge Scholars Publishing).

Emre Cetin, K. B. (2018a), 'Television and the Making of a Transnational Alevi Identity', *National Identities*, 20(1): 91–103. DOI 10.1080/14608944.2016.1247260

Emre Cetin, K. B. (2018b) 'Communicative Ethnocide and Alevi Television in the Turkish Context', *Media Culture and Society*, 40(7): 1008–23.

Emre Cetin, K. B. (2020a), 'Mediatised Culturalisation through Television, Second-Generation Alevi Kurds in London', in E. Algan and Y. Kaptan (eds.), *Television in Turkey: Local Production, Transnational Expansion and Political Aspirations* (New York, Palgrave Macmillan), 207–21.

Emre Cetin, K. B. (2020b), 'Transnational Resistance to Communicative Ethnocide: Alevi Television during the State of Emergency in Turkey', in K. Smets, K. Leurs, M. Georgiou, S. Witteborn and R. Gajjala (eds.), *The Sage Handbook of Media and Migration* (London, Sage), 563–73.

Erman, T. and Göker, E. (2006), 'Alevi Politics in Contemporary Turkey', *Middle Eastern Studies*, 36(4): 99–118. DOI 10.1080/00263200008701334

Erol, A. (2012), 'Identity, Migration and Transnationalism: Expressive Cultural Practices of the Toronto Alevi Community', *Journal of Ethnic and Migration Studies*, 38(5): 833–49. DOI 10.1080/1369183X.2012.668025

Erseven, İ. C. (2005), *Çağdaş Türk Romanı ve Öyküsünde Aleviler* (Istanbul, Alev).

Ertan, M. (2017), *Aleviliğin Politikleşme Süreci* (Istanbul, İletişim).

Ertan, M. (2019), 'The Latent Politicization of Alevism: The Affiliation between Alevis and Leftist Politics (1960–1980)', *Middle Eastern Studies*, 55(6): 932–44.

Es, M. (2013), 'Alevism in Cemevis, Religion and Secularism in Turkey', in I. Becci and M. Burchard (eds.), *Topographies of Faith: Religion in Urban Spaces* (Leiden, Brill), 23–43.

Escobar, T. (1989), *Ethnocide: Mission Accomplished?* (Copenhagen, International Work Group for Indigenous Affairs).

Eubanks, V. (2018), *Automating Inequality: How High-Tech Tools Profile, Police, and Punish the Poor* (New York, Picador).

Everett, A. (2009), *Digital Diaspora: A Race for Cyberspace* (Albany, State University of New York Press).

Faist, T., Fauser, M. and Reisenauer, E. (2013), *Transnational Migration* (Cambridge, Polity).

Fenton, S. (2010), *Ethnicity* (Cambridge, Polity).

Florini, S. (2019), *Beyond Hashtags: Racial Politics and Black Digital Networks* (New York, New York University Press).

Fraser, N. (1990), 'Rethinking the Public Sphere: A Contribution to the Critique of Actually Existing Democracy', *Social Text*, 25–6: 56–80. DOI 10.2307/466240

Gajjala, R. (2019), *Digital Diasporas: Labor and Affect in Gendered Indian Diasporas* (London, Rowman & Littlefield).

Geaves, R. (2003), 'Religion and Ethnicity: Community Formation in the British Alevi Community', *Numen*, 50(1): 52–70.

Georgiou, M. (2007), 'Transnational Crossroads for Media and Diaspora: Three Challenges for Research', in O. Bailey, M. Georgiou and R. Harindramath (eds.), *Transnational Lives and Media: Re-imagining Diaspora* (New York, Palgrave Macmillan), 11–32.

Georgiou, M. (2013), 'Seeking Ontological Security beyond the Nation: The Role of Transnational Television', *Television and New Media*, 14(4): 304–21. DOI 10.1177/1527476412463448

Gezik, E. (2012), *Dinsel, Etnik ve Politik Sorunlar Bağlamında Alevi Kürtler* (Istanbul, İletişim).

Gezik, E. (2018), *Geçmiş ve Tarih Arasında Alevi Hafızasını Tanımlamak* (Istanbul, İletişim).

Gezik, E. (2021), 'The Kurdish Alevis: The Followers of the Path of Truth (Raa Haq/Riya Heqi)', in H. Bozarslan, C. Güneş and V. Yadırgı (eds.), *The Cambridge History of the Kurds* (Cambridge, Cambridge University Press), 560–80.

Gezik, E. and Gültekin, A. K. (2019), *Kurdish Alevis: The Case of Dersim* (London, I. B. Tauris).

Ginsburg, F. (1994), 'Embedded Aesthetics: Creating a Discursive Space for Indigenous Media', *Cultural Anthropology*, 9(3): 365–82.

Ginsburg, F. (2005), 'Black Screens and Cultural Citizenship', *Visual Anthropology Review*, 21(1–2): 80–97.

Göner, Ö. (2017a), *Turkish National Identity and Its Outsiders: Memories of State Violence in Dersim* (London, Routledge).

Göner, Ö. (2017b), 'Alevi-State Relations in Turkey: Recognition and Re-marginalisation', in T. Issa (ed.), *Alevis in Europe: Voices of Migration, Culture and Identity* (London, Routledge), 115–27.

Gültekin, A. K. (2022), 'Thinking of Alevism as a 'Majority': Alevi and Sunni Communities in Dersim', in D. Özkul and H. Markussen (eds.), *The Alevis in Modern Turkey and the Diaspora* (Edinburgh, Edinburgh University Press), 101–27.

Güneş, C. (2012), *The Kurdish National Movement in Turkey: From Protest to Resistance* (London, Routledge).

Güneş, C. (2020), 'Political Representation of Alevi Kurds in Turkey: Historical Trends and Main Transformations', *Kurdish Studies*, 8(1): 71–90.

Güvenç, B., Şaylan, G., Tekeli, İ. and Turan, Ş. (1991), *Dosya: Türk-İslam Sentezi* (Istanbul, Sarmal).

Hall, S. (1973), 'Encoding and Decoding in the Television Discourse' (discussion paper, University of Birmingham), available at: http://epapers.bham.ac.uk/2962/1/Hall%2C_1973%2C_Encoding_and_Decoding_in_the_Television_Discourse.pdf, [last accessed 8 May 2022].

Hall, S. (1990), 'Cultural Identity and Diaspora', in J. Rutherford (ed.), *Identity: Community, Culture, Difference* (London, Lawrence & Wishart), 222–37.

Hall, S. and Held, S. (1989), 'Citizens and Citizenship', in S. Hall and M. Jacques (eds.), *New Times* (London, Lawrence and Wishart), 173–89.

Hanoğlu, H. (2020), 'From '*Yol*' to Diasporic Alevism: Migration and Religious Change among Alevis in Britain', *British Journal of Middle Eastern Studies*, 1–20. DOI 10.1080/13530194.2022.2052802

Hanoğlu, H. (2021), *Remaking Alevism in Diaspora: The Socio-spatial Dynamics of Migrant Alevism in the UK* (PhD thesis, University of Kent).

Haraway, D. (1988), 'Situated Knowledges: The Science Question in Feminism and the Privilege of Partial Perspective', *Feminist Studies*, 14(3): 575–99.

Hartley, J. (2001), *Uses of Television* (London, Routledge).

Hartley, J. (2007), *Television Truths: Forms of Knowledge in Popular Culture* (London, Wiley).

Hassanpour, A. (1998), 'Satellite Footprints as National Borders: Med-tv and the Extraterritoriality of State Sovereignty', *Journal of Muslim Minority Affairs*, 18(1): 53–72. DOI 10.1080/13602009808716393

Hassanpour, A. (2003), 'Diaspora, Homeland and Communication Technologies', in H. K. Karim (ed.), *The Media of Diaspora* (London, Routledge), 76–88.

Helsper, E. J. (2012), 'A Corresponding Fields Model for the Links between Social and Digital Exclusion', *Communication Theory*, 22(4): 403–26.

Helsper, E. J. (2021), *The Digital Disconnect: The Social Causes and Consequences of Digital Inequalities* (London, Sage).

Henry, N., Vasil, S. and Witt, A. (2021), 'Digital Citizenship in a Global Society: A Feminist Approach', *Feminist Media Studies*. DOI 10.1080/14680777.2021.1937269

Herrera, L. and Sakr, R. (2014), *Wired Citizenship: Youth Learning and Activism in the Middle East* (London, Routledge).

Hintz, A., Dencik, L. and Wahl-Jorgensen, K. (2019), *Digital Citizenship in a Datafied Society* (Cambridge, Polity).

Holston, J. and Appadurai, A. (1996), 'Cities and Citizenship', *Public Culture*, 8: 187–204.

Hopkins, L. (2009), '"I Feel Myself to Be a World Citizen": Negotiating Turkish and Alevi Identity in Melbourne', *Social Identities*, 17(3): 443–56.

Howard, P. N. and Hussain, M. M. (2013), *Democracy's Fourth Wave?: Digital Media and the Arab Spring* (Oxford, Oxford University Press).

Hurd, E. S. (2014), 'Alevis under Law: The Politics of Religious Freedom in Turkey', *Journal of Law and Religion* 29(3): 416–35.

Iosifidis, P. (2020), 'House of Lords Communications Committee: Public Service Broadcasting in the Age of Video on Demand', *Journal of Digital Media & Policy*, 11(1): 81–95. DOI 10.1386/jdmp_00013_1

Isin, E. F. (2002), 'Citizenship after Orientalism: An Unfinished Project', *Citizenship Studies*, 16(5–6): 563–72. DOI 10.1080/13621025.2012.698480

Isin, E. F. (2008), 'Citizenship in Flux: The Figure of the Activist Citizen', *Subjectivity*, 29: 367–88.

Isin, E. F. (2009), 'Theorising Acts of Citizenship', in E. F. Isin and G. M. Nielsen (eds.), *Acts of Citizenship* (London, Zed Books), 13–43.

Isin, E. F. (2012), *Citizens without Frontiers* (London, Bloomsbury).

Isin, E. F. (2013), 'Claiming European Citizenship', in E. F. Isin and M. Saward (eds.), *European Acts of Citizenship* (Cambridge, Cambridge University Press), 19–46.

Isin, E. F. and Ruppert, E. (2020), *Being Digital Citizens* (London, Rowman & Littlefield).

Isin, E. F. and Wood, P. K. (2002), *Citizenship and Identity* (London, Sage).

Issa, T. and Atbaş, E. (2017), 'Alevi Communities in Europe: Constructions of Identity and Integration', in T. Issa (ed.), *Alevis in Europe: Voices of Migration, Culture and Identity* (London, Routledge), 189–203.

Ito, M. et al. (2010), *Hanging Out, Messing Around, and Geeking Out: Kids Living and Learning with New Media* (Cambridge, MA, MIT Press).

Jenkins, C. (2020), '"Aspirational Capital" and Transformations in First-generation Alevi-Kurdish Parents' Involvement with Their Children's Education in the UK', *Kurdish Studies*, 8(1): 113–34. DOI 10.33182/ks.v8i1.545

Jenkins, C. and Cetin, U. (2014), 'Minority Ethno-Faith Communities and Social Inclusion through Collaborative Research', *Insights*, 9: 1–4.

Jenkins, C. and Cetin, U. (2018), 'From a "Sort of Muslim" to "Proud to be Alevi": The Alevi Religion and Identity Project Combatting the Negative Identity among Second-Generation Alevis in the UK', *National Identities*, 20(1): 105–23. DOI 10.1080/14608944.2016.1244933

Jenkins, H. (2006), *Convergence Culture: Where Old and New Media Collide* (New York, New York University Press).

Jongerden, J. (2003), 'Violation of Human Rights and the Alevis in Turkey', in P. White and J. Jongerden (eds.), *Turkey's Alevi Enigma: A Comprehensive Overview* (Leiden, Brill), 71–89.

Joppke, C. (2001), 'Multicultural Citizenship: A Critique', *European Journal of Sociology*, 42(2): 431–47. DOI 10.1017/S0003975601001047

Karademir, A. and Şen, M. (2021), 'The Case of Alevis in Turkey: A Challenge to Liberal Multiculturalism', *Southeast European and Black Sea Studies*, 21(1): 147–65. DOI 10.1080/14683857.2020.1857075

Karagöz, H. M. (2017), 'Alevism in Turkey: Tensions and Patterns of Migration', in T. Issa (ed.), *Alevis in Europe: Voices of Migration, Culture and Identity* (London, Routledge), 71–81.

Karakaya-Stump, A. (2015), *Vefailik, Bektaşilik, Kızılbaşlık: Alevi Kaynaklarını, Tarihini ve Tarihyazımını Yeniden Düşünmek* (Istanbul, Bilgi Üniversitesi Yayınları).

Karakaya-Stump, A. (2018), 'The AKP, Sectarianism, and the Alevis' Struggle for Equal Rights in Turkey', *National Identities*, 20(1): 53–68.

Karakaya-Stump, A. (2021), *The Kizilbash/Alevis in Ottoman Anatolia: Sufism, Politics and Community* (Edinburgh, University of Edinburgh Press).

Karim, K. and Al-Rawi, A. (2018), *Diaspora and Media in Europe* (London, Palgrave Macmillan).

Karolewski, J. (2008), 'What is Heterodox about Alevism? The Development of Anti-Alevi Discrimination and Resentment', *Die Welt des Islams*, 48(3–4): 434–56. DOI 10.1163/157006008X364767

Kaya, R. and Çakmur, B. (2010), 'Politics and the Mass Media in Turkey', *Turkish Studies*, 11(4): 521–37. DOI 10.1080/14683849.2010.540112

Kehl-Bodrogi, K. (2003), 'Ataturk and the Alevis: A Holy Alliance', in P. White and J. Jongerden (eds.), *Turkey's Alevi Enigma: A Comprehensive Overview* (Leiden, Brill), 53–70.

Kehl-Bodrogi, K. (2008), 'The Role of Kerbela in the (Re-)Construction of Alevism in Turkey', in I. Bellér-Hann (ed.), *The Past as Resource in the Turkic Speaking World* (Würzburg, Ergon), 43–57.

Kehl-Bodrogi, K. (2012), *Kızılbaşlar/Aleviler* (Istanbul, Ayrıntı).

Keiser, H. L. (2001), 'Muslim Heterodoxy and Protest and Utopia: The Interactions between Alevis and Missionaries in Ottoman Anatolia', *Die Welt des Islams*, 41(1): 89–111.

Keiser, H. L. (2003), 'Alevis, Armenians and Kurds in Unionist-Kemalist Turkey (1908–1938)', in P. White and J. Jongerden (eds.), *Turkey's Alevi Enigma: A Comprehensive Overview* (London, Brill), 177–96.

Keleş, J. Y. (2015), *Media, Diaspora and Conflict: Nationalism and Identity amongst Turkish and Kurdish Migrants in Europe* (London, I. B. Tauris).

Kenix, L. J. (2011), *Alternative and Mainstream Media: The Converging Spectrum* (London, Bloomsbury).

Koçan, G. and Öncü, A. (2004), 'Citizen Alevi in Turkey: Beyond Confirmation and Denial', *Journal of Historical Sociology*, 17(4): 464–89.

König, L. (2016), *Cultural Citizenship in India: Politics, Power and Media* (Oxford, Oxford University Press).

Kosnick, K. (2007), *Migrant Media: Turkish Broadcasting and Multicultural Politics in Berlin* (Bloomington, Indiana University Press).

Kosnick, K. (2011), '"To Whom Honor Is Due": Mediated Crime-Scenes and Minority Stigmatization in a Border-Crossing Context', *New Perspectives on Turkey*, 45: 101–21.

Küçük, M. (2007), 'Türkiye'de Sol Düşünce ve Aleviler', in M. Gültekin and T. Bora (eds.), *Modern Türkiye'de Siyasi Düşüce: Sol* (Istanbul, Iletisim), 896–934.

Kurban, D. (2006), 'Unraveling a Trade-off: Reconciling Minority Rights and Full Citizenship in Turkey', *European Yearbook of Minority Issues*, 4 (2004/5): 341–72.

Kymlicka, W. (1998), *Multicultural Citizenship* (Oxford, Oxford University Press).

Lee, C. T. (2014), 'Decolonizing Global Citizenship', in E. F. Isin and P. Nyers (eds.), *Routledge Handbook of Global Citizenship Studies* (London, Routledge), 75–86.

Lemarchand, R. (1994), *Burundi: Ethnocide as Discourse and Practice* (Cambridge, Cambridge University Press and Woodrow Wilson Center).

Leurs, K. (2017), 'Communication Rights from the Margins: Politicising Young Refugees' Smartphone Pocket Archives', *International Communication Gazette*, 79(6–7): 674–98.

Lievrouw, L. (2011), *Alternative and Activist Media* (Cambridge, Polity).

Livingstone, S. and Markham, T. (2008), 'The Contribution of Media Consumption to Civic Participation', *The British Journal of Sociology*, 59(2): 351–71.

Lizot, J. (1976), *The Yanomami in the Face of Ethnocide* (Copenhagen, International Work Group for Indigenous Affairs).

Lobato, R. (2019), *Netflix Nations: The Geography of Digital Distribution* (New York, New York University Press).

Lopez, L. K. (2016), *Asian American Media Activism: Fighting for Cultural Citizenship* (New York, New York University Press).

Lord, C. (2017), 'Rethinking the Justice and Development Party's "Alevi Openings"', *Turkish Studies*, 18(2): 278–96. DOI 10.1080/14683849.2016.1257913

Lord, C. (2018), *Religious Politics in Turkey: From the Birth of the Republic to the AKP* (Cambridge, Cambridge University Press).

Madianou, M. and Miller, D. (2013), 'Polymedia: Towards a New Theory of Digital Media in Interpersonal Communication', *International Journal of Cultural Studies*, 16(2): 169–87. DOI 10.1177/1367877912452486

Maksidi, U. (2002), 'Ottoman Orientalism', *The American Historical Review*, 107(3): 768–96. DOI 10.1086/ahr/107.3.768

Mamdani M. (2003), 'Making Sense of Political Violence in Postcolonial Africa', *Socialist Register*, 39: 132–51.

Mandel, R. (1989), *Cosmopolitan Anxieties: Turkish Challenges to Citizenship and Belonging in Germany* (London, Duke University Press).

Mannheim, K. (1998), 'The Sociological Problem of Generations', in P. Kecskemeti (ed.), *Essays on the Sociology of Knowledge* (London, Routledge), 163–95.

Marino, S. (2021), *Mediating the Refugee Crisis: Digital Solidarity, Humanitarian Technologies and Border Regimes* (Cham, Palgrave Macmillan).

Markussen, H. (2012), *Teaching History, Learning Piety: An Alevi Foundation in Contemporary Turkey* (Budapest, Sekel Bokförlag).

Marshall, T. H. (1992), *Citizenship and Social Class* (London, Pluto Press).

Massicard, E. (2003), 'Alevism as a Productive Misunderstanding: The Hacı

Bektaş Festival', in P. White and J. Jongerden (eds.), *Turkey's Alevi Enigma: A Comprehensive Overview* (Leiden, Brill), 125–41.

Massicard, E. (2017), *The Alevis in Turkey and Europe: Identity and Managing Territorial Diversity* (London, Routledge).

Matsaganis, M., Katz, V. and Ball-Rokeach, S. (2011), *Understanding Ethnic Media: Producers, Consumers, and Societies* (Los Angeles, Sage).

Mbembe, A. J. (2016), 'Decolonizing the University: New Directions', *Arts & Humanities in Higher Education*, 15(1): 29–45.

McCosker, A., Vivienne, S. and Johns, A. (2016), *Negotiating Digital Citizenship: Control, Contest and Culture* (London, Rowman & Littlefield).

Meghji, A. (2021), *Decolonizing Sociology: An Introduction* (Cambridge, Polity).

Michaels, E. (1987), *For a Cultural Future: Francis Jupurrurla Makes TV at Yuendumu* (Melbourne, Art and Criticism Monograph Series).

Mignolo, W. (2007), '*Delinking*: The Rhetoric of Modernity, the Logic of Coloniality and the Grammar of Decoloniality', *Cultural Studies*, 21(2–3): 449–514. DOI 10.1080/09502380601162647

Mignolo, W. (2021), *The Politics of Decolonial Investigations* (London, Duke University Press).

Miller, T. (1998), *Technologies of Truth: Cultural Citizenship and the Popular Media* (Minneapolis, University of Minnesota Press).

Miller, T. (2007), *Cultural Citizenship: Cosmopolitanism, Consumerism, and Television in a Neoliberal Age* (Philadelphia, Temple University Press).

Mohamed, E. and El-Desouky, A. (2021), *Cultural Production and Social Movements after the Arab Spring: Nationalism, Politics, and Transnational Identity* (London, I. B. Tauris).

Mossberger, K., Tolbert, C. J. and McNeal, R. S. (2008), *Digital Citizenship: The Internet, Society and Participation* (Cambridge, MA, MIT Press).

Nigam, A. (2020), *Decolonizing Theory: Thinking across Traditions* (London, Bloomsbury).

Okan, N. (2016), *Canların Cinsiyeti: Alevilik ve Kadın* (Istanbul, İletişim).

Okan, N. (2018), 'Thoughts on the Rhetoric that Women and Men Are Equal in Alevi Belief and Practice (*Alevilik*) – to Songül', *National Identities*, 20(1): 69–89. DOI 10.1080/14608944.2016.1244936

Öktem, K. (2008), 'Being Muslim at the Margins: Alevis and the AKP', *Middle East Report*, 246: 5–7.

Omarkhali, H. (2014), *Religious Minorities in Kurdistan: Beyond the Mainstream* (Wiesbaden, Harrassowitz Verlag).

Omarkhali, K. and Kreyenbroek, P. (2021), *Yezidism between Continuity and Transformation* (London, Blackwell).

Ong, A. (1996), 'Cultural Citizenship as Subject-Making: Immigrants Negotiate Racial and Cultural Boundaries in the United States' [and Comments and Reply], *Current Anthropology*, 37: 737–62.

Orhan, G. (2019), 'Religious Freedom Governance or Institutionalization of a Heterodox Religion? Turkey's Urban Policies with Respect to Alevi Population', *Peace Human Rights Governance*, 3(2): 193-214.

Özkan, N. (2019), 'Representing Religious Discrimination at the Margins, Temporalities and "Appropriate" Identities of the State in Turkey', *PoLAR: Political and Legal Anthropology Review*, 42(2): 317-31.

Özkan, N. (2022), 'The Mediatised Reproduction of Alevism: Alevi Television Networks and Their Audiences', in D. Özkul and H. Markussen (eds.), *The Alevis in Modern Turkey and Diaspora* (Edinburgh, Edinburgh University Press), 272-89.

Özkul, D. (2014), 'Emotive Connections: Insider Research with Turkish/Kurdish Alevi Migrants in Germany', in L. Voloder and V. Kirpitchenko (eds.), *Insider Research on Migration and Mobility* (London, Ashgate), 117-32.

Özkul, D. (2015), 'Alevi "Openings" and Politicization of the "Alevi Issue" during the AKP Rule', *Turkish Studies*, 16(1): 80-96. DOI 10.1080/14683849.2015.1022722

Özmen, F. A. (2011), 'The Alevi Identity and Civil Rights in the Twenty-First Century', in R. Ö. Dönmez and P. Enneli (eds.), *Societal Peace and Ideal Citizenship for Turkey* (Plymouth, Lexington), 71-94.

Pakulski, J. (1997), 'Cultural Citizenship', *Citizenship Studies*, 1(1): 73-86.

Pawley, L. (2008), 'Cultural Citizenship', *Sociology Compass*, 2(2): 594-608.

Ponzanesi, S. (2019), 'Migration and Mobility in a Digital Age: (Re)Mapping Connectivity and Belonging', *Television & New Media*, 20(6): 547-57. DOI 10.1177/1527476419857687

Ponzanesi, S. (2020), 'Digital Diasporas, Postcoloniality, Media and Affect', *Interventions*, 22(8): 977-93. DOI 10.1080/1369801X.2020.1718537

Portes, A. (2000), 'The Two Meanings of Social Capital', *Sociological Forum*, 15(1): 1-12.

Postman, N. (1992), *Technopoly: The Surrender of Culture to Technology* (New York, Vintage).

Postman, N. (2000), 'The Humanism of Media Ecology' (keynote address delivered at the inaugural Media Ecology Association Convention Fordham University, New York, 16-17 June).

Poulton, H. (1997), *The Top Hat, the Grey Wolf, and the Crescent: Turkish Nationalism and the Turkish Republic* (New York, New York University Press).

Poyraz, B. (2005), 'The Turkish State and Alevis: Changing Parameters of an Uneasy Relationship', *Middle Eastern Studies*, 41(4): 503-16. DOI 10.1080/002 63200500119233

Poyraz, B. (2007), *Direnişle Piyasa Arasında: Alevilik ve Alevi Müziği* (Ankara, Ütopya).

Poyraz, B. (2013), 'Bellek, Hakikat, Yüzleşme ve Alevi Katliamları', *Kültür ve İletişim*, 16(1): 9-39.

Punathambekar, A. and Scannell, P. (2013), 'Back to the Future: Media and

Communication Studies in the 21st Century', *Media, Culture & Society*, 35(1): 3–8. DOI 10.1177/0163443712465316

Reiter, B. (2021), *Decolonising the Social Sciences and the Humanities: An Anti-Elitism Manifesto* (London, Routledge).

Rennie, E. (2006), *Community Media: A Global Introduction* (London, Rowman & Littlefield).

Richardson, A. V. (2020), *Bearing Witness While Black: African Americans, Smartphones and the New Protest #Journalism* (Oxford, Oxford University Press).

Rodríguez, C. (2001), *Fissures in the Mediascape: An International Study of Citizens' Media* (New York, Hampton).

Rodríguez, C. (2011), *Citizens' Media Against Armed Conflict: Disrupting Violence in Colombia* (Minneapolis, University of Minnesota Press).

Rosaldo, R. (1994), 'Cultural Citizenship and Educational Democracy', *Cultural Anthropology*, 9(3): 402–11.

Rosaldo, R. (1997), 'Cultural Citizenship, Inequality, and Multiculturalism', in W. V. Flores and R. Benmayor (eds.), *Latino Cultural Citizenship: Claiming Identity, Space, and Politics* (Boston, MA, Beacon Press), 27–38.

Şahin, S. (2005), 'Alevism as a Public Religion', *Current Sociology*, 53(3): 465–85.

Şanlı, Ş. (2016), *Women and Cultural Citizenship in Turkey: Mass Media and 'Woman's Voice'* (London, I. B. Tauris).

Salman, C. (2019), *Lamekandan Cihana: Göç, Kimlik, Alevilik* (Ankara, Dipnot).

Salman, C. (2020), 'Diasporic Homeland, Rise of Identity and New Traditionalism: The Case of the British Alevi Festival', *Kurdish Studies*, 8(1): 113–32.

Salman Yıkmış, M. (2014), *Hacı Bektaş Veli'nin Evlatları: "Yol"un Mürşitleri Ulusoy Ailesi* (Istanbul, İletişim).

Santo, A. (2004), '*Nunavut*, Inuit Television and Cultural Citizenship', *International Journal of Cultural Studies*, 7(4): 379–97.

Savaşal, S. (2021), 'Londra'daki Sivas Anıtı'nın Öyküsü', https://sonhaber.ch/londradaki-sivas-anitinin-oykusu/ [last accessed 22 June 2021].

Sen, M. (2020), 'Redefining the Minority: Alevis in Turkey', in S. T. Jassal and H. Turan (eds.), *New Perspective on India and Turkey: Connections and Debates* (London, Routledge), 127–37.

Sen, S. and Soner, B. A. (2016), 'Understanding Urban Alevism through Its Socio-Spatial Manifestations: Cemevis in İzmir', *Middle Eastern Studies*, 52(4): 694–710. DOI 10.1080/00263206.2016.1176919

Şentürk, B. (2017), 'Urbanisation, Socialist Movements and the Emergence of Alevi Identity in the 1970s', in T. Issa (ed.), *Alevis in Europe: Voices of Migration, Culture and Identity* (London, Routledge), 82–95.

Sevli, S. G. (2019), *Ötekinin Ötekisi: Etno-Dinsel Bir Kimlik Olarak Alevi Kürtlüğün İnşası* (Istanbul, İletişim).

Shankland, D. (2010), 'Maps and the Alevis: On the Ethnography of Heterodox

Islamic Groups', *British Journal of Middle Eastern Studies*, 37(3): 227–39. DOI 10.1080/13530194.2010.543307

Sinclair, C. and Smets, K. (2014), 'Media Freedoms and Covert Diplomacy: Turkey Challenges Europe over Kurdish Broadcasts', *Global Media and Communication*, 10(3): 319–31.

Sinclair-Webb, E. (2003), 'Sectarian Violence, the Alevi Minority and the Left: Kahramanmaraş 1978', in P. White and J. Jongerden (eds.), *Turkey's Alevi Enigma: A Comprehensive Overview* (Leiden, Brill), 215–36.

Smets, K. (2016), 'Ethnic Media, Conflict, and the Nation-State: Kurdish Broadcasting in Turkey and Europe and Mediated Nationhood', *Media, Culture & Society*, 38(5): 738–54.

Sobande, F. (2020), *The Digital Lives of Black Women in Britain* (Cham, Palgrave Macmillan).

Soğuk, N. (2008), 'Transversal Communication, Diaspora, and the Euro-Kurds', *Review of International Studies, Cultures and Politics of Global Communication*, 34: 173–92.

Soileau, M. (2005), 'Festivals and the Formation of Alevi Identity', in H. I. Markussen (ed.), *Alevis and Alevism: Transformed Identities* (Istanbul, The ISIS Press), 91–108.

Soileau, M. (2017), 'Hızır Pasha Hanged Us: Commemorating Martyrdom in Alevi Tradition', *The Muslim World*, 107(3): 549–71.

Sökefeld, M. (2002a), 'Alevi Dedes in the German Diaspora: The Transformation of a Religious Institution', *Zeitschrift für Ethnologie*, 127: 163–86.

Sökefeld, M. (2002b), 'Alevism Online: Re-Imagining a Community in Virtual Space', *Diaspora: A Journal of Transnational Studies*, 11(1): 5–38.

Sökefeld, M. (2004), 'Religion or Culture? Concepts of Identity in the Alevi Diaspora', in W. Kokot, K. Tölölyan and C. Alfonso (eds.), *Diaspora, Identity and Religion: New Directions in Theory and Research* (London, Routledge), 133–55.

Sökefeld, M. (2008a), *Struggling for Recognition: The Alevi Movement in Germany and in Transnational Space* (Oxford, Berghahn Books).

Sökefeld, M. (2008b), 'Difficult Identifications: The Debate on Alevism and Islam in Germany', in A. Al-Hamarneh and J. Thielman (eds.), *Islam and Muslims in Germany* (Leiden and Boston, MA, Brill), 267–90.

Soner, B. A. and Toktaş, Ş. (2011), 'Alevis and Alevism in the Changing Context of Turkish Politics: The Justice and Development Party's Alevi Opening', *Turkish Studies*, 12(3): 419–34. DOI 10.1080/14683849.2011.604214

Squires, C. R. (2006), 'Rethinking the Black Public Sphere: An Alternative Vocabulary for Multiple Public Spheres', *Communication Theory*, 12(4): 446–68.

Stavinoha, L. (2019), 'Communicative Acts of Citizenship: Contesting Europe's Border in and through the Media', *International Journal of Communication*, 13: 1212–30.

Stevenson, N. (1997), 'Globalization, National Cultures and Cultural Citizenship', *The Sociological Quarterly*, 38(1): 41–66.

Stevenson, N. (2003), 'Cultural Citizenship in the "Cultural" Society: A Cosmopolitan Approach', *Citizenship Studies*, 7(3): 331–48. DOI 10.1080/1362102032000098904

Stevenson, N. (2010), 'Cultural Citizenship, Education and Democracy: Redefining the Good Society', *Citizenship Studies*, 14(3): 275–91.

Stokes, M. (1992), *The Arabesk Debate: Music and Musicians in Modern Turkey* (Oxford, Clarendon Press).

Tagg, J. (1988), *The Burden of Representation: Essays on Photographies and Histories* (Basingstoke, Palgrave Macmillan).

Tambar, K. (2010), 'The Aesthetics of Public Visibility: Alevi *Semah* and the Paradoxes of Pluralism in Turkey', *Comparative Studies in Society and History*, 52(3): 652–79.

Tambar, K. (2014), *The Reckoning of Pluralism: Political Belonging and the Demands of History in Turkey* (Stanford, CA, Stanford University Press).

Tanikella, L. (2009), 'Voices from Home and Abroad: New York City's Indo-Caribbean Media', *International Journal of Cultural Studies*, 12(2): 167–85.

Taylor, C. (2004), *Modern Social Imaginaries* (London, Duke University Press).

Tazzioli, M. (2018), 'Spy, Track and Archive: The Temporality of Visibility in Eurosur and Jora', *Security Dialogue*, 49(4): 272–88.

Tekdemir, O. (2018), 'Constructing a Social Space for Alevi Political Identity: Religion, Antagonism and Collective Passion', *National Identities*, 20(1): 31–52.

Temel, H. (2021), 'Alevi Hatırlama Kültürü, "Canlarımızı yaktınız anmamıza izin vermiyorsunuz"', *Birikim*, 392: 97–108.

Tufekci, Z. (2018), *Twitter and Tear Gas: The Power and Fragility of Networked Protest* (London, Yale University Press).

Turner, B. S. (1993), 'Contemporary Problems in the Theory of Citizenship', in *Citizenship and Social Theory* (London, Sage), 1–18.

Uçar, M. (2017), 'Migration and the Invention of Tradition: A Socio-Political Perspective on Euro-Alevis', in T. Issa (ed.), *Alevis in Europe: Voices of Migration, Culture and Identity* (London, Routledge), 131–44.

Uldam, J. and Vestergaard, A. (2015), *Civic Engagement and Social Media: Political Participation beyond Protest* (London, Palgrave Macmillan).

Uslaner, E. M. (1998), 'Social Capital, Television, and the "Mean World": Trust, Optimism, and Civic Participation', *Political Psychology*, 19(3): 441–67.

Van Dijk, J. (2020), *The Digital Divide* (Cambridge, Polity).

Vega, J. and Hensbroek, P. B. V. (2010), 'The Agendas of Cultural Citizenship: A Political-Theoretical Exercise', *Citizenship Studies*, 14(3): 245–57. DOI 10.1080/13621021003731773

Venkateswar, Sita (2004), *Development and Ethnocide: Colonial Practices in the Andaman Islands* (Copenhagen, International Work Group for Indigenous Affairs).

Vorhoff, K. (1998), 'Academic and Journalistic Publications on the Alevi and Bektashi of Turkey', in T. Olsson, E. Özdalga and C. Raudvere (eds.), *Alevi Identity* (Istanbul, Swedish Research Institute in Istanbul), 23–50.

Waltz, M. (2005), *Alternative and Activist Media* (Edinburgh, Edinburgh University Press).

Wang, L. (2013), 'Towards Cultural Citizenship? Cultural Rights and Cultural Policy in Taiwan', *Citizenship Studies*, 17(1): 92–110. DOI 10.1080/13621025.2012.716213

White, P. J. (2003), 'The Debate on the Identity of Alevi Kurds', in P. J. White and J. Jongerden (eds.), *Turkey's Alevi Enigma: A Comprehensive Overview* (Leiden, Brill), 17–29.

White, P. J. and Jongerden, J. (2003), *Turkey's Alevi Enigma: A Comprehensive Overview* (Leiden, Brill).

Williams, R. (2002), 'Culture Is Ordinary', in B. Highmore (ed.), *The Everyday Life Reader* (London, Routledge), 91–100.

Wimmer, A. and Schiller, N. G. (2003), 'Methodological Nationalism, the Social Sciences, and the Study of Migration: An Essay in Historical Epistemology', *The International Migration Review*, 37(3): 576–610.

Wodak, R. and Meyer, M. (2001), *Methods of Critical Discourse Analysis* (London, Sage).

Yalçınkaya, A. (1996), *Alevilikte Toplumsal Kurumlar ve İktidar* (Ankara, Mülkiyeliler Birliği Vakfı Yayınları).

Yalçınkaya, A. (2005), *Pas: Foucault'dan Agamben'e Sıvılaşmış Gelenek ve İktidar* (Ankara, Phoenix).

Yalçınkaya, A. (2014), *Kavimkirim İkliminde Aleviler* (Ankara, Dipnot).

Yalçınkaya, A. (2020), *Aleviler de Bildirir: Alevi Bildirilerinde Develete Kaçış 1963-2017* (Ankara, Dipnot).

Yalçınkaya, A. and Karaçalı, H. (2020), *Aleviler ve Sosyalistler, Sosyalistler ve Aleviler: Bir Karşılaşmanın Notları* (Ankara, Dipnot).

Yanardağoğlu, E. (2021), *The Transformation of Media System in Turkey: Citizenship, Communication and Convergence* (London, Palgrave Macmillan).

Yesil, B. (2016), *Media in New Turkey: The Origins of an Authoritarian Neoliberal State* (Chicago, University of Illinois Press).

Yıldırım, R. (2017a), 'A Genealogy of Modern Alevism, 1950–2000: Elements of Continuity and Discontinuity', in T. Issa (ed.), *Alevis in Europe: Voices of Migration, Culture and Identity* (London, Routledge), 96–114.

Yıldırım, R. (2017b), *Aleviliğin Doğuşu: Kızılbaş Sufiliğinin Toplumsal ve Siyasal Temelleri* (Istanbul, İletişim).

Yıldırım, R. (2019), 'The Safavid-Qizilbash Ecumene and the Formation of the

Qizilbash-Alevi Community in the Ottoman Empire, c. 1500–c. 1700', *Iranian Studies*, 52(3–4): 449–83. DOI 10.1080/00210862.2019.1646120

Yuval-Davis, N. (1997), *Gender and Nation* (London, Sage).

Yuval-Davis, N. (1999), 'The "Multi-Layered Citizen"', *International Feminist Journal of Politics*, 1(1): 119–36. DOI 10.1080/146167499360068

Yuval-Davis, N. (2007), 'Intersectionality, Citizenship and Contemporary Politics of Belonging', *Critical Review of International Social and Political Philosophy*, 10(4): 561–74. DOI 10.1080/13698230701660220

Zaborowski, R. and Georgiou, M. (2019), 'Gamers versus Zombies? Visual Mediation of the Citizen/Non-Citizen Encounter in Europe's "Refugee Crisis"', *Popular Communication*, 17(2): 92–108.

Zelizer, B. (1998), *Remembering to Forget: Holocaust Memory through the Camera's Eye* (Chicago, University of Chicago Press).

Zırh, B. (2008), 'Euro-Alevis: From Gastarbeiter to Transnational Community', in R. G. Anghel, G. R. Gerharz and M. Salzbrunn (eds.), *The Making of World Society* (Bielefeld, Transcript), 103–31.

Zırh, B. (2012a), '1980'ler Alevilik, 2000'ler Dersim, Uyanışı Anlamak', *Alevilerin Sesi*, 161: 20–5.

Zırh, B. (2012b) 'Following the Dead Beyond the "Nation": A Map for Transnational Alevi Funerary Routes from Europe to Turkey', *Ethnic and Racial Studies*, 35(10): 1758–74.

Zırh, B. (2013), 'Al-Gündem 2012, AKP'nin 10. Yılında Türkiye'nin Alevilik Gündemi', *Alevilerin Sesi*, 162: 42–50.

Zırh, B. (2017a), 'Alevi Olmayan Bir Araştırmacı Olarak Alevilik Üzerine Çalışmak, Göç-Mekanda Ama Evde Çok-Alanlı Etnografi', *Moment Dergi*, 4(1): 52–72.

Zırh, B. (2017b), '*Kırmančiya Belekê*: Understanding Alevi Geography in between Spaces of Longing and Belonging', in T. Issa (ed.), *Alevis in Europe: Voices of Migration, Culture and Identity* (London, Routledge), 157–72.

Index

access 20–1, 25–6, 64, 66, 69, 94, 104, 106, 113, 117, 119–20
activism 7, 65
  data 18
  digital 25, 27
  media 47, 65, 81, 111, 119, 128
  political 25
affordances 28, 62, 81
algorithm/algorithmic 25–6
Assyrian 60, 74, 81

British Alevi Federation 4
  the Federation 4–5, 14, 64, 84, 86, 91–2, 106, 109, 115–16, 121, 124

cem 4–5, 14, 43, 52, 57, 59–60, 68–9, 87, 89, 95–6, 101–2, 109–10
cemevi 14, 37, 39, 48, 68–9, 91, 92, 101, 110
Cem Foundation 10, 43, 47, 63, 71, 79, 104, 124–6, 131
Cem TV 9–10, 12–13, 59, 63, 71, 79, 95, 98, 104–5
censorship 28, 105–6, 117, 119
citizenship acts 11, 15–16, 18–20, 23–8, 34, 44, 47, 51–2, 56–7, 61–6, 68, 72, 81–2, 103–4, 111, 119, 122, 125, 128–32
colonial 1, 3, 11, 28–9, 33, 56–7
  colonialism 1, 28–9, 31, 62
  coloniality 29, 31, 133
community media 1–2, 10–11, 16–17, 31, 51, 75, 103, 114, 116, 119, 127, 129–33
cultural citizenship 19–23, 28–31, 34, 39, 43, 46–7, 49–50, 57, 59, 80, 90, 129
cultural identity 6, 22, 24, 28, 57, 59, 95

decolonial 1–2, 15, 17–18, 20, 28–32, 133–4
  decoloniality 2, 11, 15, 20, 28–31, 33, 132
  decolonising 1–2, 28–9, 32
dede 5, 45, 57–8, 88, 96, 101, 116
delinking 29, 134
Democratic Alevi Federation (DAF) 4, 65, 75, 101
Democratic Peace Movement Party (DPMP) 45
Dersim 4, 40–1, 59, 67–70, 77, 85, 91, 101–2
deyiş 5, 49, 54, 69, 77, 95, 124, 126, 129
diaspora 5, 43, 75, 77–8, 80, 88, 123, 132
  communities 27
  digital 24, 27, 81, 118
  media 134
digital citizenship 18–19, 23, 25–6, 81
digital divide 17, 28, 32, 112–15, 118, 127, 130–2
digital rights 19–20, 25–6
digital technologies 20, 25–7, 81, 110, 113, 132
Diyanet (DRA) 37–8, 44–5, 47

emic 1, 6, 32, 37
ethnocide 32, 98–105, 110, 119, 128
  communicative 11, 17, 98–9, 102–11, 114, 119–20, 122, 127, 130, 132–4

etic 32, 37
European Confederation of Alevi Unions 3, 10, 42–3, 64–5, 68, 74, 108, 120
Ezidi 63, 81, 133

Gazi 40–1, 45, 86

genocide 99–101, 105
  Armenian 74, 86
Germany 3, 5–9, 13, 24, 31, 37, 40, 42–5, 47, 49, 54, 56, 58, 62, 64, 68, 72–4, 77, 80, 88, 91–3, 101, 107–9, 114, 120–1, 124, 129
Global North 1, 32–3, 118, 132
Global South 32, 118, 132
Gülbang 5, 57, 95, 129

Hacı Bektaşı Veli 49, 53, 84
  Anatolian Culture Foundation 39
  Associations 44
  Festival 49, 109
  lodge 48, 102
Hamidian Era 11, 36–7
heretic 15, 35–6, 52
  heresy 37
heterodox(y) 35–7, 46

imaginary 11–12, 16, 66, 68, 71, 81–2, 128
  self- 103, 128
  social 20, 22–4, 132
  transnational 43, 76–9
  transversal 1, 16–17, 67, 76, 80–2, 90–3, 96–7, 109, 115, 122, 128, 130, 133
intersectionality 15, 19, 23, 79
Islam 4, 7, 10, 13, 24, 31, 35–42, 49, 52, 54, 71, 73, 74, 79, 101, 104–5
  Islamic State of Iraq and Syria (ISIS) 60
  Islamophobia 74

Justice and Development Party (JDP) 8, 38–9, 64, 101, 110, 114, 116, 132

Kızılbaş 35–7, 52–3
Kurdish 2–4, 10–13, 17, 24, 35, 45, 48, 59–61, 63, 68, 70, 74–6, 78, 83, 85, 90–1, 93–8, 102, 104–9, 110, 114, 120–1, 124, 131–3
  question 55, 72

local 4, 11, 15–17, 19, 23–4, 27, 41, 46–7, 49–50, 54, 56–7, 59, 62–3, 65, 67–73, 75–7, 79–83, 85, 88–90, 92–4, 96–8, 101–3, 107, 109–10, 117, 122, 129–33

authorities 61–2
communities 68, 70–2, 77, 101
programmes 67–8, 71–2, 78, 96, 122
translocal(ity) 20, 24, 91, 97
London Alevi Cultural Centre and Cemevi 4, 55, 84, 86

Madımak 9, 39–42, 45–6, 48–50, 53, 63, 85, 109, 128
marginalised 1, 21, 28–30, 32, 60, 80, 109, 118, 129–30, 132
massacre 9, 40–2, 45–6, 48, 50, 53, 63, 69, 85, 91–3, 101, 128
media studies 1–2, 10, 15, 17, 28, 30–3, 133–4
mediation 15, 17, 19, 23–4, 78
migration 3–4, 15, 24, 27, 43–4, 56, 58, 69, 71, 75, 77, 79, 81, 83–4, 92, 95, 128
millet 36
multicultural 18, 21, 28, 30, 34
mum söndü 52–4

national 6, 15–16, 23, 27, 41, 43, 47, 67, 72, 75–6, 79–81, 90, 96, 98, 107–8, 110, 128, 133
  audience 56
  borders 43, 46, 62, 67, 77, 133
  boundaries 27, 49, 76, 78–9
  community 67
  context 6, 11, 15, 19, 24, 27, 51–2, 74–6, 79–80, 117, 130, 133
  culture 23
  discourses 27
  jurisdiction 26
  identity 24, 35, 42, 48, 81, 107
  politics 8, 73, 75, 132

ocak 3, 5, 37, 40, 53, 57–8, 69, 71, 75, 82, 88, 95, 119, 129, 133
online 10, 17–18, 20, 25–8, 32, 56, 71, 104, 106, 110–11, 113–17, 119–20, 122, 131–2
oppression 6, 21, 24, 27, 43, 49, 61, 82–3, 86–7, 89, 98, 128–30
Ottoman 11, 15, 35–6, 40, 42, 52, 74, 107

participation 18, 20–3, 25–6, 28, 48, 132

Peace Party (PP) 7, 48, 53
persecution 3-4, 9, 15, 40-1, 50, 73-4, 82, 84-5, 99, 102, 130, 134
 persecuted 3, 8
Pir Sultan Abdal 41, 49-50, 84, 110
pluriversal 32, 134
public 30, 39, 41, 44-5, 48-57, 59, 61-3, 69-70, 74-9, 87-8, 104, 109-11, 121, 122, 124-5, 129, 131-2
 broadcasting 48, 52-3, 55, 124, 132
 counter- 121
 discourse 53, 62, 129
 sphere 9, 12, 18, 57, 77-9, 104, 109-11, 125, 129

Radio Television Supreme Council 13, 48, 55, 96, 98, 104
Ramadan 52, 61-3, 102, 130
recognition 1, 7-8, 19, 21-4, 28, 38, 40, 47-8, 50, 58, 70-1, 84, 86-8, 95, 125, 131, 133
Red Apple 54-6, 88
Republic 6, 37, 42, 44, 52, 84, 94, 105
Republican People's Party 44, 62
regional 8, 11, 15-16, 23-4, 26-7, 34, 43, 47, 72, 79-81, 90-1, 128, 133
regulation 28, 48, 101, 105, 117
representation 16, 21, 47-50, 52, 54, 60, 75, 87-8, 103, 105, 132

secular 6-8, 35, 38, 42-4, 46-9, 60, 64, 74
social media 10, 17, 27, 71, 75, 103, 106, 112-17, 119, 121-2, 125, 131
spatial 1, 11, 15-16, 19, 20, 23-4, 26-7, 29, 50, 57, 66-8, 72, 80-2, 91, 93, 114, 122, 128
state 3-4, 9, 13, 17, 22-3, 31-2, 35, 37-9, 41, 44, 45, 47-9, 54-5, 63, 69, 71, 84-6, 90, 98-105, 107-8, 110-11, 125-8, 130

 of emergency 9, 12-13, 17, 90, 98, 107-8, 120-1
 nation- 18-19, 21, 23, 31, 34, 37, 59, 78, 81, 110
 Turkish 6, 17, 63, 78, 101, 105, 107, 110, 119, 121, 126-7, 133
Sunni 6, 31, 36-7, 42, 52, 54, 63, 74, 85, 88, 92, 101, 105-6
Sürgü 61-4, 67, 79
syncretism/syncretic 35-7

talip 5, 88, 96, 129
Tatort 54, 56, 65, 130
transnational 5-6, 8, 11, 15-16, 23-4, 27, 30-1, 34, 39-41, 43, 47, 56, 65, 67, 72, 75-6, 79-81, 87, 90, 96, 108-9, 111, 115, 128, 133
 community 18, 46, 56, 78, 80, 98, 109, 129
 connection 19, 43, 71-2, 78, 93, 98, 133
 context 8, 15, 79, 107, 110, 128, 130
 media 62, 67, 77
 networks 31, 40, 51, 65, 80-1, 114, 128
 politics 42, 64, 80
 public sphere 12, 77, 110
 social space 15, 31-2, 40, 43-4, 77-8, 91, 133
 television 78, 107
 ties 68, 93, 96
Turkish-Islam synthesis 105
Turkish Radio Television Broadcasting Company (TRT) 48, 53-5, 105, 126
Turkish Unity Party 7, 45

Valley of the Wolves 54-6

Young Turks 36

Zaza 3, 55, 68-9
Zazaki 4, 59, 74